From Cowboys to Cockpits

by Douglas Hargreaves

From Cowboys to Cockpits   First Edition
Copyright by © "The Cowboy Publications", 1998
Illustrations and art work are copyrighted by
Matrix CompuServices.©
Editors: Robert Haugen and Brian Grams
Photographs of the Norsman credited to
Colleen Robinson
Cover Design by Edgar & Miriam Ambrosy-Ruiz
Book Layout & Production Matrix CompuServices

Cowboy Publications
102 - 32988 South Fraser Way, Abbotsford, B.C.
CANADA V2S 2A8
Tel. (604) 855-4541
Fax (604) 855-4538

Printed by
Matrix CompuServices
(604) 855-4541
(604) 855-4538
E-mail : matrix@uniserve.com

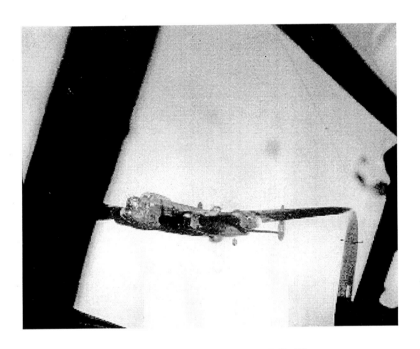

LANCASTER BOMBER Mk. V.
September 1944 - February 23, 1945
Assigned to R.A.F. Three Group,
Stradishall 90 Squadron and 186 Squadron
43 Bombing Missions
Pilot: Sergeant Skipper Hargreaves

Sgt. Skipper Hargreaves

PROLOGUE

The author, named "Skipper" by a relative since his early years, spent 4 years of his pre-adolescence life living on a ranch Southwest of Calgary, Alberta, in the mid 1930's. He lived with a young bachelor rancher by the name of Ken Wills. Ken's mother, father and sister lived within 5 miles of the Bar U Lazy Y ranch. That was the name of the cattle brand.

Ken's father and mother were like real grandparents to Skipper and treated him like one of their own. Peggy, Ken's sister was like a mother to Skipper, caring for him when Skipper was hurt or ill. Ollie, Peggy's husband was a very caring father to his children Eileen, Jhonny and Mark. They were part of Skipper's newly extended family.

Johnny, Gordon McKray and Phillip Wilson were Skipper's best friends and Ken's father called them " The Four Musty Steers."

After 4 marvelous years on the ranch, Skipper had to return to Winnipeg, to live with his parents and to finish the last two years of highschool education.

This book is a follow up to the author's autobiography beautifully written on "The Cowboy", the first part of his life on the ranch.

DEDICATION

From Cowboys to Cockpits is dedicated to all those airmen who gave everything they had for their country, even their lives.

In particular Easy's Crew:

F/L Jack Buvan, DFC DSO (Bombaimer)

F/L Jack Mckay, DFC and Bar, KIA (navigator)

F/O Bill Baker, DFC and Bar (Radio Operator)

P/O Johnny Carr, DFC and Bar (Flight Engineer)

F/O Frank Malorey, DFC and Bar(Mid Upper Gunner)KIA

F/O Hank Simms, DFC and Bar (Rear Gunner) KIA

Also to those Bush Pilots who flew through the worst weather imaginable to save lives.

To my family   who wanted to know

To my wife   who knew

To Robert Haugen Editor

To Brian GramsEditor

To my Cowboy Dad Ken Wills

I recall standing in formation at Manning Depot in Brandon, Manitoba, when our Corporal informed us that "We must pull all together as a team because the airman standing on either side of you would not be coming home"   *Doug Hargreaves.*

Tiger Moth

FROM COWBOYS TO COCKPITS

CONTENTS

DISCLAIMER

From Cowboys to Cockpits has been composed mostly from memory and a writer's prerogative and license. The experiences and events detailed throughout the book are true but some subtitles were substituted. Some target dates may not be exact, due to the destruction of the author's log book,

Some names used in "The North" are purely coincidental and not meant to be identified with any person(s) living or dead.

THE GRADUATE

The day arrived when all the goodbyes had been said, all the tears had been shed and I was leaving home. I felt like screaming because I was so miserable yet I knew that there was no other way.I had to go back to my parents in Winnipeg. I left some of my clothes at Ken's so I would have something that I would have to come home for.

The drive in to Calgary was very uncomfortable, apart from all the noise on the rough gravel roads and the volumes of dust that seeped into the cab of Ken's half-ton truck.

Ken and I walked around the station while waiting for my train to be called for loading.The conversation was forced and rather trivial as we fumbled our way through this difficult time.I couldn't find the words to express my feelings. It had to be the unhappiest day of my life. I was leaving my ranch home and all those that I loved and cared so much about.

My parents, having returned from England, insisted I return to Winnipeg to finish my high school.I hadn't seen them for four years and now I was returning to the big city to be reunited with them.I was devastated at the thought of our reunion.I felt that I was starting life all over again with people I barely knew although I was looking forward to seeing my brother.

In the weeks preceding my departure, I must have cried buckets.I tried to hide my emotions, after all, I was fourteen and boys my age didn't cry.They were supposed to act like men.I was also a rancher and cowboys don't cry.Well, that may have been how I was supposed to act but it sure wasn't how I felt. I knew that Ken was also holding his feelings in check. \We spent nights sitting and talking, each one trying to keep the conversation away from my departure.

Johnny, Gordy, Phillip and Lynn didn't help matters much. We were all walking around with long faces.Not at all our usually happy selves.We had become very close over the years and I

would miss them.

Peggy, Grandma and Grandpa were trying very hard to make my leaving like an adventure into a new world where I would be very happy once I got settled. They didn't sound very convincing. Everyone was trying to make it easier for me.

I tried to convince my parents to allow me to stay and finish my education here, then I'd return home. What would another couple of years mean after all this time? I could visit them in the summer.

"Ken, can I come home for Christmas?" I asked. I realized that I shouldn't have mentioned Christmas. Ken looked away from me as he tried to hide the tears in his eyes. I wept unashamedly and hugged him.

"You be a big man now, you hear. You know I'll always love you Skipper. You'll always be my kid and you'll always have a home here. You work hard at school and try to adjust to your family. They'll learn to appreciate and love you. It won't be long until Christmas and we'll be together again. Why, by that time you'll probably have grown half an inch and be ready to take on the world. You'll be all settled in and doing great," Ken kidded me.

"I can grow here just as well," I replied.

Finally the boarding call came and we walked to the train. I climbed the steps and Ken followed me into the car and to my seat. He helped me store my luggage in the racks above and then sat down beside me. He put his arm around my shoulders and we looked at each other. We were silently saying goodbye. The train conductor called "All Aboard!". Ken stood up and without another word walked out of the car. Two days later I arrived in the big city.

My parents were at the station to meet me. It was an awkward situation which consisted of a formal handshake and "My, how much you've grown". I felt they were as uncomfortable as I was. We were strangers. The only real welcome came from Nancy, our maid and my old nanny. She hugged me and welcomed me home. "Skipper, you'll be surprised to see the new house and your special room," she offered.

Billy, my young brother, stood awkwardly in the background while all the welcoming was going on. I couldn't believe how much bigger he was than me. I walked past my parents and shook hands

with him. He was like a complete stranger and it was very difficult.

On his way to work the next day my father dropped me off at Kelvin High, my new school. I had been told that it was a very good one.I felt as frightened as I had on my first day in the one room school in Millarville.

I stopped to ask some students for directions to the secretary's office but was greeted with "You're in the wrong school, aren't you kid?"

"I just need to know how to get to the office," I answered.There was no need to get into any discussion about why I was there. They directed me down the hall and continued on their way, looking back over their shoulders to see if I really was going to the office.

With my report cards and a letter of introduction from Turner Valley school, I entered the office. "What's on your mind today, young fellow?" the secretary asked.

"I'm here to enrol in grade eleven," I announced. I was trying to act braver than I felt This place was huge and certainly nothing like Turner Valley High. I could easily get lost.

"Young man, I think you're in the wrong school. The junior high is two blocks away. Did you say grade eleven?" she asked, failing to hide her scepticism.

"Yes Ma'am. It's all here in my papers," I said, reaching into my bag. She examined my report card and the accompanying letter.

"My word, this is most impressive. Will you take a seat while I see if the principal can see you?" she instructed as she left the counter and entered a side office. She wasn't in there a minute when she reappeared with a tall heavy set man.

"Well there young fellow, your report card is outstanding but I think we may have a problem here," he announced. I knew exactly what the problem was as I had been through all of this before.

"Don't worry sir, I won't make any trouble. I'll stay clear of sports and I won't upset my classmates," I tried to put his mind at ease.

"It isn't going to be easy for you with all these young adults. I'm afraid that they won't understand."

"Sir, let me try and if things become too difficult then I'll find another school," I said, trying to make it easier for him.

"We'll give it a try and see how things go. Do you know anyone

in the school?"

"No Sir, I've been living in Alberta for the last four years." I answered, hoping that might explain everything.

A new kid entering a classroom for the first time almost feels like throwing up.I think my heart was about to burn out that it was pumping so fast.I felt like a skunk at a garden party as I entered my new classroom.The principal introduced me to the teacher, who looked incredulously in my direction and motioned me to take an empty desk at the back of the room.The teacher and the principal became engrossed in a spirited conversation in front of the entire class.They suddenly realized where they were and the principal left the room.

The teacher introduced me to the class, explaining I was from Alberta and that should be sufficient to explain my size, my grade level and I suppose, to a certain extent, my appearance.

"Another hay seed from the West, huh?" one student yelled. He reminded me of Billy Wilson. I sat down at my desk and tried to hide my embarrassment.

It seemed that I was to start my first day at Kelvin High with more than one traumatic experience. I had forgotten that my previous school had given me credits for music. I enjoyed playing the piano and Miss Snowdon had felt I had a real ear for music. She taught me to chord and showed me how to read melody lines. Not what you'd call formal music training but we did have a music program in our school.

My room teacher, noticing the entry on my report card, advised the principal, at a school assembly, that I was a piano player. I wondered if he was trying to embarrass me.He'd been quite successful at accomplishing that so far.I tried explaining my way out of the situation, which just made things worse.

I wound up playing the Skater's Waltz in front of the whole assembly.I guess they liked it because I was asked to accompany the school chorus.Things went better for me after that and my size and age wasn't upsetting my classmates any longer.

Mother had insisted I leave all my ranch habits where they belonged, on the ranch. She was determined to "Clean Me Up" so to speak. My constant references to Ken and the ranch upset her, so I

promised to alter my attitude. I really was trying to adjust.

Everyone at home was trying to pick up where we had left off and that I couldn't do. I couldn't remember where we had left off.I became edgy and stayed to myself as much as possible. I was finding fault with everything and everyone. Father had a long talk with me, suggesting that I had a big chip on my shoulder and the sooner I realized that, the better things would be.Outside of my sleeping and eating, I spent little time at home.

One Sunday I attended services at a Baptist church.My parents were not church going people but I was used to attending regularly. I enjoyed the service and in particular the great pipe organ. After the service I waited until everyone had gone then introduced myself to the lady organist, a Miss Agnes Forsythe. I told her how much I enjoyed hearing her play and of my interest in the instrument. She invited me into the choir loft to look at it.

It was huge, with pedals running from one side to the other. She explained there was another keyboard to be played by the feet. Talk about being intimidated. Hoooolly!

"Do you play?" she asked.

"I took lessons and I play for our school chorus", I replied, hoping she would let me try the instrument.

"Come over here and sit up on the bench. I'll start it up and we'll see what you can do," she said. Hooolly! I almost fainted from my excitement.

It was one of the greatest thrills of my life as the music soared through the empty church. I had never heard anything so beautiful. It was like having fifty horses in one team I had so much power in my fingertips.

"Try the pedals Skipper." For some reason neither one of us could explain I had no trouble locating the right notes. I found the pedals quite easy to use even though I had to rest my bum on the edge of the bench in order to reach them.

"You're doing just fine. I'm quite surprised." I was wishing I could stay here all day I enjoyed it so much.

"Would you consider teaching me?" I asked, almost apologetically, feeling she wouldn't even think of it.To my surprise, she agreed. "Skipper, you're a natural and I think you show great

promise. Yes, we can give it a try for a while and see how it goes," she suggested. That was how I came to learn to play the organ and how I became part time organist at Trinity Baptist church in Winnipeg.I knew Grandma would be proud of me.

I think my parents were relieved to know where I was in my spare time and they readily agreed to pay for my lessons.Eventually I was paying for them with the money I earned playing part time for Agnes.

Christmas was approaching so I decided to broach the subject of my going to the ranch.To my surprise, they agreed.I think they were almost relieved. They were going to Corpus Christi for Christmas as guests of some business associates.Children were not included, as usual.

Ken had already invited me home for Christmas but I wondered if it was still okay. I wrote to Ken asking if I could come and his letter soon arrived telling me that it was okay.

I was very busy with Christmas programs both at church and at school and time passed quickly. I found my mid-term exams easy and was sure I had done well. I would have my results when I returned from holidays.

The train ride to Calgary had to be the longest ride I had ever taken. It seemed to take forever to cross the white, snow covered Saskatchewan prairies. They looked even more desolate in the winter time.

The train was loaded with young service men from all branches of the military returning home for the holidays. I tried a couple of times to strike up a conversation with a few of them, however they weren't too interested in talking to a kid.

A Chinook wind was blowing and the weather was warm as I stepped off the train. Water was running everywhere. I looked around the packed station searching for Ken. I could hardly contain myself as I thought of what I would say to him or how I would act.

Where were they? I had told them what time I was arriving. They were probably on their way but just a little late, I tried explaining their absence to myself.

"Hi Skipper! Just had to get back to God's country, huh?" a voice yelled at me. It was Pete Sylvester from Millarville. I went to school

with some of his kids and used to visit them every now and again.

"Hi Mr. Sylvester, have you seen Ken or anyone from home?" I asked.

"Nope, and I don't expect you're going to either. They ain't expecting you 'til tonight. I hear there was a whole bunch coming in to meet yuh," Pete explained.

"Hooollyy! how did that happen?" I asked myself. I must have made a mistake about the time of my arrival.

"Want a ride home?" he asked. "I'll be glad to give you a lift. Otherwise you'll be waiting a long time Skipper. Golly boy, I think you grew some," Pete laughed. "Pete, if it's okay I'll come with you," I said.

I shocked Peggy when I walked in the door and she nearly dropped her baking. "Skipper, you young scamp, what are you doing here so soon? And look at you, you've grown some too," she laughed. "You're not due in here until tonight. The kids were planning on going into Calgary with Ken to give you a welcome," she explained. We hugged and I cried because I was so happy to be back and, of course, I got my usual pinch on the bum. I guess I hadn't grown too big for that.

"Skipper, we really missed you and looked forward to your letters. It was good of you to write so often. It sounded as though things were not too good at home."

"You're right Peggy, it was a difficult time and it didn't go all that well. School went just fine, better that I expected, and I think I did okay on my mid-terms.

"Where is everybody? Where's Ken?" I asked.

"He's over at Wilson's. He bought more cattle for feeding this winter and he's going to move them tomorrow. He was waiting for you to arrive. He figured you'd want to help."

"When's he coming home?" I asked.

"He'll be here for supper. He was going to take the kids to pick you up. They'll sure be surprised."

"Leave your coat on and haul me some water, it won't be all that long before the kids are home," she said.

"Where are they?" I asked.

"They went over to Sylvester's. They'll know you're here when

they talk   to Pete. They're probably racing home now," Peggy laughed. "They're sure excited about your coming and Christmas and all. I think you're the only Christmas present they really wanted," Peggy smiled at me. "You're our boy and we're just so happy to have you home." I was getting a lump in my throat again.

"Peggy, after I haul the water, can I borrow Olie's horse? I want to see Grandma and Grandpa.I just have to see them," I asked.

"He's in the corral Skipper, you know where the saddle is.Go ahead if you think you can still ride," she joked.

"Peggy, I'll never forget how to ride," I answered."You have about an hour or so before supper.You better be here when Ken arrives you hear," Peggy warned.

"Sure Peggy," I answered, taking off out the door.

Grandpa was in the living room and Grandma was in the kitchen doing some baking.The house smelled wonderful and was all decorated in the Christmas style with spruce boughs and tinsel and candles everywhere. I didn't knock, I just walked in.

"Skipper! Oh dear me, you scared me almost to death. You were not to come until tonight," Grandma said, hugging me to her ample bosom.

"Who's out there Mum?" Grandpa shouted.

"No one special Grandpa, just your Grandson," I answered.

"Oh, my boy it's you." Grandpa came into the kitchen and we hugged. "My oh my, you have grown. I recall when you were almost up to my elbow," he chuckled.

"Ah Grandpa, I've grown quite a bit don't you think?" I pleaded.

"Yes my boy, you really have. They must be feeding you out there.Well we're going to feed you even more. This is going to be the best holiday we have ever had. Does Ken know you are here already?"

"No Grandpa. He and Peggy's kids were going to pick me up tonight at eight. He'll sure be surprised to see me."

"I had better get going Grandpa, I told Peggy I'd come right back."

"All right son, we'll see you tomorrow. Gosh but it's good to have you home," Grandpa chuckled. I rode back to Peggy's feeling incredibly happy.

I was in time to meet the kids just as they were going through

the gate.

They knew the minute they saw me who it was and came racing over. We almost tore each other apart. Our whoops and hollers could be heard all over the valley. We rode home to Ken's all talking at once and asking all sorts of questions.

I was taking the saddle off Olie's horse when Ken came in. He just stood looking at me. "Gosh all Friday boy, can't you do anything right and get here when you're supposed to?" he laughed. We just stood there hugging and crying. Our reunion was just too much for me. I had waited so long for this moment that I couldn't find the right words to say to him. As had happened many times before, the look in our eyes said it all.

Christmas was the best celebration we had ever had, at least that was the way everyone described our holiday. I met all my old school chums and the four "Musty Steers" were together again. I was so very happy that I hated the thought of having to return to school.

The school term had come to an end and I passed with honours into grade twelve. That pleased both my parents and the school. I was preparing for my fifteenth birthday and had been pondering what I was going to do when I finished school. I still had another year to make up my mind.

The church Pastor had mentioned to my parents that I would make a good preacher. They thought that was hilarious but told him it was up to me. Mother was more concerned about what I was going to do during the summer holidays. They wanted me to come with them to their "Summer Cottage" as they called it, in Kenora by The Lake of the Woods. It was almost as big as our city house. I informed them that I couldn't. "I suppose you're planning on going back to the ranch for the summer, are you?" Mother asked.

"Yes ma'am. I have a lot to do and they need the help," I said.

"Oh sure, you'd rather sit around with those hillbillies than be with your own family," Mother remarked. Ha! That was funny. Where had they been for the last four years of my life?

"I shudder when I think what the ranch has done to you already. You look and dress like a boughunk," she claimed. Whatever a boughunk was.

"Mother, I still own that quarter section and I have twenty head

of steers to look after. I have all the money I need," I reminded her. It always made me feel badly when she'd talk about the only people I really cared about. I told her that I wouldn't listen to any more talk about Ken and the ranch.

"Well young man, as long as you're living under this roof you'll do as we say and that's that. You're too young yet to be on your own," she stated.

"Well, I want to go west for the summer anyway," I said.

I was disappointed when I received a letter from Peggy telling me that Ken had enlisted in the Army, in the armoured tank division. Now what was I going to do? Well, it only made my decision to go west easier. Grandpa would need me even more with Ken away.

I worked very hard that summer and when I returned to Winnipeg I had grown some and had put on a bit more weight. My muscles even looked like muscles for a change, at least so Grandpa had told me.

Grandpa caught me trying to shave one day and he laughed so hard, telling me I was about to cut my throat and I should leave the shaving for grown-ups.

"Ah Grandpa, you always say that. I want to grow a beard," I explained.

"My son, it'll be a few years yet before you get enough hay to mow so just leave it to Mother Nature," he chuckled as he handed me a towel to wipe the shaving soap off my face.

I decided that I was going to go into the service and spent the next year trying to make myself look and act older. I graduated from grade twelve second in my class. My parents had nothing to complain about, other than I should be heading to university. "All that talent going to waste," they claimed.

I returned to Millarville and worked hard helping Grandpa. Peggy was there for me like she had always been. "You sure you want to join up little man?" she asked.

"Peggy, I want to join the Navy and see the world," I replied.

Skipper, you're too young yet, you're only sixteen and you know you're still my baby. You're too little yet," she said.

"Well, I want to enlist and I'm going into Calgary with Grandpa

and see what they can tell me about joining up," I stated. I thought my good marks should get me in easy. If only I wasn't so small. Well, I was going to try anyway, I could tell them that I was seventeen already. I had just celebrated my sixteenth birthday. Peggy just laughed. She didn't think they'd believe that.

Ken was furious when he heard of my plan and told me he was going to lay a good lickin' on my behind when he came home. I knew he couldn't do that because he was at the military base at Camp Wainright. He and Morris were together.

I returned to Winnipeg with a definite plan in mind to enlist in the military. I was going to be a sailor and no one was going to talk me out of it.

THE DECISION

You ain't nothing but a kid. Come back when you're dry behind the ears." Those were the words still ringing in my ears as I left the Naval Recruiting Office.

I had made up my mind that one way or another I was going to join the services. I was walking down Portage Avenue in Winnipeg when I passed a young man in Navy uniform. He had just come out of the Navy's downtown office. Here was my chance. It was now or never.

I walked into the small office where an old Navy Chief Petty Officer sized me up and down. I told him I wanted to join up. He decided not to see it my way. He threatened to call my parents. "Get out of here sonny or I'll call the truant officer and he'll haul your little ass back to school," he said. Obviously, my size didn't impress him.

"Horse Pucky," I thought.

I had been this route before and knew when to back off. I even opened my briefcase hoping to show him my birth certificate, my graduating diploma and my final report card. These had no effect on the burly Chief. He laughed as he told me there was no place in the Navy for midgets. I was so exasperated when I left the office that I yelled back. "Go sit on your hat you big oaf." I then beat a hasty retreat into the street. I guess I sure told him.

I was angry and disappointed but even more determined to join something. I was now committed. It was going to be the military or else. I was not going to go home until I had this thing squared away.

A few doors away on the same avenue, I came across the Airforce Recruiting Office. "Come in and sign up for a future in aviation," the sign read. Well that looked interesting. I walked into the office and laid my papers on the desk before anyone could comment or ask any questions. "These your papers kid?" the officer asked.

"Yes sir, they're mine," I answered.

"You intending to apply for enlistment in the Airforce?"

"Yes Sir, I'm serious," I replied in my most grown up falsetto voice, trying my darndest to sound older but my face gave me away.

"Hold on a minute while I get someone to talk to you," and away the officer went. In a few moments, he returned with another officer of even higher rank. The papers were reviewed and the officer motioned me to come into his office. "Sit down son." he pointed to the chair. "You certainly have the papers and academic standing to make aircrew," he said. He told me I was quite small and really too young for the services unless perhaps I could get my parents authority to enlist. I assured him that I could get the necessary authorization.

"You know kid, this will be really difficult for you because of your size and your age. It isn't going to be any picnic and you might not make aircrew training depending on what your medical shows," he told me.

"What they didn't know about my medical condition wouldn't hurt them," I thought.

He called the other officer into the office and they discussed the matter in front of me. I was feeling very uneasy and totally embarrassed. They kept talking about my size and my age like I wasn't in the same room. Finally, they told me to get my Father or Mother into the office for another interview and their written consent. They would process me at least as far as Manning Depot (Basic Training Centre). There I would have my medical, my classification tests and my indoctrination. If I made it past that phase, I would be accepted into the Airforce. As to what I would be doing, they couldn't tell me.

"It all depends on how you do on your medical and aptitude tests. With your academics you could easily qualify for pilot training." I left, feeling much better and knowing that I was going to make it.

I walked down Portage Avenue to my Father's office located in the big department store in the midst of downtown Winnipeg. He happened to be in his office and was just preparing to go to lunch. I was about to upset his appetite.

"I have joined the Airforce," I announced.

"You can't, you're under age," he replied.

"Well, they agreed I'm just who they're looking for and all I need is your signature," I replied, as convincingly as possible. He knew I was not "Just what they were looking for" and talked to me for a few more minutes. I think he knew all along that I was going to try to enlist and not attend University.

"I don't suppose there is any way I can talk you out of this, is there? What do you think your Mother is going to say when she hears of your decision? We don't have to sign your papers you know," he stated.

We went to the recruiting office and I am certain my Father expected I'd be turned down. He, like everyone else, still saw me as a young boy. The officer seemed impressed with the way I conducted myself. I explained the reasons why I wanted to join and I felt I was suited for the Airforce. The officer told my Father that ordinarily, with my academic standing, I would have been recommended for officer training, however in view of my very young age and lack of maturity, this avenue would not be open to me at this time, perhaps later. The officer was certain I'd have a career in the service, providing I got through basic training. My Father assured the officer that I was capable of taking care of myself and probably would make an excellent member of the service. I could hardly believe my ears. My Father, speaking up on my behalf.

"You sure this is what you want Skipper?" my Father asked.

"Yes Sir. I've made up my mind that I want to join," I replied.

"All right young man, you sign here and your Father signs along with you," the officer instructed.

"You will be leaving in two days. I'm having your orders typed up right now and your train ticket will be included," the officer went on. "Don't be late and take only the few things of a personal nature that you will require." He handed me a typed list of instructions. "You'll be issued a uniform after you arrive at Manning Depot. Remember, this doesn't mean that you are being accepted, it all depends on Manning Depot," the officer concluded. Hooolly! This was it. I was going to be an airman.

MANNING DEPOT

For any young person joining the service, their initial reaction to Manning Depot is one of utter confusion and awe. People are milling around wondering what to do and wondering who will tell them where they should go. It appears there isn't anyone in control, until a voice shouts over all the other sounds.

"Recruits! I am Corporal C. W. Morrow. I will be your counsellor, mentor and guide for the next few weeks while you are in my care. You will come to me with your every concern and I will put them at rest," he shouted. He didn't need a megaphone, his voice was so loud. Apart from the fact that he got red in the face when he yelled, he was a rather pleasant looking man in his late twenties.

We were in a large Airforce drill hall. I think it must have been a hangar at one time. The building had hardwood floors and there were basketball courts and other sports facilities throughout the place. We milled about carrying our suitcases and various other personal effects until Corporal Morrow started talking to us again. We stopped in our tracks and listened, afraid that we might miss some vital information regarding our futures.

"Gentlemen and boys." (Already he was singling me out.) "You will form up in three lines in front of me on my command and place your luggage in front of you," he barked. I only had one suitcase and it was heavy. I heaved it around so it was in front of me. With all the shoving and pushing I found myself in the back row. My friend, whom I had met on the train from Winnipeg, was in the second row at the opposite end to me.

"From this moment on you will address me as Corporal Morrow and nothing else. When I speak no one else will talk. Ever! I can be a very pleasant and happy man or I can be most unhappy and make your lives hell on earth. You will wish to be anywhere but near me. Do you all understand?" he continued.

"Yes Sir, Corporal Morrow," we all answered, more or less in unison.

"You will not call me Sir under any circumstances. Do you understand me?" he barked.

"Yes, Corporal Morrow," we answered. We were getting the hang of it already. Two other corporals joined him as he walked along the ranks looking us over. I stood, at what I thought was attention, and waited for the onslaught I knew would come when they got to me. They passed right by me, looking over my head. I could hardly believe my good fortune. There were remarks made up and down the line, questions asked, replies made and even some laughter. Things were very serious indeed. I felt the tension in the air. We didn't know what to expect or how far we could go with this new boss. Most of us had never taken orders in such a formal manner before. We were new and it certainly showed. Our corporal knew it, that's for sure.

We came from every walk of life, from ex-jailbirds, to city business types, to farmers and labourers. We were all here ready to be moulded into a fine example of "Military Might".

"You are being allotted bunk space in the new billet facility nearby. You will take your luggage to these quarters where you will stay until I or my assistants order otherwise. You will not shift your allocated bunk positions from one to another unless you are authorized to do so. You will then be sent for your medical examinations and your inoculations. From there we will go to the supply depot where you will be outfitted with uniforms and all the necessary gear that you will require while in my care. Do you all understand me?"

"Yes, Corporal Morrow." I was getting the feel of the situation and, in my enthusiasm, my soprano voice pierced the building above all the others. I realized what had happened the minute I answered but it was too late.

"Who is the smart person with the falsetto voice?" he screamed. I slunk down even lower than my ordinary height and waited for him to seek me out. It wouldn't be hard with everyone looking at me. He found me and had me step forward. "You are testing me, aren't you little one?" he asked.

"No, Corporal Morrow, Sir," I replied in my normal voice. He did not like my normal voice either.

"Are we having a problem little man? I sincerely hope we are not. And what are you doing in my flight?" he asked.

"I was told to stand in this row by you corporal," I replied. Everyone was chuckling quietly at my dilemma. They felt I was putting the corporal on. I assured the corporal that I was where I was supposed to be and that my voice hadn't completely changed yet.

I see. We must keep close tabs on you little man," he replied and moved back to the front of the line. Hooolly! Was I ever shaking. Anyone in the second row who turned to look at what was going on had their name listed on a pad for further action, whatever that might be. We would soon find out. To be in the corporal's note pad was to be in deep crapola as everyone put it.

We were dismissed and told to follow each of the three corporals to our billets. My bed and locker were on the second floor of a brand new billet and I had a top bunk. It was located right beside the emergency exit and fire escape. The fire escape was a long chute-like slide that led to the ground outside the main door. The door to the fire escape could only open from the inside. There were two pump fire extinguishers, filled with water, located on each side of the door. The red exit sign was lit and cast an eerie dull glow over my bunk. I had no idea who was going to be in the lower bunk but I'd find out soon enough.

There was a double locker assigned to each of us and these were located between the bunks. You had to make your personal effects fit. There was no other storage. This presented a problem for many fellows who, I am sure, brought along all their worldly possessions. They looked for additional space from their fellow recruits.

"When you are completely installed gentlemen - and child," he was looking right at me, "you will stand at the foot of your bunk and wait for me to come around. Do you understand me? Junior! Do you understand my request?" he asked.

"Yes Corporal Morrow."

He looked at me and shook his head as he moved along the rows of bunks. "All right. Now hear me! You will follow my assistants to the hospital. You may be there for some time. When you have completed your examinations, you will proceed with my assistants to the supply depot for your equipment and uniform. I

want you all completed and in uniform before supper time. Do you hear me?" he shouted.

"Yes, Corporal Morrow," we answered. I was learning to answer quietly and to lower my voice as much as I could.

If the fifty men in our flight had been issued numbers, I'm sure I would have been number fifty. I was virtually a non-entity, redundant. I don't know how it happened but every time I'd get in line everyone would walk in front of me as if I wasn't there. I tried to protest and to shove back. All that got me was a cuff on the head. I didn't feel I was in any position to make a scene. Corporal Morrow would not see it my way I was sure.

I was still waiting for my medical when several of the recruits were marching off for their uniforms. They made passing remarks about what we were in for. "Oh boy, you guys don't know pain until you go through those MOs (Medical Officers)."

"Cough hard you guys." Whatever that meant. Most of us had never had a full medical before in our lives so this was a new experience and it showed. We were all nervous and fidgety and asked those who were coming out how it was and if it hurt. There were some pretty wild stories too. Tales of big guys keeling over when it came time for their needles.

I finally came to a desk where an elderly MO sat making notes. "Well son, what can we do for you?" he asked.

"I've come for my medical. I'm a recruit for Flight Crew, Sir."I answered.

"You are a what for what?" he chuckled.

"I am a flight trainee coming for a medical."

"My God sergeant, what is this child asking of us?" he asked his clerk. "Sit down son," he ordered. "Fill out the questionnaire and I'll ask you some questions." I finished the questions and was asked to undress down to my shorts. Then along came another doctor who gave me a needle, an inoculation by scratching and then another needle. I felt like a pin cushion. They listened to my lungs and heart, tapped my chest, pushed on my stomach, and made me cough while squeezing my testicles. I now knew what the guys meant when they told us to "cough hard". I had never done this before.

"What the hell goes here? I can't find your nuts child," he

laughed. So did everyone else standing in line. How humiliating. "Bend over and touch your toes lad," he instructed me. I bent over while he inserted his index finger up my behind.

"Ow," I squeaked. It was like getting an enema with a broom handle.

"This examination is to determine if you have a prostate problem or haemorrhoids," he explained. I had never heard of such a thing and I suspect the others hadn't either, judging from their grunts and groans. Well they sure knew now.

"What is this about your "Lazy Colon Syndrome"," he asked, reading from my file.

"Sir, I have had this since I was a very small child and ordinary medicines and laxatives make me very ill," I told him.

"Does this occur often?" he asked.

"No sir, not often," I told him, only partly stretching the truth. He made me lie on his table while he pushed and shoved on my stomach again.

"Sergeant, take him to x-ray for a barium enema. I want the results as soon as possible. In the meantime tell the Flight Corporal that this boy will be delayed a short time." I was told to pick up my clothes and move on down the corridor with the sergeant. I knew what was coming and tried to act as nonchalant as possible. Two fellows were coming out of the x-ray room while I was waiting. I wondered what they had x-rayed. They left for their uniforms. Obviously they had passed. I hoped I would pass too. "Please God, let me pass," I quietly prayed.

I was ushered into the change room and told to undress and put on the smock they handed me. Then a nurse came in. She looked familiar somehow. Hooolly! It was nurse Nora Burchill, the nurse I had in the Calgary hospital four years ago. She had given me my barium x-ray when I was thirteen. She recognized me. "Well, Skipper! Dear boy, we meet again after so long a time. Still got your little problem I see?" The doctor asked her about it and she told him what it was and that my bowel was perfectly healthy, no disease.

"Well, in that case little man you will be spared the x-ray on Burch's recommendation," he said. Nurse Burchill told the doctor what was prescribed for me because I couldn't hold down medicine.

"Burch, how come you can remember this little guy from so long ago?" the doctor asked. "Is he actually old enough to be here?"

"He was such a nice boy how could I forget him? He's a cowboy you know, in fact a rodeo cowboy," she said. I was embarrassed.

"Okay, make arrangements with the infirmary to look after him whenever he comes in. I'll make it a standing order."

"Thanks doctor, the nurse replied." I also thanked him and then hurried to dress and get out of there. Nurse Burchill said she was happy to see me and was glad she was able to help. I thanked her and departed. I knew I would be seeing her sooner or later.

I ran over to the supply depot because I was afraid I would be late and knew what that would mean. I was late but Corporal Morrow stood patiently by as they tried to find a uniform to fit me. This was not going to be easy. They tried all sizes until finally he said. "That's it. He will take that last one. Fit or not, he wears it until you can get him his right size. Understand me?" he yelled to the clerks in the depot. It was obvious they understood.

I took the parts of my uniform that fit and struggled along the parade square to my billet. Hooolly! I couldn't find it. I was lost. There were usually lots of people walking around but not now. No one. Panic was about to claim me. Hooolly! I knew it was the new building but in my haste not to be late, I had forgotten its location. I was paralysed with fear. There was no one coming along except, you guessed it, Nurse Burchill.

"Hi Ho, Skipper Boy, what's the trouble?" she asked.

"I can't remember where my billet is ma'am," I answered, embarrassed at my stupidity. When I told her it was a new billet, she took me right to the doorstep.

"Okay Skippy, don't get lost again, I might not be around," she smiled. I did appreciate what she had done for me and I told her so. "Did you ever expect to see me again after your visit to me in Calgary?

"No ma'am. Meaning no disrespect ma'am but I hoped not. "I understand Skipper and good luck. It really is a small world, isn't it?" she said, walking away. She was a big woman and wore her officer's uniform with great pride. She was a warrant officer and looked very smart.

I entered the building and climbed the stairs to my quarters. I really struggled with all my gear, dropping it on my bunk. To my surprise, Mark, my friend whom I met on the train, had taken over the lower bunk. He helped me get my things stored away. "We have to get into our uniforms or we can't go for supper," he explained. I rushed to get into my uniform and although the shirt and the underwear fit, the uniform did not.It was way too big and the pants dragged on the floor. Even wearing suspenders didn't hold them high enough. My wedge cap fit though. I could have fit two of me into my tunic it was so big. The boots and socks fit so, all in all, if you didn't have to look at me, I might pass for a service man.

We were called to attention and once again we were inspected. The corporal assisting Corporal Morrow looked me over and suggested I stand behind the others so the corporal wouldn't see me. I was only too willing to oblige.

We marched haphazardly to the mess, where we ate. I knew that I was not a very good cook but I could sure do better than these guys. Ugh! What a meal. They must have taken instruction as to how to ruin perfectly good food.

We were marched back to our billets and dismissed for the evening. We were told to read our manuals on discipline and drill and other things like that. I sat on my bunk reading and memorizing everything in the book while Mark and some of the others decided they would walk around the base. I decided to join them. The base was huge and there were airmen everywhere. Transport trucks and other vehicles raced around carrying out their specific tasks. We were told that every time we passed the main flag in the parade square we were to salute it the way they had instructed. We practised on everyone we passed, officer or not.   Each day we marched and drilled either inside or outside, depending on the weather and availability of space. We learned how to pack our backpacks so they weighed exactly 38 lbs. We also learned how to pack these heavy weights on our backs around the parade square several times. It was called duty discipline. We carried rifles, practised rifle drill and even got to shoot at targets. I usually got knocked on my arse by the recoil of the damned thing.

We marched miles and miles with the corporal calling cadence.

Someone or maybe even all of us had goofed off and we were being punished by being made to march around the parade square with full packs. It was midnight when we finished. I just about collapsed. We were not alone as it was quite common to find recruits marching the parade square at all hours of the day or night.

We were given evening passes after our first week and could go off the base and into town if we chose. We were to report for duty at 0700 hours Monday. I had no place to go and I sure didn't want to be seen in that terrible fitting uniform. My new uniform had not yet arrived so I decided to stay on base. I changed into my shorts and a T-shirt and decided to wander around the base and familiarize myself some more. I was questioned everywhere I went by MPs (military policemen) and asked to produce my ID card. What a bore. Most of the airmen once they got their uniforms on, hardly ever took them off. I think they even wore them to bed. I chose to stay close to base as I did not have a proper fitting uniform and besides it itched terribly so it didn't bother me not to wear it.

One time I was being questioned by an MP, when who should arrive but my friend, Nurse Burchill. "Any problem here corporal?" she asked.

"No ma'am, just checking that this boy is allowed on the base," he replied.

"Oh, he's allowed on the base all right, he is Aircrew personnel." She smugly ordered him to be off.

"What are you up to Skippy, all dressed up and no where to go? No wonder they stop you, you look like a school boy," she laughed.

"I was just looking around. I didn't want to go into town with that terrible uniform, so I thought I would stay here," I informed her.

"You'll do nothing of the sort. Come with me," she ordered. We checked out through the gate and I followed her to her car.

"Get in Skip, I'm going to show you where I live, then you'll have some place to go," she smiled. I\ got in and we drove about two miles to the house she was renting. Brandon was not a very large city and I could easily find my way here.

Her house was a bright two-storey home. The living room reflected Burch's taste for plain homey furnishings. She took me on a tour throughout the whole house and told me I could have the

spare bedroom to sleep in if I ever wanted to stay overnight.

"Your home is very nice ma'am," I said.

"Look Skippy, when we're off the base you can call me Burch like all my friends," she said, putting her arm around my shoulder. "I think we've known each other long enough to be called friends, don't you?" she asked, chuckling at the curious look on my face. "I'm going to make some hot chocolate, want some?" she asked. I thanked her for her hospitality. She was being very friendly and kind. We sat and ate cookies and drank hot chocolate on her front porch until late. We talked about Calgary and her job with the government, and how it turned into an Airforce appointment. "He's rather like you in a lot of ways." She told me her husband was overseas as the head maintenance officer with Six Group Bomber Command. He had been over for almost two years. She really missed him but then it was war and she felt she was doing her part. "My son George is in Winnipeg visiting his Grandmother. He'll be home tomorrow evening.

"Ma'am?" I started.

"Skipper, I'm Burch, remember?"

"Burch, how come you're being so nice to me and everything? We only met that one time in Calgary?" I recalled.

"Oh Skippy, that's where you're wrong. I watched you win the Junior Boys calf roping contest in High River at the Little Britches Rodeo and your very first event at the Millarville Races and again in Calgary at the Stampede. You see, George and I are rodeo nuts. I remembered who you were when I first heard your name called to ride. I was really proud of you when you won your trophies," she bubbled over with her enthusiasm. "I told my friends that I knew you very personally. I had x-rayed your little posterior," she laughed, recalling the occasion. I blushed.

I had been issued a weekend pass so Burch insisted I stay the night. She ran a bath for me and after the showers in our billets this was heaven with no harassing to go with it. I had good reason to hate the showers. The other airmen were always making remarks about my not having any body hair and about what they called "My Boyhood". I usually waited until everyone was through and this made me late for breakfast, which I sometimes had to miss, and then

I would be late for parade.

It was nice and quiet at Burch's. I never heard anything all night until I awoke and heard her downstairs, rummaging in the kitchen. She had a beautiful breakfast prepared, the best I had eaten since leaving home.

It was so peaceful here, much different from the billets where every nasty trick in the book had been thrown my way. The jokesters had even thrown me naked out of the fire escape chute. Some WDs (women's division) had been passing by and one of them gave me her jacket to cover up with until I got to the door. If it wasn't one thing it was another. So being here at Burch's was almost my salvation. I did make the best of it.

The guys were asking me where I went on evening passes or on weekends. I told them I had family here and would visit them. Only the Senior Medical Officer knew I was Burch's young visitor. Actually, she helped me over this terrible transition period like no one else could have.

Burch had rank and used it where necessary. She was a big woman with a heart of gold. I didn't know that when I first met her in the Calgary General Hospital. I remembered how ill I felt and my frame of mind was far from the best as were the circumstances of our meeting. She had been quite friendly as I remembered her and I had been scared and unhappy.

I was usually in my summer shorts with either a sweater or T-shirt. I don't think anyone knew I was an airman. A man asked me one day, when I was mowing the lawn, if I was one of Burch's sons. "Well, sort of," I replied.

Burch overheard our conversation and told me she would have been proud to have been my mother. Things were being made tolerable in an otherwise unbearable situation.

I was truly being spared when I knew I should be going through all the growing-up agonies like everyone else. I would have to stand up for myself if I were ever going to mature. Well, the other recruits weren't small and didn't have to endure all the rotten tricks and abuse I did. They seemed to handle things a lot better than I could. I was blaming all my misfortune on my being small when in fact it was my own attitude. I was so used to being intimidated that I had

come to expect it.

My uniform came and surprise, surprise, it fit! Burch was there when I first put it on to make sure they had fit it properly. I spent a lot of time with George and Burch as it got me away from the base for awhile.

I was making out just fine on the written exams, in fact I was second in the course. Ten of the top students were slated for Officer Training but not me. I was told I qualified but I was too small and too young. Burch felt unhappy for me but there was nothing she could do about it.

"Burch, I'm being cheated. Every time I turn around it's the same thing. I hate it. How can I ever measure up?" I asked.

We were into our third week when my stomach started acting up. I knew it was only a matter of time but I had been hoping against hope that it wouldn't start until I had been posted elsewhere. I told Burch that I was going to the infirmary in the morning.

I went to report in to sick parade. This is where all the malingerers came to get out of their daily duties and drills. Not me though, I really had a stomach ache. I didn't see Burch anywhere so I presumed she was busy elsewhere.

I was ushered into a treatment room and told to wait. An orderly would be in to look after me. To my annoyance, who should be the orderly but one of the guys who had been bugging me in the billets.

"Well, hello little one, we meet again and under almost the same circumstances, huh? You know I really am sorry about what we did to you that night. (He was referring to the soaking they gave me with the fire extinguishers.) "I was really drunk, I wouldn't have done that otherwise," he apologized.

"It's done, let's get this over with,"I said. He finished and then left me alone.

One day, during a drill session, we were made to climb a heavy rope that hung from the roof. The rope was slung over one of the roof beams about 30 feet above the floor. The idea was to climb hand over hand to the top then slide down again. Some guy, when he got to the top, untied the rope and slid down the rope on the other side, pulling the climbing rope with him. "Okay, who's the smart jockey who has disrupted my drill?" Corporal Morrow shouted. No

one owned up to the misdeed. "Then we shall simply stay here until the rope is either tied back up again or the smart guy owns up."

I spotted a small rope used to support a volleyball net. "Corporal Morrow, I can get your rope back up again," I said.

"Well, you just come over here and tell me how you plan to do this. It had better be good hadn't it little man?" he remarked sarcastically. I was wishing I had kept my mouth shut.

I untied the net rope, tied it to the end of the larger climbing rope and coiled it for a throw. It was long enough to sail over the beam but the tough part was getting it through the narrow space between the roof joists and the roof. I tossed the rope easily between the trusses, under the roof and over the beam. There was enough of the coil to carry over the beam and down to the floor. This had certainly been my lucky day. What if I had failed? I thought.

Everyone applauded my effort as a bit of entertainment. We tied the end of the heavy rope to the end of the smaller line and pulled it up. Another guy climbed the rope to the top and made it fast. Hooolly! Now maybe they would know I was around. The corporal, as well as several recruits, wanted to know how I learned to throw a rope like that. "I'm a rancher," I explained. It seemed my little exploit had added a few inches to my stature. I wasn't just a little kid any more.

I had completed each day without having missed any duties or drills and was told I had the week end off. Some chaps talked about getting hotel rooms and others about taking in the big town. Others talked about taking the train into Winnipeg. I said I was going to visit friends and told Mark I would see him on Monday. As luck would have it, I was slated for Duty Flight on Friday night. I had to be on call. I couldn't leave base until Saturday morning. I'd have to let Burch know.

I got up bright and early the next morning and left. I loaded my backpack with jeans, shorts and a sweater and headed out to Burch's. She wasn't home when I got there. It seemed she had pulled DUTY OFFICER that night. George had already laid out breakfast for us. We ate and then I decided to catch up on a little reading. Burch always had lots of reading material around.

I was lying out on the balcony enjoying the beautiful sunshine

and getting a tan, when Burch arrived home. "I heard something about you today, young man," she whispered.

"Now what have I done, Burch?" I asked.

"You surprised the daylights out of a few of your drill instructors, I hear. Pretended you were back in the Stampede, huh?" she laughed. "I heard you saved the day for a few guys in your drill squad. Nice going there Skippy boy. Good for you, that'll show them." She had a big grin on her face.

We started talking about Ken and Peggy and my friends as well as my music. She wished she had a piano for me to play but suggested we walk down to her church and she would let me play their organ. She told me she knew all about my organ playing from Ken.

"We'll go down town for supper. How about that? My treat."

"Only if you let me pay. I would like to Burch, please?" I pleaded.

"Can you afford it? George and I are big eaters."

"Yes ma'am, I can afford it. You never let me pay for anything," I told her.

"You're our guest and we love having you here," she said. She was so thoughtful and kind to me. I was truly being spoiled. This is not how the military works. It tries to make men out of raw material and train them to fight wars. They are not to be babied or mollycoddled. Burch was very good to listen to all my tales of woe and would sit and talk me through my problems. These mostly concerned my relationship with the rest of the flight. They called me a smart-ass. All my boot licking wasn't going to get me my commission.

"Skip, I've been meaning to talk to you about what happened to you in the billets," she said. I knew what she was referring to but tried to make out I didn't understand.

"What do you mean Burch? What are you talking about?" I replied.

"Skippy don't play dumb with Burch, huh. The fire extinguisher episode," she said.

"How do you know about that?" I asked.

"Well you know how people talk and especially big mouths. I overheard them talking the day you came into the infirmary. I was in the operating theatre right beside the desk. I overheard the corporal telling another guy about what they had done to the little kid in the

new billets. I knew they were talking about you."

"Oh, that time," I said.

"The orderly is no longer on this base. I had him moved to Davidson, Saskatchewan, the worst base on earth. That will teach him. Did those drunks hurt you?" she asked.

"I was really afraid Burch, but they didn't hurt me although I was sure soaking wet," I replied.

She laughed. "You are sure some sort of kid. I'm sorry, I don't mean to call you a kid all the time but you are just a little kid to me," she chuckled.

I dressed and we went out to dinner and a long walk. We dropped by her church and I played the organ for half an hour. I enjoyed myself and Burch was delighted. George was bored.

Burch towered over me although I had grown almost another two inches since spring. "Burch, can I ask you a sort of personal question?" I asked.

"Go ahead, shoot," she replied.

"Why have I not grown like most other guys, why am I so small? I don't shave or have any hair on my body like I should," I asked.

"Because you're just late starting into puberty. You know what puberty is don't you Skip?" She asked. "Well Skipper, you're barely starting. You're just a late bloomer. One day you'll just take off and you'll wonder what hit you," she said.

"Yeah, well I wish it would hurry. Will it make me grow in my body too?" I asked.

"Yes Skipper it will, or at least a little. It may be you'll just be a short man," she laughed.

"Ah, come on Burch don't say that," I pleaded.

"You're going to grow just fine, you wait and see," she assured me.

It was dark when we got home and the sky was bright with stars. It was so beautiful we decided to sit on the porch and talk some more. George and I were both nodding and she told us to get away to bed.

"Goodnight Burch and thank you for everything," I said. I was laying on top of my bed because of the heat and was just dozing off when Burch came to the doorway. I pretended to be asleep. She tiptoed over to the bed, leaned over and kissed my cheek. I was

ready for her. I suddenly reached up, put my arms around her neck and kissed her back.

"You crazy kid, I thought you were asleep.

"I wasn't asleep, just kidding. I knew you were going to do that. I just wanted to kiss you back." She grew red and hugged me. I said goodnight and went to sleep.

Burch really was some kind of lady. She was my friend when I needed one most. I have never forgotten Burch nor did she forget me. We wrote to each other all the time and we were to run into each other on several occasions, professionally and otherwise.

I was posted out two weeks later to Trois-Rivieres Quebec for Elementary Flying Training. I was going to be a pilot.

I did not go home to Winnipeg on my leave before going east. My family was at the lake anyways, so I stayed with Burch. She was happy to have me and I was content to be there.

When my leave was up, she came down to the train to see me off. We both shed a few tears. Most of the other recruits from my course had long gone and new fellows were being ushered into my old billet. I knew what they were to go through and I knew too that they would make it. I did, even if I did have a lot of help. I was lucky to have Burch enter into my life at a time when I needed someone.

THE PILOT

I had never been in an aircraft before and the thought of learning to fly one was both exciting and more than a bit frightening.

At Manning Depot all airmen wanted to be aircrew. There were many who were not selected and were assigned other duties in the Airforce. I was thrilled and relieved when my name appeared on the bulletin board. Not only had I been selected for aircrew but for pilot training. I was one of the lucky ones as there were only a few that fell into that category. The others were to go to gunnery, navigation or wireless training schools across the country.

There were several EFTS (Elementary Flying Training School) centres and I was posted to Trois-Rivieres, Quebec (Three Rivers). I had never been to Eastern Canada before and I looked forward to it. Someone joked that either you learned to speak French or you didn't learn to fly.

There were five of us posted to Trois-Rivieres and the next course was starting in three days. This meant travelling to the East as fast as we could get there. We boarded the train in Brandon with Winnipeg being our first stop. We were only there long enough to load more military recruits, then headed East. I didn't call my parents as I just wanted to get away and on with my training.

Our flying training would be done on the ancient Tiger Moth built by the De Havilland Aircraft Company in England. This was a two place open cockpit bi-plane. My first familiarization flight left me at a loss for words. It was hard to put anything into words while my heart was in my mouth. The instructor who took me up was a little concerned about my legs being too short and my not being able to apply full rudder.

I could reach the rudder pedals all right but had to admit that I had to shift forward in my seat to be able to push the pedals to the fullest extent of their travel. I wondered why that was so important until he did a demonstration spin. I think he was trying to see if he could frighten me. I learned later that it was one of the ways to get an idea on how the student might manage his course.

Having never been near an aircraft before was one thing but to suddenly find myself in the air, high above the ground with the wind blowing in my face, was another. I suddenly found my body wanting to propel itself out of the cockpit. The plane tumbled through the air heading for the ground and, I was sure, my demise. I had the distinct urge to relieve my bladder.

I felt the rudder pedals push my right foot back and the control stick in between my legs almost yank me into the instrument panel. Luckily, it was padded with sponge rubber. I presumed this was for just such an occasion as this. I was glad it was there as my face was mashed into the rubber.

The plane straightened itself from its twisting and headed straight down, presenting another problem for me to face. I was happy when I felt the nose of the plane coming up, at the same time I was being pressed down into the seat. The muscles in my face started to pull downward so much that I was certain my cheeks would be permanently located in my neck. I had given up trying to see what was happening as my eyes had disappeared into the space vacated by my cheeks. Hoooollyy!

The instructor had me follow through on the controls as we did lazy eights and a few other manoeuvres. When we landed he seemed pleased and informed me that I had passed this first flight. "How did you ever get into Pilot Training? You really are too short for it. You must have done well in your exams for them to allow you to come this far. I'm going to try something before you start your flying training. I'm going to make you a couple of pedal blocks that will build them up so you can get full use of the rudder," he said. "I'll be your instructor so I'll have them ready for you when you start. Keep this to yourself for awhile," he said, checking around to see if anyone had heard us. I liked him and it was obvious he liked me.

As was the case in Manning Depot I was subjected to the same sort of treatment. Too young, too small, too almost anything. In spite of it all I passed all my ground school courses and my flight training, in particular my aerobatic skills. In March '44 I was posted to No. 3 SFTS (Service Flying Training School) in Calgary for the next phase of my training.

I was ecstatic when I heard the news because I would be close to my friends and the ranch.

We were about to start the final stage of our training where we would be flying more sophisticated aircraft and engaging in more advanced flying. We flew Harvards (AT6), Cornells and Chipmunks. All were low wing mono-planes with two cockpits and the instructor usually flew in the rear seat.

We flew cross-country navigation flights and learned instrument flying. I did quite well and had no trouble with either the flight or ground school classes. I still used my wooden rudder blocks and thought I might always have to use them.

I went to the ranch on my few day passes and on my one week's leave before graduation. It was a very happy time for me. Ken was away in the army and that rather spoiled my visit but everyone else was happy to see me home.

On the day before my graduation, my Father called to tell me that the Commanding Officer was a personal friend of his and that he had been invited to present me with my wings if I wanted him to. I was flattered that he would want to do that but I would much rather have had Ken do it.

I was very surprised but decided that this would be good for both my Father and me. I hoped it would help our relationship which, until now, had almost been non-existent.

The ceremony went off well and my Father made the presentation, as did several other parents. June was a happy month for me. I had finally turned eighteen and only two weeks later received my wings.

The biggest disappointment for me came when several of our course's top students were promoted to Pilot Officer. We had heard that the top ranking students would be chosen for officer training. I was one of three students in first place and it appeared I was headed for a commission. I was interviewed and complimented on my high marks and excellent airmanship however, because I was so young and didn't appear to be officer material I was denied the promotion. Even my course mates couldn't believe what had taken place.

I was very discouraged at not getting my commission. To me it was just another part of a long list of disappointments. It bothered

me that discrimination not only existed in civilian life but also here in the military. It seemed to me you were judged on not what you knew or your ability but by how you looked.

My father discussed the matter of my commission with the Commanding Officer who was very sympathetic but felt, as the selection board had, that I looked like a school kid and therefore couldn't command the respect required of an officer. The course members were all excited as we read the postings sheet. Several were being posted overseas right away. Some were going to transport command while others were sent to coastal command. Some were categorized as Service Pilots and would be going to Bombing, Gunnery, Navigation and Wireless Training Schools. They would then fly the aircraft that the various trades would learn on. I nearly cried when I found my name was on that list. Hooolllyy! I didn't want to do that kind of flying. I wanted to be in the war.

In July I was informed that I was being posted to No. 9 Bombing and Gunnery School in Mont-Joli, Quebec. I would be flying Fairey Battles that had a gun turret mounted on the top of the fuselage behind the pilot's cockpit. It looked like a big brother to the Hawker Hurricane, a front line fighter from the first days of the war. I couldn't help thinking that my Father had something to do with this posting away from the war as I was sure he was trying to prevent me from going overseas.

Mont-Joli proved to be the most desolate training base in Canada. It was located on the Gaspe Peninsula in Quebec. In fact, it felt like we were in another country where everyone spoke French. I was not impressed and already was making plans on how I could get out of there.

The British built Fairey Battle carried three gunnery trainees. They'd crawl into the aircraft through a hatch in the underside of the aircraft. One would go into the turret for his turn while the other two would sit under the turret on the floor. The fumes from the engine poured into the compartment almost suffocating the poor airmen. Most of the time they got sick and puked on each other. It was awful and the poor gunners had to clean up their own mess. I felt very badly for them until one day I heard a few of

them complaining to the Operations Officer. They were objecting to being flown by a "Kid". I stopped feeling sorry for them after that.

I called my Father and told him I knew he was responsible for my posting and I wanted out of here as fast as he could arrange something. He sounded shocked that I would think of such a thing but three days later my orders came through sending me to Halifax for embarkation aboard the Dutch Steamship "New Amsterdam".

I had never been aboard a ship before and the talk amongst the troops and airmen was on how to keep your rectum from being puked up over the side of the ship from seasickness. I was lucky, I didn't throw up but I sure felt like it as we had bad weather all the way across.

We were informed that the weather would keep the German U Boats from attacking us. No one cared about the bad weather after that. All in all it was a very exciting and new experience for me and I was even getting so I could tolerate all the wise cracks about the "Junior Airman". They weren't going to get to me.

Six days later we arrived at the port of Gurrock in Scotland. I was glad to have finally arrived and able to get off the ship. I think everyone had had a belly full of mountainous waves and seasickness.

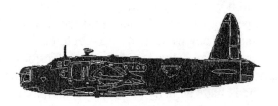

Vickers Wellington

BANFF TO OTU

Our trip from Gurrock in Scotland to Bournemouth, a resort town on the south coast of England, was a most interesting one as at each stop the train was inundated with children clambering for chocolate and cigarettes. "Hey Canada, how about some sweets for me Mum and Dad." Every station brought forth the kids. It had been a long time since they had seen chocolate, gum or candy of any kind. The Americans and Canadians presented too good a source for these scarce commodities. The Americans, of course, were a much better supplied group than the Canadians but I don't think the kids had too much to complain about.

On arriving in Bournemouth, we were greeted by the Luftwaffe, which was not quite what we had expected. A greeting party yes, but with ME 109s, hardly. They came racing in from the Channel, over the pier and up the little valley leading to the park. The beautiful coastal gardens were their targets.

Mothers and nannies were wheeling their prams around the square while children played on the grass nearby. No one saw or heard the planes rushing in and this was my first sight of the enemy I was about to fight.

They shot up the entire garden and square area, killing hundreds, mostly women and children. From a tactical point of view, Herr Goehring must have considered this a major coup in the annals of psychological warfare.

The entire city was in chaos and mourning. A major depression hit everyone. There was no joy or happiness as was usually the case in this major resort town. It was a disaster. This was the real thing and not just a game. What a cowardly thing to do using helpless women and kids as targets.

We were billeted in the most elegant hotels that normally housed the rich and famous. Mind you, they had all been boarded up to protect the windows and the finer ornamentation but still they were beautiful buildings.

We were told we would be here for a week or so and would be indoctrinated into our new surroundings. We would eventually be assigned to the various training squadrons throughout the country.

The next day, after familiarization, we were given medicals to ensure our new masters that we were indeed of good Canadian stock. The way the MOs prodded and jabbed us with everything from needles and wooden tongue depressors to gloved fingers, there could be no question that they would uncover all of our deepest secret illnesses and they soon discovered mine.

Once again, I provided the laughs for the group I was in. "Did your nanny leave you at the hotel by mistake?" or " When is your mother coming for you?" or "Where did you get the uniform kid?" and so it went. I was really developing a hard shell to protect me.

Whenever it got too bad I'd just walk away and be by myself and this helped. If I spoke up or fought back I got a punch in the face or worse.

"Where had I obtained the Pilot's jacket?" one Officer questioned.

"I am Sergeant Pilot Skipper Douglas Scott, those are my sergeant stripes and those are my Wings, care to see my ID card-- Sir?" I snarled in my worst soprano voice. This only brought on more laughter. Oh well, so be it.

The MO apologized and told me he had heard about the boy who was passing through their hallowed halls and that he only wanted to have a little fun.

We would parade in the mornings then do a phys. ed. program followed by a three mile run. Then we would all rush to see who was on the DROs (Daily Routine Orders) for postings. These came out each morning at 1100 hrs. You looked for your name and then read your orders. After four days, my name appeared on the DROs.

It was October and I was being sent to the ATU (Advanced Training Unit) in Banff, Scotland. Banff lay almost at the northernmost part of Scotland, on the Moray Firth, and it was beautiful. The air base was nestled in amongst the rolling hills. It was from this base we would be trained in flying SBAs (Standard Beam Approaches), night missions and bomb runs. We would be training on the twin engine Oxford. It looked a lot like the Cessna

Crane or T50 that we flew at SFTS in Calgary.

This was great flying and the airplanes we had were superb performers. Not like the Cessna in this regard at all. This airplane could fly on one engine and in many cases that is exactly what we were required to do. Shut down one engine on the Cessna Crane and you were going down.

Aircraft recognition was another major undertaking. We had to know what a German aircraft looked like and how to tell it from our own. I guess too many of our own aircraft had been shot down by mistaken identity.

Throughout the winter, we flew many cross-country missions amongst the hills and valleys and sometimes in marginal weather conditions. It was quite nerve racking to say the least. I got along well with my instructors and gave them no trouble. They were all Royal Airforce types with funny British accents that reminded me of Michael and Eric Stacey-Barnes.

The instructors gave me a large cushion to put behind me to keep me from sliding too far back in the seat. The closer to the controls the better control I had. Everyone seemed to think I was destined for fighters because of my size and they felt I had the skills to make it. I even had a couple of blocks made to fit over the rudder pedals because they could not be adjusted any closer.

The major discussion at meal times was about who was going to be posted where, and when. There were fourteen of us and I think we guessed every posting except two and these chaps were failing the course.

Two were going to Coastal Command and ten were going to Bomber Command, as they seemed to have the greatest need due to their heavy losses at the time. Two were slated for fighters and I was happy when they chose me as one of them. We were delighted when the postings actually appeared in DROs. I took some ribbing about how much I had paid the brass to give me a fighter assignment. I was so thrilled with the posting that I was beside myself. I tried to act nonchalant about the whole matter but failed miserably. I was so happy I couldn't hide it. Ken had always told me that when we got a little too high and mighty we could sure as "All Friday" expect an "Almighty Fall".

We all graduated shortly after the postings and soon we were all packed up and heading out. The month had gone by very quickly. It seemed that we had just arrived and here we were on our way again. Usually the time was about five weeks, however, our group did very well and made it in four. The weather never once turned so bad that we couldn't get our flying assignments done.

I had packed all my things and was heaving away on my flight bag when a big guy came along and offered to carry it for me. "Thanks a lot. I sometimes have one heck of a time moving all my stuff," I explained.

"It's okay kid, I just can't stand to see little guys getting screwed around that's all," he said. I wondered who he was. He wore pilot's wings but I couldn't place him. Then it came to me. He was one of the "Washouts" who was being reassigned to navigator school. He wished me luck and said he really envied me being small and having been selected for fighter training. I thanked him again and we walked slowly to the transport that was to take us to the rail station. For once, I was feeling that being small did have its advantages now and again.

I was just getting on board when a sergeant policeman called my name. He informed me that there had been a re-assignment and that I was not going to fighters. I was being posted to R.A.F. Three Group Bomber Command at Chedburgh. This was an O.T.U. (Operational Training Unit). My heart dropped right through my feet. "There must be some mistake," I complained.

"Take it to the brass, don't complain to me Chumly," he said, not the least bit sympathetic. Well, I sure as heck wasn't his CHUMLY and I was furious. What could a little punk like me ever do to make a case for myself?

I went to the officer in charge and asked whose authority had reassigned me. "Well chappy, it appears that Three Group Bomber Command needs your outstanding expertise immediately and so it is there you will go, correct Chum?" he smirked sarcastically. I was so disappointed, I had to get away by myself for a while. I had really wanted to join a fighter wing. All my course mates and my instructors claimed I was fighter pilot material. I wiped my eyes as the sergeant in charge of the pool trucks told me to get my stuff and

get aboard the transport headed for O.T.U. I didn't have much time to wonder what was going on because they soon changed their minds, again. Now instead of O.T.U. Chedburgh, I was being sent to O.T.U. base Chipping Warden. This was an operational drome as well as a training unit. They were operating Wellingtons (Wimpys) on mine laying operations.

There were seven of us and it took us about two hours to reach the base. As was usually the case, these other pilots were much older than I was. I think most were in their mid-twenties.

We arrived and were ushered into the main drill hall where we milled around waiting for billet assignments. We were told we could, at some early point in our stay, get together with other chaps who would like to fly together and form a crew.

On December 15 the pilots or captains, as we were called, were to get together with navigators, bomb aimers, radio operators, engineers and gunners. It was a case of everyone looking for the most qualified and available crewmembers. The captains were to check the credentials and log books of each member but I don't think anyone checked anything. It seemed a strange way to form a crew but the system worked and most crews stuck together for their entire tour of operations. The various trades would search around for a pilot they liked the looks of and ask if he had need of a gunner or engineer or whatever his trade might be. The pilot would look them over, go for a beer or two in the mess and so a crew was born. This plan worked well and for the most part the crews were harmonious in nature and attitudes.

On the day, we were to be formally recognized as crews the pilots gathered at one end of the drill hall while the other crewmembers milled around in the centre. Some were still looking for positions remaining to be filled but no one looked to me. The fact that I had lost my kit bag containing my uniform and personal effects didn't help my appearance much. All I had to wear was my T-shirt and a pair of jeans. I guess I didn't look much like a captain. No one approached me nor did anyone I talk to want to fly with me. "Sorry, but I'm crewed already," they would say.

I was standing with the rest of the pilots when I heard the adjutant shouting out the names of the captains. He called my name

and I shouted "Here Sir." All eyes turned towards the soprano voice and the laughter started. "What the hell are you doing there?" he shouted, as he sent an assistant to check me out. I explained the situation regarding my lost kit bag to the corporal and he seemed convinced. He returned to the adjutant and whispered in his ear. I was pretty sure of what was being said. The officer just shook his head. The laughter had stopped as he continued calling out captain's names.

"When I call your name," he shouted at the pilots, "I want you to go over to the west wall where your crews will form up on you." He then addressed the remaining crewmembers. "Gentlemen, please seek out your captain and wait until we have recorded the crewmembers. Here was where I was having another problem. I was embarrassed, as I stood alone as everyone I had approached had already joined another crew. There didn't seem to be anyone willing to join me.

As it turned out, I was there for almost two weeks while course after course came and went and each time I was left alone feeling terrible and wondering what I was going to do.

I wasn't the only one left after all the crews were completed. There were others who had not found a crew to join. If one was to be in a position to develop an inferiority complex then come and stand by me for a while.

It appeared that most of those left were much older men and several officers were mixed in the group. The adjutant came over to us one day and said, "Gentlemen, your vacation is over, we can no longer provide you with this holiday. Either you team up as a crew with what is available or we will have to reassign you to other aircrew trades. Is this clear chaps?" No one wanted this.

Flight Lieutenant Jack Buvan, a 56 year old bomb aimer from Devonshire, came over and asked me if I really was a pilot and would I be interested in a father for the remainder of the war? "God you are a wee shaver, how did you ever get this far lad?" he asked. He introduced me to Flying Officer Jack McKay, a navigator who had been a high school teacher in Australia.

"I'll fly with you lad, as long as you promise to bring me back home each time." Jack McKay was 53 and not married. Jack Buvan was married with three daughters all of whom were married. Flying

Officer Bill Barker came over then and volunteered to fly as radio operator for us. He was 48 years old and was married with a young family. In fact his son was my age and in the Navy. Good grief, another father which made three so far. Pilot Officer Johnny Carr, a flight engineer, was a Yorkshireman whose accent was to be almost the death of us. He was 30 years old, married and had a young family. The only crewmembers left to join were the gunners. There was a young chap, Flight Sergeant Hank Simms who was 26 and from Canada, Toronto to be exact, while Flight Sergeant Frank Malory was 48, a mid upper gunner, also from Toronto. Frank owned and operated a collection agency there. Unbeknownst to us, Frank was an alcoholic. A truly died in the wool lush. From the sublime to the ridiculous. These men were as desperate for a flying position as I was. Over half of my newly found crew was old enough to have fathered me and in a couple of cases to have fathered my father. I didn't need another Grandpa as I had one already. I wondered if I would ever see him again. Well, if I was to survive, these were the guys who were going to help me do it. I would do the best I could and I was to learn later that their years of wisdom and decision making would save our backsides more times than I care to remember. I grew to love them all and we really did hit it off. Desperation and determination often made strange bed partners.

We flew our way through the OTU in the age old Wellington with few problems. Actually, we were one of the few crews who finished the course almost trouble free.

So far so good. We seemed to be adjusting to each other and getting along quite well in spite of our age differences. I was depending on them and they were tolerating and encouraging me. On July 24th 1944, we were posted to a Conversion Unit.

Sterling

A STERLING IDEA

Chedburgh was an RAF operational base which was slowly being converted to a CU (Conversion Unit). The Sterlings, which just a short time before had been Britain's front line bomber, were now being used to train and convert flight crews to four engine aircraft.

Chedburgh was still an operations base with half the personnel completing their tours and the other half in training. This was quite a mix when you considered that we shared the same messing facilities. We would sit around listening to the stories the operational types told us about their trips. It was frightening but exciting too.

Their operational role was slowly being diminished. They were involved in short mini-operations such as diversionary raids over the Dutch or Norwegian coasts or mine laying operations in the Channel or North Sea. We listened spellbound for hours as they related their exciting stories. Many aircraft failed to return and some came back mangled and shot up. It was certainly giving us an insight as to what lay ahead. Rather a frightening look into the future.

Our course consisted of 10 crews and we were here to learn how to fly these four engine behemoths. They truly were ugly and huge. I stood under the wing of one of them and I barely came up to the axle hub of the wheel. It was the largest aircraft I had ever seen. Doing my preliminary walk round was a chore and most of the time I needed a ground mechanic to help me. There was no way I could ever have crawled up into the engine nacelle. Johnny, the flight engineer, helped me up so I could see what things looked like inside. Even standing on the upper part of the undercarriage, "extensions" as I called them, I was only just able to see the auxiliary power connections. I would never have been able to get up there on my own. Besides, it was Johnny's job to do that.

The Sterling was never flown with another pilot so the bomb aimer sat in that seat. On the bombing run, he would go down into his

position in the nose while the engineer would take over the seat. The inside of the beast was a large, almost cathedral like, chamber. Unlike the Lancaster, there was a second set of controls for a co-pilot.

We started our familiarization flights but because they were short of instructors, we had to wait for hours until it was our turn. Unlike the Wimpy, the whole crew came along, with the instructor sitting in the right seat.

As it happened, our first flight instructor turned out be a tall, lanky fellow who, I'm sure, hated small people. The two of us walking out to the aircraft looked like Mutt and Jeff. The instructor had completed a tour of operations and was well experienced on the Sterling. He took a complete dislike to me from the start. "You're just a little kid playing at a man's serious game of war. You have no business being here at all," he lectured, trying to put me down.

He treated me like a child, showing me everything in detail five or six times. I felt really put down and told the crew that I didn't know whether I was going to make it or not. Jack came to my aid. "Why don't you give the kid a chance. He's just as good as any pilot on the base. Just sit back and let him do his job instead of pounding him down all the time." Jack, being an officer, could talk to him that way. I thought Jack had overstepped his bounds but realized he was the senior officer.

Our first take off went quite well and the wheels were still under the aircraft after the landing. So far so good. It seemed we were still a hundred feet in the air when the wheels tweaked the ground. The crew said it wasn't bad for my first time. The instructor never screamed or grabbed the controls.

The Sterling stood very high off the ground because of its unusual under carriage. It was designed to raise the aircraft so the props wouldn't touch the ground during take-off and landing. The instructor pointed out that any amount of drift on landing was a no no as this would certainly spell the end of the undercarriage and probably the aircraft too. I saw a couple of aircraft lose their gear from crosswind landings and this made me more apprehensive than ever.

Our landings went okay. The crew yelled their approval through the intercom. "Yeah! Way to go Skipper," they yelled.

"Shut up you blokes, you know you're not supposed to make idle

conversation on the intercom. Once more and I'll pack it in," the instructor barked. I felt he was a rotten type but maybe it was just war nerves.

I made two more touch and goes both of which seemed acceptable. Jack then took over the co-pilot's seat and was now acting as my second in command. The instructor was pleased with the engineer's performance and told him so but never said anything to me.

We took courses throughout the day learning everything there was to know about the bird. Then we would go out and practice what we had learned.

Each trade had their respective training sessions. The gunners went into aircraft recognition courses and armament training while the engineers went into maintenance, the radio operators went to communications and I went into general familiarization courses on bomber operations, navigation and operational take off and landing procedures. We also received the latest tactics to evade German fighters.

I was in the NCO's mess one day with Hank, our rear gunner. We were just finishing lunch when our instructor came and sat down at our table. He started right in by telling me I should quit before I killed my crew. The bird was just too big for me and he thought that I was positively overwhelmed by the plane. "You can never fly any bird chappie if you're afraid of it. Either you fly it or it will fly you into the deck. Major prang, Chappy." I resented him calling me Chappy as I had done just as well if not better than most of the other pilots. He knew he was getting my goat. He suggested I must have been babied throughout my whole training career and had got here only through special consideration and favours. Well, bull crap to him too.

He informed me that he had asked to have my files brought to him for a review. "Why are you doing that?" I asked.

"Because Chappy, I don't think you know what the hell this is all about nor do I think you have what it takes. Besides you're just a child," he lashed out at me then got up and left. I thought I was used to this kind of "Put Down" but each time it hurt and my self esteem sustained another blow.

My size, I was convinced, was still at the root of most of my

problems. I wouldn't have had to go through this kind of CRAP if I hadn't been so small. All through my flying training, I was within the top three in all the courses. The reason that I didn't get a commission upon graduation must have been because of my size since I had performed as well as most other pilots. Perhaps I really was too young for all this. Would I wind up killing the men who had put their lives in my hands by flying with me?

Maybe the instructor was right that the plane was too large for me. I hadn't had any trouble so far. I admit I had my hands full but then so did all the others. I was getting the feel of the aircraft and growing to like the way she handled.

I was to have my final check ride with the Chief Flying Instructor (CFI) of the course who would okay me for night flying. These would be the last sessions we would spend on the Sterling and then hopefully we would be posted to a Lancaster Squadron.

I was so shaky the day of our ride that the crew spent most of their time assuring me that we were going to do just fine. "Don't think about it," they'd say. That was all well and good for them to say. They weren't in the hot seat.

We were waiting by the plane ready to get aboard and the CFI drove up in a jeep. Sitting in the front seat beside him was "Double Ugly" himself, my instructor. I could imagine what he was telling the CFI. I was doomed. This was it. Finally, after what seemed a lifetime, he got out of the jeep and "Double Ugly" drove away.

The CFI introduced himself to us. He seemed quite pleasant. "Well, you boys certainly seem to be the talk of the course. What's so special about a crew full of officers and a child pilot?" he chuckled. I wasn't sure if he was joking or was just being sarcastic. "Well chaps I'm ready if you are. Come along junior," he called and we got aboard.

X-Xray was the aircraft. I had good reason to never want to fly in a bird marked "X-Xray." Definitely, a bad omen.

There was a slight crosswind but nothing we hadn't handled before but one thing did bother me. What would he think of my cushion? It was usually carried and stowed behind the radio operator's bulkhead so I wouldn't be seen carrying it or be leaving it behind.

The CFI told us to carry on as if he wasn't there. He would sit in

the co-pilot's seat. I crawled into my seat as the CFI was climbing into his. Bill came forward and shoved the cushion under my behind. The CFI, observing the procedure, remarked, "Hmmm, I see you enjoy a little comfort in your flying lad. Good thinking. Might as well be comfortable while we can. Is that a regulation cushion?" he laughed. I was feeling a little more at ease when he gave me the okay to start up. Once again he told me to forget he was there. How in blazes did he ever think I could ignore his presence as he was sitting there watching everything I was doing?

Well, as luck would have it, "X-Xray" started first off. Sometimes over-priming and flooding would cause a fire. Then there would be an enormous belch of flame when she finally caught. This time the start went perfectly and with the engines ticking over, we got permission to taxi on the perimeter strip to the runway in use.

We did our pre-flight and engine run-up without any problems then waited for the green light from the control caravan located at the approach end of the runway. After about five minutes, I received the green light and started my roll to the runway. Still the CFI sat watching, not saying a word. He dug in his pocket and came out with an old briar pipe, which he shoved into the corner of his mouth. If ever I needed a tension breaker, it came when that pipe went into his mouth. I could see Grandpa sitting beside me and giving me his usual wink. Thank goodness for memories.

I got the second green and opened the throttles to take off setting. It was my practice to get the tail off the ground as soon as I could to get rudder control. This was a lot easier than trying to steer by the engines. No sense in tempting fate with any swing on take off. " X-Xray" rose off the runway like a gazelle. It just couldn't have been better. We flew out over the coast after clearing the anti-aircraft batteries with our IFF (Identification Friend or Foe). Over the North Sea we practised evasive action, some engine failures and so on. The CFI wanted to see how we coped with emergencies and how well we co-operated as a crew. We performed well and managed these procedures satisfactorily. Once, he cut three of our four engines. A Sterling will not fly on one engine and started to drop like a stone. He okayed me to restart the engines and we were once again heading for home.

The gunners fired bursts on their guns and the bomb aimer gave us a dummy bombing run on a little fishing boat. We arrived back at base and got a straight in clearance to land. This would either be my finest hour or my final hour. The intercom on this airplane was experiencing heavy interference from electrical circuits cutting in and out. Every time we deployed flap or lowered the undercarriage, the servo power units would create a terrible static in the intercom. The CFI was trying to say something but I couldn't hear him. Besides, I was just flaring for touch down. He was watching me and making motions with his hands. Well, ready or not, I was committed. "X-Xray " touched with a squeak just like the book called for. I thanked my lucky stars and my guardian angel for once more watching over me.

"What you say sonny?" the CFI asked.

"Nothing Sir, just talking to myself."

"Very nice flight indeed. You certainly do have a feel," he praised. "I am, I must admit, very impressed and surprised, to say the least. Your performance was not what I had come to expect." I was getting red as we taxied to the dispersal pan. The CFI gave us "a thumbs up" motion as he left the aircraft. "A delightful trip chaps," he said, walking towards his waiting jeep. I almost fainted from the release of the pressure and the tension I had been under. I had wanted this to be perfect, if for no other reason than to show them I could do it. My crew was proud of me too, pounding me on the back in support. When a crew is checked out okay, the officer's mess buys drinks on the house and everyone else buys a round. There were no such celebrations in the sergeant's mess.

In the officer's mess, my crewmembers were celebrating the success of the check ride. They had as much at stake in a successful flight as I had since it might have been their last chance for operations as well.

In spite of this successful flight, things were not so rosy elsewhere. We had tried for several nights to get our check ride for night flying but we were the last on the list. It seemed all the instructors were committed until early hours in the morning and we were the last ones to be checked. Finally, this one night, we had drawn "X-Xray" for our night ride with the plan being that the

instructor would make a couple of circuits with us then be dropped off at the control van. We would then fly two or three more circuits and turn in ourselves.

We were scheduled to take off at 2000 hrs. but it was 0200 hrs. before our instructor showed up. We could hardly keep our eyes open and thought about cancelling but figured if we ever wanted to be checked out we couldn't miss this flight.

I had dozed off in my chair while waiting. Jack shook me awake and said "Come on Skipper, it's finally our turn." Jack swore a lot and he was sure cussing when the instructor finally came over to us and told us to get our gear and move.

The lorry took us to the aircraft and the instructor advised he was going to make one circuit with us. He claimed he had a heavy day tomorrow and would need his sleep. What the heck did he think we were needing?

"X-Xray "lifted off as smoothly as usual into a bright clear sky. Our first circuit came off without any problems. "Drop me off at the tower," he said. I stopped in front of the tower and he jumped out. I got clearance and we started to move around the perimeter, for what seemed about three miles, to the active runway. There wasn't another aircraft anywhere in sight. It appeared we were the last flight making circuits. Here was just another case of discrimination against my crew and me. I was too young and my crew was too old so we could fly whenever they chose to schedule us. I think the tower was asleep as it took a long time to get my green clearance light. Finally, we took off, made a short, close-in circuit of the field, and landed. The instructor had told us to make a couple more circuits after we let him out. We were on our second circuit and I was truly sleepy. "God Skipper, are you still able to keep your eyes open?" Jack hollered through the intercom.

"I'm okay Jack, I can make this one," I assured him.

We took off and I detected a slight crosswind developing as daylight was coming on. The tower had not changed the runway so I felt it wasn't going to be too serious if the wind didn't get much stronger. A change of runway would have taken almost a half-hour to relocate the van. I decided it was okay.

On our final approach the flight engineer was in the co-pilot's

seat and would normally handle the flaps if I required any. The wind by then had swung around again and was blowing right down the runway. What a piece of good luck, particularly as I had been worrying about the crosswind and our undercarriage. I wasn't going to require any flaps at all.

The intercom started to squeal then abruptly cut out. Johnny was reaching for what I thought to be the flap lever and I made a motion "No flaps". He had in fact been reaching, rather blindly, for the locking nut on the throttle quadrant. Thinking he was about to deploy flap on me, I yelled "No Flap!" Johnny couldn't make out what I said but decided I had asked for full flaps. He thought that my shaking head meant that I was impatient that the flaps were not being deployed soon enough. Once again I yelled and we were just about to set her on when the flaps finally dropped. The aircraft ballooned a hundred feet into the air and there was no way I was going to save her with power. X-ray dropped her port wing in the initial stall and then the undercarriage hit and was immediately torn off. The aircraft dropped onto the wing tip and port outer engine. I had cut all switches by then, knowing we were doomed to crash. I was too busy trying to steer X-ray by rudder but there was nothing I could do about it. We were starting into a full blown ground loop when the starboard undercarriage came off allowing "X-Xray" to settle down onto her belly and start skidding sideways at about 75 miles an hour. "Hold on!" I yelled, but no one heard. The intercom was dead. There was a building located on the edge of the field which housed the power transformers for the runway lights. It was heavily reinforced with concrete and bricks. The aircraft hit this little structure right between the port inboard and outboard engines, severing the wing like butter. We hardly felt it but it did straighten us out so that our slide was now taking us parallel to the runway and into a swamp at the end of the field.

Many pilots, who have endured a crash, will verify that there is nothing more devastating than the helplessness you feel when you have absolutely no control over what is taking place. You just have to sit there and wonder if you are going to die within the next few minutes.

We scraped along over the road, over the perimeter track and into the swamp. Water splashed up over the windscreen and over the

entire fuselage. Finally, with one great flop, "X-Xray" raised her tail high in the air and came down with an enormous wallop. I was sure I had broken the gunner's backside, we hit so hard. There wasn't a sound except for a radio generator winding down. We were so stunned we just sat there. I tried the intercom and it worked beautifully. Why didn't it do that when I needed it? "Is everyone okay?" I called. Each position gave me their assurance that they had survived, no thanks to me. I was devastated. I knew this was the end of my flying career. "PILOT ERROR" they would call it.

The next voice we heard was that of the engineer. It is his job to inform the crew, in the event of a ditching at sea, when the dinghy has been deployed from its compartment in the starboard wing. He alerts the crew that they could exit from the top hatch and climb aboard the raft. He announces this by calling "DINGHY! DINGHY!"

Our dinghy, having been activated by the impact, was sitting on top of the wing. "DINGHY! DINGHY! " Johnny called. That broke the spell we were in and we started laughing. It was what we needed to break the tension and shock we were experiencing. The water in the swamp couldn't have been more than a foot deep, so the craft couldn't have floated anyway. No one, other than the rear gunner, was even remotely shaken up. "You didn't make a very good job of this Skipper," Johnny yelled. "We're still alive but how are you going to explain this to the brass?" he asked.

I tried to call the tower but there was no response. I wondered if our radios had been damaged but Bill assured us that they were sending out a signal. There didn't seem to be any action or life anywhere about. No rescue trucks, any ambulances, nor fire tenders, no one at all. Just us, sitting by ourselves in a busted airplane.

We got out and slopped our way to the perimeter track. Still no one around.

"God Skipper, you sure wrote this one off," Jack said. It was then I started to shake. I was starting to realize the gravity of my situation.

We walked the two miles to the tower only to find there was no one on duty. The place was empty. Having aircraft traffic demanded duty staff. "This had to be a real FUBAR deal if you ask me," Jack said angrily. I found a phone and called the duty officer. He too had been sleeping.

"Why the hell are you calling at this time of the morning?" he yelled.

"Sir, I have just pranged "X-Xray" on the south end of the field. I haven't been able to find anyone to report to," I informed him, advising there were no injuries and we are all okay.

"Good God man what are you saying? Are you telling me you pranged and there is no emergency crews at the sight?" he screamed into the phone. I think he was experiencing some shock as well.

"Yes Sir, that's right," I informed him, feeling sorry for myself.

The sun was coming up and the airport started to come to life, especially the ground crews and the heavy lift operators. The duty officer told us to get breakfast and to report to him afterwards. "I wish I was dead," I moaned.

"I'll bet you do, Skipper," Jack said. "Tough luck son," he said. "We'll all pull for you."

The enquiry was over in about two hours. Not soon enough for me. It seemed I had almost committed murder the way everyone was treating me. I had destroyed one of His Majesty's most prized possessions, as if this was the only aircraft we ever lost. I was feeling like I was going to be sick. Several of the staff was walking around with that "I told you so" look on their faces. My reputation of being a kid had got around and I had finally screwed up.

The incident was hushed up and very little was said about it. I don't think many on the station knew about the crash or the subsequent enquiry. They decided that things were too straightforward to require a court martial. It was definitely pilot error but there were a few other factors to consider, particularly the base's responsibility in the emergency. A court martial would have unearthed the lack of duty personnel at the time of the crash and this would reflect badly on the Commanding Officer.

There wasn't going to be a court martial for Skipper Scott. The enquiry verdict? I was to be posted to a replacement centre for a month then rescheduled for evaluation as a pilot on the Sterling. I would not lose my crew but they would have to carry on their operational flights with another pilot or as a spare crew. I was to lose three months pay and my promotion was cut back six months if I was due for one at that time. In spite of how badly I felt at not being

able to continue on with my crew, I knew I had squeaked through a very bad situation. I would still fly or at least it looked that way.

On August 5th I was posted to a replacement centre where operational crews could find temporary crews as they required them. It was better than being grounded or worse, court martialled.

My crewmembers were not very happy with the outcome and were most supportive of me during the enquiry. No one ever asked as to how we were doing. It seemed no one gave a damn whether we had lived or died. The crew and I felt the only reason I was not court martialled was that the courts would have discovered the "cover up" of the operations the night of the crash. There was no one on duty when I pranged X-Xray. This would have created quite a stir and some heads would definitely have rolled and not necessarily mine.

I was not sent to a Sterling retraining centre. I was sent, instead, to an aircrew replacement centre. I was being re-evaluated for competency. I complained but to no avail. I would not see my crew again for several weeks. I was devastated and wondered if I could carry on. I wished I had someone to talk to about my problem. There didn't seem to be anyone around interested in talking to me. At the centre there were chaps from every branch of aircrew, from gunners to navigators to pilots like myself. We were told that we would be on operational call for any crew, which needed replacements.

I wrote a letter to the C.O. of the RCAF. He replied that I was not in their jurisdiction any longer and that I must go through the RAF office of their Chief of Staff. That too got me a polite "carry on for now old bean" answer. I would be reconsidered at a later date. I would still have to requalify on the Sterling and then possibly be assigned to an operational squadron. I would never get through this in time to join my crewmembers. They would have completed their tour. Many of the crews at the centre had been in trouble and this was a sort of clearinghouse for the misfits, so to speak.

My first assignment was as a gunner with Three Group. I guess I was as frightened of this assignment as I was of my crash. Because of my size I was required to replace a rear gunner in "L-Love". The crew were all young chaps and were happy to have me. They all wanted to know why I had been grounded and were very sympathetic. My wings gained me a degree of respect I might not

have had otherwise.

The crew of "L-Love" had lost a gunner to anti-aircraft shelling and had a new turret mounted on the plane. "L-Love's" crew were all British types and were quite interested in the Canuck from the Canadian Prairies. They wanted to know all about the West. They liked me so much that I completed nine operational flights with them. They didn't want to see me leave but didn't want to stand in my way of flying again.

During this time the captain, Flight Sergeant Bill Marchand (Willie) and I became good friends. He was someone I could talk to, although he was a lot older than I was. He encouraged me to be patient and to roll along with the deal. He was instrumental in getting me back into the main stream again. He assisted me with my letter writing and introduced me to the CO of our squadron who went to bat for me. He felt I had more than served my penance under the circumstances and should be allowed to fly again. He had all of my records to verify my status and was most interested in what I had to tell him of the enquiry. I was to learn later that it was the information I gave him that got me reinstated. It helped to have someone pulling for me.

In all of the nine trips with Bill's crew we were only damaged twice and then only slightly. A few holes in the main plane. They told me I was good luck because prior to my joining them they seemed to have nothing but bad luck. It really worried them as they had six more trips to complete their tour when I left them. They wished me all the best and we went into Banbury for a meal to send me off. They were really very nice chaps and didn't care how big I was. They did laugh at my squeaky voice over the intercom. L-Love went on to complete her tour of operations with the crew intact.

I was to fly a refresher course on the Sterling and then I would have to take another crew from wherever, perhaps even the replacement centre. My old crew remained in touch, telling me of how unlucky they were. They were having problems of one sort or another. Such things as having a trip scrubbed because of aircraft trouble or a change of captains who didn't want to fly with them. Sometimes the crew was not happy with their assigned captain. It was one thing after another. There always seemed to be something.

When they heard that I was returning to the squadron, they asked to be reassigned to me as they had been promised. Here again the CO of the replacement centre came to my rescue and wrote a note or two. Then, on September 1st '44, we were posted to 90 Squadron of Three Group. We were re-united and assigned a brand new Mk. 5 Lancaster carrying the letters "E-Easy".

We were checked out on the airplane and I knew I was back in my element. What a plane and my crew and I were like new people with a whole new outlook on life. We couldn't have been happier. There was only one thing that bothered me. My crew would be completing their tour before me. When they were done I would be left with eight more trips to do. No one seemed to know whether I could count my trips with the replacement group. They assured me that things would work out in the end and it did. My crew volunteered to fly the additional trips with me if it came to that. They would have flown forty-three missions over enemy territory and I thirty-five. I was happy when the awards committee credited them with two tours. That would give them a bar to their "Ops Wing". They deserved it.

We discovered, after we had completed our tour, that my trips as a gunner with "L-Love" could have been counted. I wound up being credited with a tour and a half. I could not express my feelings of gratitude to the men of my crew. They had made a major commitment on my behalf.

It was only superstition but everyone believed that you would die either on your first two or three missions or on your last. Too often, the superstition proved to be true. Just as a crew was completing its tour, they failed to return. In view of these statistics these "Old Men", as I called my crew, went beyond their required duty so that they would be with me when I finished. They must have had terrible concerns over their decision. They had talked it over with family and relatives and decided to fly the extra trips. I will always be grateful to them. They were prepared to give their lives for me, by doing this unselfish thing.

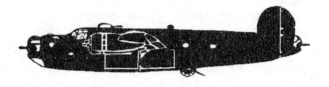

Consolidated BJ24 Liberator

MILDENHALL

Most of the operational bomber bases in England were of wartime type construction. They were built in a great hurry and at the least cost to the war effort. The buildings were of galvanized steel and looked much like a huge pipe that had been cut in half and laid on its side with concrete blocks in the ends. There was a door and a window built into each end. They were to be our homes for the duration of our operational tour. They were usually set in an "H" form with the centre section being the washrooms for the billets and the kitchen in the case of the mess. The sleeping quarters were in the rest of the building. These were strictly utilitarian with absolutely no frills of any kind.

A short distance away, at a base called Mildenhall, there was the most beautiful group of permanent Airforce buildings anywhere in the world. They were constructed of red brick and each crew member had a room of his own with an enormous mess for both Officers and SNOs (Senior Non-commissioned Officers). It was built before the war and had been a permanent base for the Royal Air Force.

The runways were superb with full lighting and gas lit runways for fog dispersal called "FIDO" (Fog Investigation Dispersal Operation).

The control towers were separate buildings and were completely outfitted. Our towers were built into the corners of a hangar, which had been built with a second floor so that the control operators could see over the field. Their equipment consisted of a radio, an Aldis lamp and some flares--barely enough to qualify as a control tower.

Everyone wanted to be posted to a permanent Airforce base. These chaps lived in utter luxury. No leaking roofs or wind blowing through the windows and doors. However, it seems that the British Government was committed to making sure our new American allies were accommodated in the very best manner as Mildenhall was occupied by the 389th Squadron of the 8th Airforce of the

USAAF.

My crew and I, along with "E for Easy", were attached to 90 Squadron based at RAF Bomber Command Three Group Tuddenham in Suffolk. We were not too far from Mildenhall and often would watch the Americans returning home in their ragged formations. Mostly they were shot up with various pieces of controls and other parts dangling from the fuselage. We knew they had been through hell.

The Americans lived much better than we did and we were jealous. We often heard of the great food they had and the wonderful theatre shows that were provided for them. On occasion, we were invited to these affairs. Their USO shows featured movie stars and big bands. Sometimes we would get to watch a first run movie.

I think Mildenhall provided me with the only real link to home while I was overseas. It was responsible for helping bomber crews forget the war around them. By now, we were veterans of eight operational flights together making us survivors, as we were called.

My first operational flight was to Bottrop, an oil refinery in the Ruhr Valley. It was a shocking experience, being shelled by anti-aircraft batteries, enemy aircraft all trying to knock us out of the sky. It was terrible to see one of your own aircraft blowing up right in front of us and seeing no debris. There was only just a mighty flaming explosion then a huge black puff of smoke. That was all that was left of seven men and their four engine Lancaster.

I wanted to scream I was so frightened. Staring out of the windscreen at the target area ahead with searchlights probing the sky and watching other aircraft being blown up, and seeing and hearing the crack of anti-aircraft shells bursting all around, held me virtually spellbound and almost incapable of movement. I could easily have broken had it not been for the calm and casual manner the crew went about their duties. This experience would remain indelibly etched in my brain forever.

After a while I found I was too occupied flying the aircraft on our bomb run to feel the full significance of what was taking place around me. It wasn't until we were on our way back that I started to shake and found it difficult not to cry. I couldn't help thinking about the crews who were not returning home. My crew handled it like the

veterans they were, settling me down and offering encouragement throughout the trip. "You okay Skip? You did real well and we're proud of you," Jack said. I had survived No. 1.

Three Group had been selected to become a daylight operational unit and some were already doing daylights. However, we were required to fly several night missions due to heavy losses to No. 86 Squadron (Night Bombers) also stationed on our base. We had very little experience flying night missions and this was another challenge. "What you don't see, won't hurt you". I wondered who dreamed that one up? Aircraft were colliding with each other and sometimes even dropping their bombs on lower flying aircraft. It was a nightmare and much more frightening than daylight missions.

We flew eight of these night affairs and were surprised that we came away fairly unscathed. We were very lucky. Many did not do as well and were not around to discuss what went wrong.

It was with great delight and some apprehension that I noticed my name and those of my crew were on the DROs (Daily Routine Orders) for a temporary posting to Mildenhall, the operational base for the 8th USAAF bomber group. We were to help with a training exercise with the 389th Squadron. Several people came up to me asking me what we were up to and whose behind had I kissed to get this assignment. I left the whole thing for my crew to explain. Jack was good at that. Gil Evers, my best friend, told me the details of the assignment. He seemed to know everything and told me to pay no attention to the "sad acres" who were complaining. Besides it was just for a short time, two weeks or so.

The Americans were losing aircraft faster than they could build them. What was even worse, was the human loss and crews were getting scarce. Jack told me that some crews were flying two men short.

The American strategy was to fly formation in groups of five or six aircraft. There would be several formations to each division with three divisions to a raid. The idea was the combined fire power of the aircraft's .50 calibre machine guns would drive off the enemy aircraft attacks. In principal it should have worked. Certainly many enemy aircraft were lost to this sort of firepower but there were five times as many American bombers struck out of the sky as

Commonwealth Bombers. They actually lost three times as many bombers to anti-aircraft fire than they did to fighter engagements. The cost was just too high.

It was decided by USAAF High Command that the 389th Bomber Group would investigate the RAF's approach to fighter tactics as our losses on a percentage basis were much less than theirs. It was in this regard that 90 Squadron was to provide an aircraft and crew along with cine-camera photos of actual air attacks. I was not inclined to argue against such a break in our normal routine. The hassling we had taken as to how come we got the job got to be a little much. We persevered and, of course, my older crewmembers were certainly up to anything any of the young crews could offer in the way of rebuttal and subsequent put downs. It seems we were riding on top. I wondered if there had been a mistake. The CO assured me that because of our outstanding gunnery exercises, we must be doing something right and that was why he gave the job to us.

Before we left, Gil Evers, my mentor, cornered me and instructed me to keep my nose clean and stay out of harm. "I don't want to have to go all the way over there to pull your coals out the fire," he chuckled. I assured him that I would keep things on an even keel and the other crewmembers told him that his fears were unfounded.

We flew EASY to Mildenhall and were impressed by the enthusiastic welcome we received. It seemed they were looking forward to the forthcoming exercise as much as we were. I wondered if they would still be enthusiastic when they discovered it was me flying the demos. Well, they'd just have to get used to it. After much fanfare we were ushered into the tower administration office to meet the Commanding Officer and his assistant. The crew left me to enter the office alone while they waited outside, smoking and answering questions from the ground crews. The CO (Commanding Officer) came in and said. "Hi young fella, what can I do for you? You with the visiting RAF group?" The sergeant had been trying to get the CO's attention and finally caught his eye. I saw the byplay and waited for the results. "Don't tell me you're the head honcho of this expedition?" he said, hoping he was wrong but fearing he was right.

"Sir," I replied in my deepest voice, "I am the Captain of E for Easy and we're here to do exercises with you."

There was a contemplative pause then, "Go on, you're joshing us, huh kid?" I smiled. "No Sir, I'm afraid not, I'm really it and I am not as young as I look."

His assistant asked me, "Well how old are you son?"

"I'm almost nineteen," I answered.

"Well, I'll be go to hell Jim, the times must be tougher than we thought. Wow! Robbing the cradle, I'd say. You know what the whole thing is about, huh?" the Captain asked.

"Yes Sir, I do and we are ready to start whenever you're ready. I tried to sound as professional as I could.

"Jim, I think we may have a little trouble with this one." the CO commented. He wondered if my looking so young would prevent these seasoned bomber crews from believing that I had the experience to be in charge of this exercise. All I could do was shrug my shoulders and say, "I hope not."

"Sergeant, will you take three of our Group Leaders for a familiarization flight in your flying machine, just to break the ice so to speak?"

"Sure thing Sir, do you want to do it now?"

"Yes, let's get on with it, the weather is CAVU (ceiling and visibility unlimited) and we aren't going to be able to stand down for too long." I saluted and walked out the door.

The crew had already gone through the baby brother routine in the outer office and had apparently been able to create a degree of mystery about me. They always enjoyed doing things like that.

The three Squadron Commanders had been outside waiting by the control tower, smoking and inspecting E-Easy. The CO came out, gave them their orders, and told them that they would be flying with the "boy wonder" here. They looked at me and then at one another and I didn't have to be a mind reader to know what was going through their minds but they were very courteous and held their remarks.

As we weren't going to be going too far or for too long we decided that full flying gear would not be required. Besides, the captains were wearing only their sheep-skinned jackets.

While "EASY" had been parked alongside the tower many visitors had taken the opportunity to have a look, especially at her bomb bay which looked cavernous with the bomb bay doors open. They seemed very impressed when I gave them some of the Lanc's specs. The Lanc would fly at 295 MPH with thirteen thousand lbs of bombs, one hundred and fifty gallons of oil and twenty five hundred gallons of petrol. The B17G flew at 285 MPH with thirteen .50 caliber machine guns and ammunition and carried about 5,000 lbs of bombs. The B24J flew at about 300 MPH had ten .50 caliber machine guns with ammunition and carried about 9,000 lbs of bombs. Johnny walked out and gave the ground handlers a word on the auxiliary power supply hook up. The boosters were put in place and plugged in as we climbed aboard.

The three officers would ride in the cockpit. Jack, the navigator, agreed to stay behind to provide another seat for observers. Jack had frequently complained that he never got to see outside. He got up from his position once to have a look out and he never asked to look out again.

Our guests were impressed when the throaty Merlins cranked up and burst into life. I always felt the moment of starting was awesome. I gave the pilots a brief run through on all I was doing, including the run-up.

We got a green light from the tower to taxi. I think the officers were starting to believe that I knew what I was doing. They wondered how I was able to see out the windows. They laughed when I pointed to my cushion.

I released the brakes and eased the throttles forward. "EASY" started to roll smoothly along Mildenhall's super smooth perimeter taxi strips. I got another green light and turned on to the runway and opened the throttles. With no load, "EASY" literally jumped off the runway and was airborne in seconds. I remembered that Gill had advised not to show off, especially on take off but "EASY" was so impressive in beautiful climbing turns just off the deck. I got a thrill every time we did these. We pulled a few Gs to stimulate the adrenalin and headed for the coast. We would do a few minor corkscrews, just to give them an idea of what the evasive action was all about.

I climbed to twelve thousand feet and let the rear gunner give us an imaginary commentary of an attacking fighter. He called, "Enemy aircraft at ten o'clock low, four hundred yards, prepare to dive starboard. Dive Starboard, Go! Go!"

"Hang on." I yelled to our passengers as I pushed the yolk forward and dropped the starboard wing. "EASY" dropped like a rock. I turned sharply to port, pulled back on the yolk and we soared around and upwards. The three passengers were hanging on for dear life but not wanting to miss any of the action they watched everything. They Ooohed and Aaahed all through a couple more of the corkscrews and I knew "EASY" had won them over. We dropped about 3,000 feet each time and then pulled "EASY" around in her climbing turn to resume height. I dropped down to about two hundred feet off the water as we headed home, skimming along at almost three hundred miles per hour. We were really moving.

If I needed any convincing about our guests' impressions, I only had to look at the huge grins and affirmative thumbs-up signs. I think they were converted.

We crossed the coast and Bill reported receiving an "Intruder" warning. We were informed there were enemy aircraft circling the base looking for unsuspecting bombers straggling down for a landing. Mostly these attacks came at night but occasionally enemy fighters would cross the coast, hidden from radar, flying undetected above the returning aircraft or low, right off the water.

"Keep your eyes open everyone. We have an enemy intruder in the circuit," I announced over the intercom. That was all I had to say and everything went quiet as we searched the skies for the unfriendly. The tower frequency came alive with a transmission from a landing B-24 Liberator. The aircraft was not attached to the base and was asking permission for an emergency landing. He also announced that he was being followed by an ME 210, which looks like a Mosquito Bomber. We spotted the Lib as she was preparing to touch down with the enemy fighter hot on her tail.

The Lib was a sitting duck and would surely cop it if we didn't do something. I heard the tower advising the Lib to overshoot. The reply came advising they were unable to go around. This would be his only chance.

I only had one option open and that was to fly an intercept course across the ME's track, before he got into a firing position. We were closing fast and in a good position to do some good. The enemy pilot was so intent on claiming the disabled Liberator that he failed to see us on his port beam. We had the advantage of surprise.

"You're not going to attack him, are you?" our visitors queried. I nodded my head and at the same time, the front and mid-upper gunners opened fire. Both gunners were scoring hits on the enemy fighter and he quickly banked away from his target, climbing, as Easy's guns tracked him out of range. I saw a few pieces of the Lib's tail break off but he was soon on the ground and rolling. The enemy disappeared empty handed.

Our observers were so shocked by what we had done that they couldn't contain themselves. I had to tell them to quiet down while I got clearance to land. I was quickly cleared and landed behind the still rolling Lib. We both taxied to the tower. The Lib was shutting down as we parked alongside. I couldn't believe the reception we received when we crawled out. The crew of the Lib almost kissed me as they carried me around on their shoulders. I was embarrassed.

The CO and the Adjutant had come running over from their office to compliment us on the job we had done. The three officers who had flown with us got into the story telling and it was bedlam all over again. In the meantime, we were soaking up the glory like a sponge. We would never receive a welcome like this again.

Jack, F/L Jack Buvan, came over to me and said, "Skipper, I think we have established some credibility. Let's make the most of all this flying crap while we have the opportunity." I was a bit uncomfortable with all the bragging and told him I wished that he wouldn't continue.

The crew was wined and dined in the officer's mess until late that night. They still wouldn't allow me to drink liquor, much to everyone's amusement. I never suffered from a hangover as most of them did. The CO told me they were going to put us up for a medal. I sure didn't think we deserved that but the Americans were quick to reward people for jobs that were well done.

Three days later the exercises were still going on. We were also giving classroom instruction, showing films and lecturing.

Our gunners did the best job of presenting the corkscrew tactic, describing how it gave them the opportunity they needed to hit the enemy as he passed through their line of fire. All this while the bomber was heading down on the first leg of the corkscrew and the fighter, with its fixed guns, was unable to turn quickly enough to fire upon us. Everyone seemed interested in what we had to say.

In my leisure time I often changed from my heavy woollen battle dress uniform into a t-shirt and shorts. It wasn't that I didn't like the uniform but it was just that it was hot and itchy on my skin. Then I'd get hold of a bike and pedal into town along the country roads. I was exhausted from all the flying we had been doing and needed some time to myself. All the attention we had been getting was just too much for me. I just wanted to get away. My crew knew I liked to do this and knew where I was.

One day I was pedalling along a narrow path when a group of kids came riding along. There were two boys and a girl and they were joking and laughing, especially when they nearly ran me off the pathway. "Ho Ho chumly, nearly gotcha didn't we? Sorry about that. You from around here?" they asked.

"I'm just visiting." I said. They caught my accent and asked me if I was American. I told them no, I was a Canadian and I was visiting the airbase.

"Your Father works at the base?" the boy named Matthew asked. I told him no. They introduced themselves and then asked if I would like to pedal along with them. They were going down to the river and then into town. They would be pleased to show me around. Matthew was 15 years of age, while his sister was 14. Her name was Sally. Their younger brother, Mark, was 13 and reminded me a bit of Johnny back home. They seemed quite nice. I realized they thought I was their age and were treating me just like another friend.

I rode along with them, enjoying their company. I guess I wasn't getting too old after all. It also felt good to act and feel young again. I laughed when they poked fun at my accent.

The river was beautiful and wound majestically through the rolling meadowland. It looked like a scene from a fairy tale. We sat and talked and they asked me about Canada, school and things

like that. Matthew asked me if I wanted to swim. I told him I had no suit. He said they didn't either. "Are you some kind of a prude Skipper?" Matthew asked. Without even waiting for me to answer, they all three undressed and were in the water before I even had my shoes off. Now where had I experienced this before? It was the thought of the ranch and when I was a kid that made me forget all modesty as I undressed and dove in.

We fooled in the water for about fifteen minutes, then dressed and rode back. We were getting along real well and they seemed to like me. I liked them.   They still didn't know how old I was nor did they ask. They thought Matthew and I were about the same age, perhaps I was a bit younger. His voice was deeper than mine. They asked me home for supper and I accepted.

They lived in a nice two-storey cottage, just the right size for their family. Their parents were just as nice and friendly as they were. I think you can tell the parents by their kids.

The supper conversation was all about Canada and why I was over here. I knew that eventually it would get around to that. Well, I decided I would tell them only if they asked specific questions which they did.

Mr. Brown asked me what I was doing at the base. I told him that I was in the Airforce. "How old are you Skipper?" Mrs. Brown asked.

"I'm eighteen going on nineteen," I replied. I was getting a little red and uncomfortable. I felt badly that I might have led them on. I knew they thought I was telling them a whopper.

"Skipper, is it the truth that you are in the Airforce? You look so terribly young, like Matthew's age for certain," Mr. Brown said. "What on earth do you do there, Skipper?" Matthew asked.

This was going to be my downfall and I decided not to tell them the truth. I knew they were not going to believe me. "I, well I," I hesitated and then said, "I deliver messages around the camp."

"Hey Dad, wouldn't that be neat for me to do?" Matthew shouted enthusiastically.

"Well Skipper, you are a very nice young man, to be in the services doing your part, at least your duties are out of harm's way. I'll bet you miss your Mum and Dad," Matthew said.

"Mostly my Dad," I replied. I told them that he was in the Army and was soon going to Germany with a Tank Repair Unit.

We helped with the dishes and it was almost like being home again. I guess that's why I hung onto this time with them for so long. I missed being home and it was a nice break from the routine.

They decided to ride back to the base with me and made me promise that I would be back as often as I wanted, even stay over night if I could.

As luck would have it, I had come away without my ID card. It was in my battle dress pocket. A Liberty truck carrying airmen back from town arrived at the gate at the same time as we did. It was loaded with happy and inebriated aircrew. Mr. Brown was riding his bike in the lead when the truck drew abreast of us and the guys were leaning out of the truck, yelling, and throwing cigarettes at us. "Hey, that's the kid that flew the Lancaster that chased the ME off the B-24 the other day," someone yelled as he recognized me.

"Yeah that's him," someone else said and then it was all over for me. I didn't look back at the Browns but just acted as though I hadn't heard.

At the gate, the sergeant in charge wasn't going to let me in. Then the chaps in the truck vouched for my identity. "Hey Sarg, this is the kid that shot up that Me 210 the other day," they yelled. "Yeah! Well hell yes, I remember now. Well kid, welcome back, and carry your ID next time," the sergeant laughingly warned.

Throughout the whole exchange between the airmen, the gate guard and I, the Browns were standing off to one side taking the whole thing in. I went over to thank them for their hospitality and I was red faced again from embarrassment. Mr. Brown just stared incredulously at me. "Skipper, why did you lie to us. Why didn't you tell us who you really were? You told us you were a messenger."

"Were you trying to deceive us or make us look like fools?" Matthew asked. "I'm sorry Matthew and Mr. Brown and all of you. It was just that I knew you wouldn't have believed me if I told you I was a pilot in the Airforce. No one ever does. I just told you a small white fib. I'm sorry, "I apologised. They got on their bikes again and pedalled off. Matthew yelled back at me, "Good

luck," and then they were gone with not even a wave. I was heart broken. I had never meant to lead them on.

We flew the next morning and the following two days. We had two more days to go to complete our assignment. The crew were so used to the "Quality Living" that they felt like applying for transfers but they were only kidding.

The results of our demonstrations, testing and discussions proved there would be no way the B-17 could perform our fighter evasive tactic. The aircraft was just too heavy and couldn't stand the strain. They would have to carry on as before. It was an interesting exercise and we enjoyed being on the base and working with the Americans. They did learn about the German Fighter attack methods we had captured on camera films so it hadn't been a total waste of time.

For the next two evenings I stayed in my billet, wrote letters home and read a little. The Browns had been on my mind almost constantly. I felt terrible that I had deceived them and wanted to make amends.

I decided I would bike down to the river and see if perhaps the kids were there and they were. I sat down under a tree and watched. Finally Matthew came over to the water's edge and yelled to me to come on in if I wanted to. "What are you waiting for Skipper?" Mark yelled. I undressed as quickly as I could and dove in. The kids were all over me and started splashing and having a great time. Matthew told me how sorry they all were at the way they had behaved.

"Skipper you are such a hero and you never boasted or anything. We were the ones who sure made a big mistake. You were right Skipper, we wouldn't have believed you, at least not at first. We liked you and couldn't see you doing anything to make us feel foolish," Sally said.

"Mother asked us to look for you and to bring you home for supper and to stay the night. We were hoping you would come back after the way we treated you," Matthew said.

Mark threw his arms around my neck and gave me a hug. He told me they had tried to get hold of me on the base but was told I was off the station. "We really miss you Skipper and we want to be your friend."

"Just remember Skipper, I'm taller than you, even if you are

older," Matthew stated as he stood beside me looking down.

We swam some more, then dressed and returned to their home.

Arriving at their place was embarrassing for me. It was like a hero's welcome. There were even neighbours over to have a look. They were calling me their Local Hero. The newspaper carried the story of the Intruder being chased off by an RAF Lancaster Bomber flown by Sergeant "Junior" Skipper Scott at the controls. I was happy and our evening roughhouse reminded me of home and my friends Gordon and Phillip. I wondered where they were right then.

Two days later we left for home base at Tuddenham. I spent much of my leave time with Matthew and his family and stayed with them when I had completed my tour and was waiting for a posting home.

The Browns were not only instrumental in assisting me in recovering from both my wounds, but also in dealing with my severe depression. They even travelled with me to Scotland to see me board ship on my return to Canada. It was like leaving another family again.

MISSING IN ACTION

Sept. 6, 1944
"WE REGRET TO INFORM YOU YOUR SON, SGT. SKIPPER
DOUGLAS SCOTT, FAILED TO RETURN FROM AN
OPERATIONAL MISSION. FURTHER INFORMATION IS NOT
AVAILABLE AT THIS TIME." signed R.A.F. Personnel Information.

This news put the finishing touches to a week filled with tragedy for both my parents and me. My younger brother Billy had passed away a few days earlier. He was only thirteen and overcome by Infantile Paralysis - Poliomyelitis. I wasn't even aware he had been ill. The telegram arrived two days after Billy's passing.

Our bombing mission to Emden, in the northern part of Germany, had been relatively easy, at least as far as fighters were concerned. The anti-aircraft batteries were always there to plague us as we were heading out over the North Sea on our return trip. We took several hits on our underside and I was thanking our lucky stars that we didn't have our bomb load hanging under there. Then two close bursts beneath us sent "Easy" into a steep climbing turn. I knew we had been hit. There was no way we could have missed getting the shrapnel from that one. The burst was close enough for us to hear the crack of it exploding and there was a smell of cordite in the aircraft.

"Skipper, we're losing fuel from somewhere," the mid upper gunner yelled through the intercom.

"Johnny, what are the gauges showing?" I asked. "Can't see why it couldn't have been one of the empty tanks."

"We're losing a ton of fuel Skipper. The gauges are unwinding like an elevator dial," he yelled.

"Can we transfer? Get some into the port tank before we run out?" I asked. "I've already tried that Skip but there is hardly any movement in the needles at all," he exclaimed. "God Skipper, I don't like the looks of the weather up front, looks like one hell of a storm

in our path," Jack in the nose observed.

"Hoooolllyy! What do we do now?" I asked, more to myself than anyone else, trying to come up with a plan. I hadn't a clue how we were going to avoid a dunking.

"Easy" was still perking along unaware she had been critically wounded. I had started our descent and had reduced power as much as I could, trying to reduce our fuel consumption. I knew it was going to take a good deal more than that to get us home. Lightning was flashing all around us and I decided we had best try to get under the cloud cover and see what lay below.

Jack estimated that we were more than half way across the Channel with only sixty miles to go. I figured that we were headed for "The Wash", a large bay located half way up the East Coast. The strong winds from the south were driving us even further north. "I'm not looking forward to a swim, Skippy baby," Hank called from the rear turret.

"What makes you so special, neither are the rest of us," Bill laughed.

"Skipper, on our present course, we'll cross right over King's Lynn on The Wash. What are your plans? Think we'll make it?" Jack McKay sounded a little on edge.

"All we can do is pray the old girl can keep going," I answered. I had no plan, other than to take each minute as it came. We broke through the clouds and it was a very grim picture. The scene below looked very much like what we had just come through with black clouds, heavy winds and rain. It was dark and I couldn't see the water below. We were down to 3,000 feet when the engines started spluttering. We were going to have a ditching on our hands. I dropped "Easy's" nose to keep our airspeed up. We were at 2500 feet before I saw the whitecaps on the sea below. Off in the distance I could just make out the breakers on the shoreline.

I was running through the ditching procedure when Jack's voice came on the intercom. "Skipper, there is no way we're going to manage a ditching in that stuff, just no way at all. She'll bust apart on the first bounce. You had best make for the coast and we'll take our chances on the ground." At this point, there seemed no way I would have any control over where "Easy" set down. I started

praying, coaxing "Easy" along to make it to land for us.

I had been taught as a kid to always say my prayers before I went to sleep. Ken said it would give God a little time during the night to decide on whether or not to answer them. This time I knew He was hearing me as I prayed.

"Engines are going out Skipper. The needles have quit bouncing. There's no more juice left. You're on your own now," Johnny informed me. Needless to say the deathly quiet, except for the whistling wind, was the most nerve racking experience I had ever had. I knew we were going to crash and there was nothing I could do to prevent it.

Jack said we only had a mile or so to go. If we could manage to stay airborne , we'd prang in some swampy farm land, just north of King's Lynn. Hooolyy! I had to make a choice, to turn into the wind while I still had a little altitude and crash in the sea, or if we managed to reach the coast, do a belly landing on territory I didn't have a clue about and in pitch darkness.

It was very dark and we were now at 800 feet. "Jack?" I asked "Go for it son, straight in I always say," he replied.

"Brace yourselves. We just passed over the surf, we're going to make it," I said excitedly. "No baths tonight guys," I quipped, just before I felt "Easy" settle onto the ground at just under her stalling speed. I was shaking badly and wondered if this would be like the time we crashed the Sterling. With "X-Xray" it happened so fast I didn't have time to do anything but fight the controls. This time I was living every second of the ordeal and feeling badly for the crew. They had done their best and now everything was in my hands.

I have often heard other crews tell about how their lives pass before them when they are about to crash and there seems no way out. It was happening to me now and I wondered how all these things could be flashing before my eyes when I was so busy trying to guide "Easy" and survive.

The props churned up mud and water then we banged down and skidded for what seemed like miles. Actually, our speed was just under the stall when we hit. We slowly ground to a halt as "Easy" ran out of steam. We were alive and incredibly fortunate in having come out of this as we did. Everything had worked in our favour

even to the location of the trees and houses we swept through. We had made an impossible landing or rather crash.

We crawled out but soon stepped back in again out of the heavy wind and rain. "Skipper, you little bugger, you are sure something else, here we are all safe and sound and I wouldn't have given any of us a farthing for our chances just ten minutes ago," Jack joked. "I'd kiss the ground but it's too wet and I might catch a cold," he laughed. That broke the tension and we all started talking at once.

"It just wasn't our time Jack," Bill said. "If it hadn't been for my RDF (radio direction finder) fix, we wouldn't have made it, right?" Bill said, endeavouring to claim some of the credit.

"Sure mate. Skipper just sat on his bum doing nothing all that time, huh?" Jack quipped back. We were all joking now.

"Well mates, it could have been a real tragedy, if we had been another fifty feet to the port," Frank observed as he noticed a tree off our port wing.

We decided to get our bearings if only the darned rain would let up. There seemed little point in our mashing about in the mud and rain, groping in the dark.

Isn't that a farmhouse over there about a mile or so?" Frank offered as he climbed back up into his turret where he could get a better look." It looks like we're in a bit of a swamp Skip, there's water everywhere and the plane is covered in mud and straw and stuff. Man were we ever lucky," he said. I had seen the water and grass flying up over the wind screen and hadn't a clue what might be coming up in front of us.

The wind and rain finally let up. "Okay, who's volunteering to go out and find out where we are?" Jack laughed. No one moved. "Fine, as senior officer of this here assembly I order you all to get off your arses and let's tell someone we're okay. Coo, I hate to think what my Gert will say when she gets the news I might have copped it," Jack went on.

"She'll bloody well jump for joy, that's what she'll do," Bill joked. It was raining slightly as we stepped into water, which was over our boots. We waded over to what looked like an old road or pathway. I had pulled all our papers and Jack had his maps and charts and away we went. We followed along the trail towards the

house but when we got there our luck ran out.

There was no one home. There was no phone, no lights, no nothing, not even a beer, Jack reminded us. "There's a small village about three miles west so we might just as well start for it. They'll surely have a phone there," Jack suggested.

I felt like I had walked a hundred miles by the way I was feeling when we finally arrived in town. There were few people about and I guess we scared the daylights out of them when they saw us walking into town. What a rag tag bunch we must have appeared. As a matter of fact we were challenged for identification and it wasn't long before there were several people gathering around us.

"Where's your plane if you crashed? We naught heard a sound," one elderly home guard said as he frowned at us suspiciously. We told them where we had come down and they looked at one another as though we had just come from another planet. We had a hard time convincing them that we were not German aviators.

Eventually we succeeded in convincing them our story was true and that we needed to communicate with the base. This they could understand.

"Who is the Captain of the aircraft?" one lady asked. "I feel it is he that we should be talking to," she continued. As usual, Jack was the spokesman for our crew. "Are you the captain?" she asked.

"No, he is," Jack said, pointing to me.

My crew looked at me and then at the town's people who were gathering around. Some were starting to laugh. "Hmmf. I thought there was something funny about this lot," she said, seeking approval from the others.

"You expect us to believe that this boy is the aircraft commander?" the spokeswoman went on, eyeing me up and down as if I was something from outer space. Here we go again.

Jack explained, in his most eloquent manner, that I truly was the captain and I just looked very young for my age.

"Well, how old is he?" they asked.

"He's eighteen," Frank snarled at them. He had had about enough of these do gooders.

"He's nothing but a child," one old grizzled townsman remarked.

Well the "Child" just saved our lives, now let's get something done

so we can get out of here," Jack lashed out at them.

Here is where we encountered still another problem. "Where can we get the nearest phone?" Jack enquired.

"The storm took the lines down and we're without any phones. We might be able to get Charlie to send a radio message or something in code to your people," one lady said. "He's got a ham set and he works for the coast watchers."

The townspeople were warming to us and were bound and determined that the pub should open and we should be fed, courtesy of the town. It was like a small parade as we marched down the street to the pub. "The Horse and Radish" they called it. One old lady claimed it was named this because it was such a hot establishment. They did have a sense of humour after all. I was really concerned that we get word out as soon as we could. Jack had already arranged for the radio operator to come to the pub as quickly as he could. A youngster had been sent to get him.

It wasn't long before we were all sitting around a very large table with fried eggs, slices of fried Spam and freshly baked buns. We were famished and the food tasted so good. We looked a little more presentable after we had removed our muddy and filthy flying suits.

The pub had fully opened and Jack and the rest were treated to large quantities of ale while I was treated to huge quantities of milk. The pub's patrons thought that was hilarious and I laughed along with everyone else. "Laddie, you're the captain and they won't let you have a wee wet of ale?" an old man quipped.

"Well, if the wee boy is old enough to bomb the likes of Hitler, then surely to goodness he should be able to take a draft or two," another said jokingly.

Jack said, "No, he still has some growing to do and milk will surely do that for him." Everyone nodded in agreement. The radio operator arrived and agreed to get a message out for us and get us a reply as soon as he could. We had been eating and drinking for about an hour when he returned with a message addressed to F/L Jack Buvan, advising that transportation and salvage crews were being dispatched to bring us home. They should arrive sometime before five o'clock that afternoon.

We were wined and dined and were taken out to the crash scene

to view "Easy" and re-assess the damage. We still felt our initial estimate that the aircraft was repairable was right on and we hoped the salvage crews would come to the same conclusion.

The transport station wagon arrived, followed by the crane and salvage crews. We waited until they had done their preliminary inspection. They were all praises for "Easy's" crew. She was salvageable, with only the engine nacelles, props and bomb doors damaged. She was dirty but that would wash off. They would have her out of there by the following day.

One thing that had completely slipped our minds was the telegrams that had been sent out to our next of kin advising the loss of our aircraft. "WE REGRET TO INFORM YOU" and so on. We hastily set about to correct this situation by having the Airforce inform our parents that we were safe.

We were sent on a ten day leave and when we returned "Easy" was sitting on her own dispersal pad waiting for us to climb aboard and try again. It was hard to believe that just a short time ago she was laying on her belly in a swamp. She was indeed a gorgeous sight, all repaired and waiting to try again.

"Easy's" crewmembers were given King's Commendations for Meritorious Conduct while I received a bar to my DFM.

THE SURVIVORS

The briefing completed, we waited for the lorries to come and take us to the equipment area. Here we would be issued our flying suits, parachutes, helmets and goggles. The WAAF ladies were always in attendance and were very kind, always willing to help any of the chaps requiring help suiting up. They usually had a little joke or two for Easy's crew. Jack, our Bomb Aimer, was a terror at teasing the girls and would often have a dry remark about the size of this or that. I won't mention what. They would twitter for hours over his jokes.

I felt I was subjected to more than my share of attention. I usually was able to sneak past everyone to get to my locker and avoid the teasing. The staff meant well and were only joking but I didn't think it was anyone's business whether I had "dumped my ashes" or not.

"It's all right laddie, you don't even have a furnace," Jack would tease. They thought I didn't know what they were talking about.

Our crew was quite often the last to get ready and so had to wait for the lorries to return from their first run before we could leave. This was usually the case and everyone referred to us as the Grandpas and Grandson. Always slow to get started.

"E for Easy" was parked in a dispersal pan (a round circle of asphalt) located almost off the airfield. As a matter of fact, Easy was located in a farm yard. The farmhouse was about 100 yards from Easy's nose. The family who lived there were very nice people and we get to know them and care for them very much.

They were always teasing my crew about their pilot and shouldn't he be home with his Mama? Mrs. Swanson called them a bunch of bullies. She would bake scones, cookies and other goodies with the baking ingredients I received from home and the ranch. We were being spoiled and living in the lap of luxury thanks to Mrs. Swanson and her family.

Mr. Swanson worked in a nearby truck livery where he drove defense supplies. The two girls and one boy were in their early teens. The boy, Jason, was two years younger than me and he loved being

around the aircraft while we were checking her over or doing repairs.

Mrs. Swanson and her family really looked after us. She was like a mother the way she was always around when we were at the aircraft. She was concerned for our welfare.

Our ground crew had a little shack located next to the barn where they kept tools and repair items for "Easy". The battery-starting cart was kept in the shed as well. Ground crews were permanently assigned to each aircraft and were responsible for keeping the airplane in top condition and ready to fly at all times. They grew as attached to "Easy" as we did. Our lives depended on how well they did their jobs. It was most embarrassing and almost a cardinal sin if mechanical problems forced their crew to take a spare aircraft. They took it personally, blaming themselves. Unfortunately, a maintenance failure would be entered on their records and none of us wanted that.

For the flight crews, it was a devastating experience to have to fly a spare. We were superstitious and we felt it was a bad omen. Too many chaps failed to return when flying in a spare aircraft. Therefore, it was in the aircrew's best interest to have a good ground crew.

We crawled into Easy from the back door located on the starboard side near the tail plane. The rear gunner turned to his left and crawled over the Elsan Can (toilet), over the tail spar and into his turret. The rest of us had to make our way up through the fuselage and over the main spar. This is the part of the wing, which passes through the fuselage. It was a very tight fit especially in heavy flight gear. The mid-upper gunner was the next to get in. With the help of the wireless operator, he would squeeze into his turret. The radio operator would secure his seat under him; it was sort of like a little swing. Then the operator (Bill) would sit at his radios in front of the main spar on the port side looking forward.

The next crewmember in was the navigator, who sat right behind me, facing to the outside on the port side. All his equipment was on that wall. Next in was Johnny the Engineer. He had a small fold up seat beside me and sat lower down and close to his engine instruments on the starboard side. Then it was my turn. I pulled out the step and climbed up into my seat while Bill slipped my cushion under me. Jack Buvan, the Bomb Aimer, was last and he would

crawl past Johnny and down the Bomb Aimer's hatchway. He also had a gun turret mounted above him so that he could quickly crawl up into it and use it for frontal attacks if need be. We were now all in and ready to go.

Johnny gave me the signal that the aircraft was ready to commence starting engines. He and I had done a walk around the airplane checking control surfaces, undercarriage pins and tires before we got into the aircraft.

The ground crew plugged the auxiliary starting truck into the socket inside the starboard wheel well. Scotty, our chief ground crew sergeant, gave me the start sign and I began the start up sequence with the starboard inner engine first because it powered the hydraulic pumps and generator.

All engines were running and ticking over with their characteristic rumbling sound. I loved to hear them. The Lancaster was an exceptional airplane and could maintain stability on one engine. It couldn't hold altitude but you still had control and you could land. More than one Lanc had done a single engine landing. With the engines warm, we started the roll out of our pan and onto the perimeter track. We steered by using the brakes and the outboard engines.

The runway in use determined how far we would have to taxi. Sometimes we would only taxi a short distance, while other times it seems that we taxied forever. We would watch for a break in the line up of aircraft to squeeze in. Everyone was heading for the main runway, zig zagging until they came to the runway and were given a turn to take off. We taxied along looking out the side windows.

About this time, I could feel my heart beating harder and faster. Some chaps used to kid us that Easy was the only aircraft where you could never see the pilot. I sat quite low down in the seat.

We waited with some degree of apprehension as it came closer to our turn to take off. We were always aware of aircraft in trouble on take off. It usually meant instant destruction. In most cases it was caused by either a tire blow out or from engine failure. The aircraft would be seen to lift off and then gently settle back down again as it ran out of runway. We prayed for miracles. Most times, they hit the ground with their wheels up and props tearing up the ground. Then

came the inevitable explosion. The entire aircraft would completely disintegrate right where it hit, leaving a huge crater. No flying pieces, no bodies, just a great hole and a towering puff of black smoke where an aircraft had been only moments before. "There but by the Grace of God, Go I." A terrible way to begin an operation. We wouldn't know who it was until we returned.

I got the green light from the caravan to turn onto the runway and slowly opened the throttles. Now was the time. Like all other Lancs, "Easy" pulled to the port so we countered with rudder and engines to offset the torque. Some chaps sometimes didn't do well and would develop a bad swing resulting in taking their aircraft very close to the edge of the runway and sometimes off. This was not a good practice but we never had that trouble, thankfully.

The "point of no return" comes quickly. This is the point on the runway where you must continue your takeoff run or abort and brake for dear life. A pilot never realizes how short a runway is until he has to abort a takeoff.

"Easy" rolled along at 90 knots. I got her tail up quickly, as it was easier to steer that way and off she came with a good quarter of the runway left. I liked to allow a good margin of safety, just in case.

We lifted off into a clear blue sky. The weather had cleared and it was one of those splendid days where we could enjoy the view. Redding was our rendezvous point so we commenced circling at 8,000 feet. As we circled, we looked for the other aircraft that were to join our formation. They usually found us first due to the two yellow bands around our tail fins that identified us as formation "GH" leaders.

By 10:30 we had all our formation together and were headed out on the first leg across the Coast and out over the Channel. Looking down into the Channel, we could see ships. It was a convoy of freighters bucking heavy seas accompanied by destroyers, cruising back and forth protecting their charges and cargo.

"I wouldn't want to be those guys down there," Jack said. "At least we get home to a warm bed and a wee wifey every night. Well, most of us do except Junior here," he laughed. Everyone else chuckled too. I wondered where I would be now if the Navy had decided to accept my application.

I could feel the rear gunner moving his guns back and forth, as he searched the sky. It made the aircraft yaw a bit each time his guns would come out to the side positions. That was one way I could tell if he was on the bit or was sleeping. But Hank never slept.

By the time we reached the Dutch coast, flak was reaching up for us and our formation. It was easy for the various formations to form one main bomber stream as we crossed the Channel, just as the Americans did.

We crossed the enemy coast at 16,000 feet and were almost at bombing height already. We were happy that the flak wasn't too heavy and we were only running into the occasional pockets as we passed over built up areas.

We were on a heading that would take us south of the Ruhr Valley (Happy Valley). This is where the flak started up in earnest as we came closer to the industrial areas. I am sure they were relieved when we passed over them and continued on. They knew some other town was going to get it today. We saw heavy flak north of us and knew the Americans were over there getting the PP pounded out of them. Today it would be their turn to take the crap. We were on a supposed "milk run".

Our bomber force consisted of fifty-two aircraft, all from Three Group. Ninety Squadron provided eleven of those aircraft. The target was Fulda, an unprotected railway marshalling yard. The specific target was a rail line, which had been built to carry armament to the front lines. We were carrying "H E" bombs plus our usual Cooky. Six tons of death hung under our bellys waiting to destroy whatever it contacted. I never really thought about what we were bombing or what it might be like down below or that our bombs might be killing hundreds of people. I just wanted to get in and out of the area as fast as I could and get home.

"Ten minutes to target Jack," the navigator called.

"Okay! There's a heck of a lot of flak coming up from somewhere," he said. We could sure see that.

"Okay Jack we're turning inbound, what you got on the screen?" I called. "Nothing too much yet Skip but it's starting to form," he replied.

"Jeeez Skip, I thought they said we'd have no flak. The place is

lousy with it up ahead," the Bomb Aimer commented as he prepared his selector switches for the drop.

"Navigator take the time, Lancaster going down on the starboard quarter," Jack called. We were required to let the navigator know when we saw anything unusual so that he could take the time and position and mark it for the Intel people back at debriefing. The mid-upper gunner called a Lanc blowing up.

The Bomb Aimer announced two more Lancs in trouble and going down. "Jack, take the time." That was all we seemed to be hearing. We still had five minutes to target and were seeing aircraft raining out of the sky from every quarter. I told Jack I was going to turn off target and come in on an alternate leg and try to get clear of the heavy flak.

"Okay Skipper, but we only have three minutes, you better do what you got to do by then," Jack instructed. "I can't keep up with your reports, guys," Jack complained. I told them to hush up while we were on our run, we could take times afterwards. Clouds were starting to form over the target. So much for the Met briefing of clear skies and a milk run.

I asked the gunners if we still had all of our formation. They confirmed they were all there. Moments later Hank gave us a commentary on R-Roger's demise. She lifted upwards on her starboard wing then slowly continued all the way over onto her back, at which point she blew up and literally disappeared.

"Oh Jeeez Skipper!" Hank called, his voice shaking with emotion. It usually took a lot to rattle him but not this time. Jack noted a loss from our own group when Hank called that the tail end aircraft "Z-Zebra" was on fire from a direct wing hit and was pulling out of the formation. This was not ordinary flak, this could only be the dreaded "Predicted Radar Flak Guns" we had heard about. Very few random flak bursts, just all of a sudden no aircraft.

"Holy Shit Skipper, we got two fighters coming in from up ahead," the bomb aimer yelled. He needn't have opened his mouth. I saw them and hoped we could get rid of our bombs before they attacked. With our formation almost completely destroyed, I couldn't help wondering when our turn would come.

Hank started his running commentary on a rear attack from below.

"Hold her steady Skipper," Jack yelled, trying to keep the target in his sight.

"Drop them Jack, we're under attack," I yelled.

"Holy Hell Skipper, they just got "L-Love". That's the last of our formation," the mid-upper gunner said.

Hank screamed. "He's coming in on us Skipper, prepare to dive starboard. 500 yards-400 yards-300 yards Dive! Dive! Go!" Hank yelled. I held off as long as I could and then I heard Jack, who had been listening to the commentary, yell, "Bombs gone, Skipper."

I pushed "Easy" into a steep dive into our attacker and at the same time closed the bomb doors. Just then Hank, from the rear turret, screamed that there was another Lanc passing under us at almost right angles to our course. "The bugger is turning before the target," Jack advised. All of a sudden "Easy" was engulfed in a searing blast of explosives and petrol, which tossed her over on her side a thousand feet higher than she was a moment ago. We were engulfed in flames, smoke and intense heat and heard sounds of shrapnel hitting the fuselage. The Lanc below us had received a direct hit with his full load still on. I fought to get "Easy" under control again wondering if it was us that been hit and were just waiting for the moment when we too would be blasted into oblivion. I was too busy to be frightened. We entered into another dive as Hank continued his commentary advising that I not stop corkscrewing. The fighter was still trying to get into position to open fire.

For a few moments, none of us realized what had hit us or even where we were. I was struggling to keep "Easy" corkscrewing while listening to Hank's commentary on the fighter's position. We continued this action for another 10 minutes. Our assailant was determined to blow us out of the sky and persisted in doing everything he could to bring that about.

He didn't know it but had he kept his attack going for another couple of minutes he would have been successful. I could not work my aching arms and legs any longer. I was completely exhausted. The last I saw of him, he was streaking ahead of us into the clouds. I prayed that he was gone forever.

There were always disabled aircraft staggering home that provided easy targets for the enemy so we were not out of the woods

yet. The flak was terrible and I knew we had taken a couple of hits as I could see the holes in the tops of the wings. Luckily nothing vital was hit but I wondered if we had sustained any other damage from the explosion. I felt like throwing up and could not stop shaking.

We were descending through a light cloudbank and it looked like we might be in the clear. "Krikey! Skip what the hell was that all about?" Johnny asked.

I was so exhausted from having heaved "Easy" all over the bloody sky that I could hardly speak. I just kept her in the clouds and headed on our outbound leg for France. I suddenly realized that the poor Lanc below us had taken a shot that probably was directed at us. It felt awful.

"Skipper, did you see it all?" the navigator asked. I told him I had but that I still couldn't describe the whole thing. There had been just too much to take in all at one time and I was still shaking all over.

"You did good Skipper, by golly you sure did," Jack yelled from the front over the I/C. We crossed over the coast and were heading on our home-bound leg when Bill came on the I/C telling us that he had intercepted a BBC news broadcast. He reported that, "An attempt has been made on the marshalling yards at Fulda but without success. The Allied Bombers have sustained devastating losses from new Anti-Aircraft Guns". The guns were apparently mounted on the railway cars we were attacking. How could the news people have the information so soon? We weren't even home yet. How did they know about our losses? The German propaganda people were busy spreading stories about the raid.

I called home base. I wondered at the lack of radio traffic on our base frequency. "Blackadar Control from Beddar Easy, turn to land, over." (Beddar was the squadron's call sign).

The answer came back quickly. "Beddar Easy, your turn one to land, runway 26, wind nil, overcast slight 2/3rds cover." Then I heard the controller say."Blackadar to Beddar Easy, what is your condition, over?"

"Blackadar, this is E-Easy. We're fine and will do a straight in approach," I said.

"Easy. You're cleared straight in," came the reply. I should

have tweaked to something being terribly wrong when I got a straight in approach. I had never had this before and to be turn one when we were ten minutes late was something else to think about.

I lowered the landing gear and Johnny and I checked the tires to make sure they were still inflated and appeared okay. "Easy" touched down close to the button (the very beginning of the runway) and we rolled to the first intersection. "Beddar Easy from Blackadar, turn off the runway at the first intersection and stop your aircraft there. Shut down your engines and wait outside the aircraft until someone comes to talk to you," the instruction came over the radio.

"Hooollly!!"

"What now?" I asked the guys but to no one in particular.

I ran through the shut down sequence and we crawled out asking each other what we had done and who did it. "Jack, we were over the target area weren't we? I asked once again.

"Skipper, come on son, you know we were," Jack replied indignantly.

"Okay! Okay! Just checking," I said, realizing what a stupid question it was. Hooollly, I felt like I wanted to sit down somewhere. My legs were fast weakening.

A car from operations came along the runway and stopped by us. Immediately, two mechanics boarded the aircraft and removed the camera. Why was Intelligence so anxious to see our target films? We had been there and dropped our bombs properly. What was going on?

"Gentlemen, I am happy to see you but it appears there has been a terrible "Ham Up" the CO said.

My God, what a calamity this has turned out to be.

"Starting from the beginning tell us what you saw and what happened," he said. We went over all the details using Jack's log book of recorded times and events to assist our memories. We were asked to repeat the details several times. It was the practice, after an operation, to issue the crew members with a "Tot of Rum". It was black navy rum given to settle frayed nerves and was an old Navy tradition. I was never allowed this remedial substance but was given two little tablets and a glass of water. I guess they thought I was too young to have any nerves.

"Chaps, as far as we can ascertain, you are the only ones from Ninety Squadron to make it home." The CO looked terribly worried. "Did you see any parachutes or anything else to indicate survivors?" he asked.

"Hell Sir," the radio operator stated, "we didn't think there was anything out of the ordinary until 10 minutes out and then all hell broke loose."

"We still didn't see all that much to suggest such an outcome," Jack commented. "Well Skipper old son, it's a very good thing your camera was working. You got excellent photos of the bomb drop and we can't fault you on a thing. Your bombs hit the target right dab on," the CO stated.

"How in God's good earth did you get through the area relatively unscathed? You do live a charmed life. Gentlemen you're on leave until further notice.

Get your passes and take off will you? You will be reassigned when you return from leave. We have to reorganize the entire group after this. There are only five squadrons left," he said. "It seems, Little Man, that you were not slated to fly your "last" mission yet," he added. No one laughed as the significance of what the C.O. had said started to sink in.

Our Officers took off for their own mess while I went to my billet, laid down and wept. No one was around to see. All the bunks were now empty, their occupants either dead or captured. This business was truly for grown men and not children. How often I had been told those same words throughout my training?

For returning safely and being the lone survivors, the officers of the crew; Jack the Bomb Aimer, Jack the Navigator, Johnny the Engineer, Bill the Radio Operator and Frank the Mid Upper Gunner received the Distinguished Flying Cross. Distinguished Flying Medals went to Hank the rear gunner and me. We went on ten days leave and returned to start the whole damned business over again. We were now starting trip 17. I wished I had been able to talk to Ken or Peggy, I think it would have made things a lot easier for me. I wondered who was going to make it easy for the Wives or Mothers and Dads of all the crews who died today. I cried especially for those in the Lanc who died in place of "E-Easy" and I didn't even know who they were.

AND THEN THERE WERE NONE

Sitting in the hospital waiting room with six other guys seemed old hat to me, a veteran of the place. I was feeling like an old timer. Unfortunately, I had been here too often over the past months. I knew everyone on staff and had learned every trick in the book used by my fellow flight crewmembers. They would try anything to avoid a particularly frightening operation. I could sympathize with them but could never do anything like that.

I was here with my usual bellyache. Those who attended the sick parade were referred to as "SICKIES" and were watched closely for malingerers who might be faking illnesses just to be excused from an operation.

The fakers, when discovered, were classed as LMFs, "Lack of Moral Fibre". These were chaps too frightened to fly any longer.

I looked at each of them sitting there and could almost tell what was going through their minds as they waited their turn. Some truly looked ill and it showed. One man was shaking so badly that I thought he was going to croak right then and there. There was another young man who looked too young to be here. He was slightly taller than me and seemed genuinely in pain. He was a sergeant pilot like myself but I hadn't seen him around before. I thought he might be new on the squadron.

I moved over to a seat beside him and introduced myself. "Hi, I'm Skipper Scott, I don't remember seeing you around before," I said, trying to be friendly. I asked him if he was new on the squadron. Looking at him, I felt that at long last I had found someone who looked as young as I did and with whom I could relate. He replied in a baritone voice with a decidedly Scottish accent, "Pleased to meet you Skipper, I'm Trevor McDonald. I've just been posted here from the Conversion Unit at Tuddenham," he

said. We both sat looking around the room at the others.

Another fellow just sat with his head in his hands not looking one way or the other. I think I knew why he was here. Another crewmember unable to carry on. It was sad but they were generally ostracized by their fellow crewmembers and virtually turfed out in disgrace. I could never agree with this sort of dehumanizing treatment. They were human beings like us. How could we treat them so badly? Once you were frightened there seemed no way to undo the feeling of utter despair. They just plain and simply could not go on any longer. They would report sick and then the MO would write in his report, "LACK OF MORAL FIBRE" because there was no other description for it. I think it took more courage to do this than it did to actually fly the operation.

The other chaps sitting and waiting were very fidgety and looked like they would rather be anywhere else. The staff were accustomed to my visits which only took a half-hour or so. I never once missed an operation due to my bellyaches. Usually I was hustled into the treatment room right away. "Elloe Skippah, come for another ozin' have yar?" the orderly asked, kidding me in front of everyone. They called my treatment a "Hosing". I suppose that in a manner of speaking, it was. I was used to their ribbing.

The staff were all English types and made light of almost everything. Making jokes, I guess, to keep from going bonkers.

My crew was aware of my stomach problems and would tell everyone they just couldn't understand why I got so constipated when every time we went on an operation, I sure frightened the crap out of them.

"Trevor McDonald," the doctor called out the young pilot's name. He stood and moved to the desk, whispered his problem to the clerk and was ushered into the doctor's office where he was examined. He was kind of bent over so I presumed he had a belly ache. Soon he came out and sat down beside me.

"Do you like it here?" I asked.

"Ach Aye," he replied, "my crew and I have just arrived from a CU (Conversion Unit). We haven't been on Ops yet but I think we're scheduled for this afternoon," he replied nervously. "As you can guess, everyone calls me Scotty. I'm glad to know you Skipper, how

come you're called Skipper, aren't all pilots called Skipper? Is that your real name?" he asked.

"Yes, I've been called Skipper ever since I was a little kid," I told him. He looked at me and laughed like I must have been joking when I referred to my once being a little kid.

"Och, you're still a wee one aren't you?" he laughed. "Are you in operations?" he asked.

"Yes, I'm in 186 Squadron." I replied. Scotty had a hard time figuring out just what I was doing there as I was in my blue jeans and sweatshirt. I usually dressed that way, as it was more comfortable.

I admit I didn't look like an operations type. Very few knew what I was doing on the base and I liked it that way. "Why are you here Skipper? What's wrong with you?" he asked.

"I have stomach problems and have to visit these guys every once in awhile," I replied, trying to avoid any further discussion.

"Well, I don't know what they're going to do to me. I guess there are others with more serious illnesses than mine," he laughed, half-heartedly. He was plainly worried.

He was in pain and suffering just like me. "Maybe I'm just so frightened about our first operation that it has made me ill. I really am scared of this first trip. They tell me that you either cop it on your first or your last. Ach, what a thing to look forward to. We're all afraid of going for a Burton Skipper. I just don't know how to stay calm, if you know what I mean," he confided. I knew exactly what he meant.

"How old are you Skipper? You look too young to be in the service. What do you do anyway?" he questioned.

Just then my name was called and I said goodbye. "See you around Trevor, I have to go now and Good Luck. It isn't all that bad," I said, walking into the treatment room for my "Hosing".

My cramps were gone and I was feeling a good deal better. I was laying on a cot in the treatment room when I heard Trevor complaining. "Ach, you must be daft if you think you're going to stick that thing up my arse!" he exclaimed in no uncertain terms. His accent was so broad it was really funny and I started to laugh. "Ach, what the hell are you laughing at junior? You should see what

they're trying to do to me," he yelled so everyone could hear him.

"Just settle down lad, Skipper knows all about these," the orderly told him.

"That's supposed to make me feel better, is it?" Trevor snorted. Misery does like company and I was feeling better already.

I was entering the briefing room, along with the rest of my crew, when the CO motioned me to the front. "Yes Sir."

"Skipper, I'm going to shock a few of the lads today. I want you to give the H2S briefing today. Shake a few of the senior bods a bit. Will you do it?" he asked.

"Yes Sir," I said and returned to my seat. The two Jacks were busy laying out what they thought our target was going to be. They always tried to guess our destination before it was officially announced. They would discover what the bomb load was going to be, how much fuel we were carrying and what time we were leaving. With these facts they were quite uncanny in determining the target. This trip was to Bottrop, an oil refinery in the Ruhr Valley.

The briefing went through the normal routines with the Met officer, the Intelligence officer and the Armament officer taking turns providing information needed for the trip. Then the CO called me to take over.

"Way to go Junior, you tell 'em chappy!" the crews yelled and applauded.

This part of the briefing primarily concerned only those crews who were equipped with the H2S equipment and who were designated "GH" leaders. These aircraft would each lead a formation of three or four aircraft. The "GH" leaders were identified by twin yellow stripes painted on their fin and rudders. I gave the crews all the pertinent information regarding our target approaches and what aircraft were being assigned to which leader. I also gave them alternate leaders in the event they lost their own. There was also an alternate target if that became necessary.

I noticed Scotty sitting with his crew wearing a look of complete bewilderment and apprehension on his face. I was thinking how surprised he must have been to see me. He truly was surprised and it showed.

"For you new crews who are just making your first operation, this should be an easy one. All you have to do is follow the leader. Stick to him like he was a magnet and you'll be okay. If you somehow can't keep up then select another leader and follow him in. Remember the dropping procedure. You drop on the fifth bomb of the aircraft in front of you. You also know that if fighters engage you you're on your own. Don't stick around your buddies as you might just take them with you. I turned the briefing back to the CO and returned to my seat. I bumped into Scotty as we were leaving and he looked at me in the strangest way. "You made me feel like a blithering idiot today Skipper, I never knew you were a pilot let alone a GH Leader, shows how daft I am doesn't it? Also shows how scared I am," he said.

"Scotty, you're going to be just fine. How are the rest of your chaps making out?" I asked.

"About like me I'm thinking. They're all too quiet and sort of spooked if you ask me. They usually are quite funny but not today. They're just as frightened as I am."

"Scotty, don't think of it as your first trip. Just go and do the job each of you have to do, don't think of anything else. When you're over the target area you'll be too damned busy to worry about it being your first or your last trip," I said, patting him on the back.

"Well, I'll do my best Skipper and, by the way, how are you feeling after your hospital visit this morning?" he asked.

"About the same as you," I laughed.

Scotty had a smile on his face now. "Skipper, they tell me you're only eighteen. Good grief you're just a child," he said.

"Well, you don't look very old yourself," I replied.

"Ach, that's true but you see, I'm twenty one or at least I will be tomorrow. I just look younger. I'm always taken for being about seventeen or so and I have a lot of fun with it sometimes," he said. "Skipper, you look like a fifteen year old. You're just a child." He tried making light of the situation but I knew what was on his mind. His idle attempts at humorous conversation just proved how strung out he was.

"Well Scotty I'll see you when you get back. Remember, just don't think of it as being number one, and you'll do just fine," I

advised. I knew what he was feeling and my words were not too convincing.

"I'll just do the best I can Skipper and, with any luck, we'll celebrate my birthday tomorrow with a bang on party. Good Luck Skipper. See you." He went out and got onto their crew bus. My crew was waiting for me and asked where I had been. "Probably too busy sucking up to the CO after his surprise briefing," Jack quipped.

"Thought I couldn't do it, didn't you?" I kidded. Jack stared at me for a moment then, in one of his humorous moods, grabbed me and hoisted me into the air. Everyone was laughing now as they did every time Jack did this to me. Well, they were in a good frame of mind and that was a good way to start an Op. At least they weren't worried about the trip.

I told Jack about Scotty and how terrible he was feeling about this trip. "Are the rest of the crew holding up okay?" he asked.

"No Jack, they're not. They're just as spooked as Scotty. I'm really worried about them," I said.

"Not your problem junior, you just fly Easy and keep your mind on us," he kidded.

We were putting nine aircraft up for this operation, six of which were GH leaders. We would be picking up our formations from the various groups at the rendezvous point and then start our first leg when everyone was formed up.

Scotty was flying "D-Dog" and was taxiing along right behind us. "Boy! That guy behind us is sure brake happy, he keeps crawling up on us, then jamming on his brakes, then crawling up again, I wonder what's eating him?" our rear gunner exclaimed over the intercom. I knew what was eating Scotty but was not about to make further conversation about the matter.

Thank goodness that the take-off went well for the whole squadron. Circling the rendezvous point, we would often see smoke rising from the various aerodromes as luckless bombers met their end. Take-offs were a very apprehensive time for all crew. You silently pray that your aircraft will lift off just as it has done every time before. "Easy" very rarely took the whole runway and would lift off about two thirds of the way down and climb out like a rocket. I loved her power although everyone claimed she was just the same as

all the other Lancs on the squadron. I begged to differ. She was a gazelle and I rode her like old Bossy back on the ranch, hanging on for dear life and afraid to let go.

Climbing out, I banked to starboard and glanced back at the runway and was able to watch "D Dog" lift off and become airborne. "So much for the first part Scotty, we'll have your birthday party yet," I thought to myself.

The rendezvous went well and we picked up our formation easily and headed out on the first leg. This part was uneventful until we reached the Dutch coast and then we had our usual greeting from the Ack Ack batteries. They were shooting high above us, which indicated they were after our fighter escort.

Looking up, I saw our fighters leaving their vapour trails as they searched for enemy fighters, all the time keeping an eye on us. We were being covered by three squadrons of Mustangs. That made us feel more secure.

The intelligence officer told us that we shouldn't have too much to worry about as far as enemy aircraft were concerned, just the Radar Flack units near the Rhine River. They would be increasingly heavy as we got closer to the industrial areas and Bottrop.

They weren't kidding when they said there would be lots of flak. At first, it looked like it was going after the fighters high above us but they soon got down to more serious targeting and started peppering us in what looked like a solid mass of steel. The expression goes, "The flak was so thick you could land on it." We could land on it today, that's for sure.

It's funny what sometimes runs through your mind on trips like this. I wondered what Scotty was thinking at this moment. I wondered if he would be as overwhelmed on his first Op. as I was or would he be petrified as so many others were.

Jack was busy logging times of aircraft reported blowing up or falling out of formation. That was scary and it worried all of us. You were certain the next aircraft to blow up would be you.

HOOOOLLLY! I was looking ahead at a Lanc. It was literally blown upside down from an aircraft exploding beneath it. I recalled the same thing happened to us once. You're positive that you have taken a direct hit and are doomed. It gives you an awful feeling

when you see a Lanc in a flying attitude it shouldn't be. It just isn't supposed to do that. I knew how the pilot must have been feeling, trying to recover control. It isn't easy hauling a fully loaded aircraft around the sky.

Our formation was still all together when we started our bomb run. Hank informed us that "D DOG" was the aircraft that had been doing the aerobatics after the Lanc blew up under him. Poor Scotty, he didn't need this to happen on his first trip. "He's forming up on us Skip," Hank informed me. I said a prayer for Scotty and his crew.

Jack guided us to the target and we dropped our bombs and continued on through the flak. We kept on the same heading until all our formation had dropped and was clear of the area.

The flak was the heaviest I had seen for a long time. I heard the rear gunner starting a running commentary on an enemy aircraft coming in on us and another on Scotty who was at the rear of the formation. "Five hundred yards, four hundred, three hundred, Dive Starboard, Dive!" Hank barked. I leaned on the yolk and "Easy" dropped like an elevator for about three thousand feet and we weaved at the bottom as we started our climb back to altitude. The fighter broke off the attack, probably looking for easier pickings. "Don't see him Skipper but there's a Mustang flying up on us on the port quarter. I think he must have scared the bugger off," Hank yelled over the I/C.

I heard cannon firing but couldn't tell if we were being hit or not. "Skip, the bastards are sure giving "D DOG" a run for their money, good heavens he's all over the sky. It looks like he's being hit hard," Hank went on in his excited voice. "Here he comes again Skip, prepare to go PORT. Dive! Dive! Go!" he yelled and this time we were taking lead on the starboard wing, Hooollly! Was it ever bad. I could feel heaviness on the ailerons. I knew we had taken a hit and Frank confirmed this when he told me we had lost the entire wing tip. There was some aileron sticking out unsupported. "Easy" still responded well although I could tell she was injured.

The fighter passed over top of us and I heard Frank drilling away at it with his .303s, then right in front of us the ME 109 disintegrated. That was a positive kill for the pursuing Mustang. He broke off his attack. It was beautiful to see but we nearly caught the whole blast right in our faces. That was too close.

Our escorting fighters were running short of fuel and had to depart while the enemy fighters continued harassing us across Belgium and the Netherlands. Finally, we crossed the coast. I was wondering where the rest of our fighter escorts were. We learned later they had been there all the time and their presence had probably "saved our bacon" so to speak. Our losses were going to be high. I could tell by the number of aircraft we had streaming out behind us and from the number of aircraft Jack logged in his book. Several were flying too low and would fall prey to the coastal Ack Ack batteries. "D DOG" was no where to be seen so we just continued on home. We had lost one of our formation but the others seemed to have made it okay.

Over the English Channel I gave our formation permission to break up and head home on their own. They drifted out of formation and headed for their own bases. "Blackadar control this is "E for Easy". Turn to land, over?"

"Beddar Easy you are turn five maintain four thousand feet." We circled and watched as the Lancs ahead of us came in to land. We could tell some of the Lancs were having trouble and we could hear them getting their clearances. We could also see problems on the runways.

One Lanc ground looped and, with a wing dragging on the ground, tore off into the bushes alongside one of the hangars.

"Our tires look okay Skipper but take it a little easy just to make sure," Johnny said. Having been hit as we had, it was quite likely we had a tire blown although they appeared to be inflated. It was hard to tell until the weight of the aircraft came down on them.

The sun was just setting and the shadows cast by the sun's reflections made everything look shadowy and sinister looking. Finally, after being monitored down by numbers the radio broke in with "Beddar Easy, you are cleared to land, you're turn one." came the tower.

"Roger control," I replied.

"Blackadar Control this is D Dog, require straight in approach, I have injured aboard and it is critical that I have clearance now." I heard Scotty's accent rolling over the airways.

Good! Scotty had made it home. We would have our party and he had worried for nothing. His first trip was over and he was home. "Blackadar Control to D Dog, you are cleared for a straight in approach, understand you have injuries, over." There was no acknowledgement from D Dog.

I touched down and luckily there were no flat tires and Easy rolled to the first intersection and we turned off. I could see D Dog was just about to touch down. Everything seemed in order. D Dog touched down perfectly and passed our intersection and came slowly to a stop just at the end of the runway.

"Blackadar Control to D Dog, please clear the runway and taxi to the tower, we have ambulances waiting, over." There was no response from D Dog. The airplane just sat at the end of the runway with its engines idling. The brakes were obviously set. I could see emergency vehicles heading for D Dog.

"Come on Scotty, please come on," I cried out loud, feeling that something terrible was wrong. "Why are you still sitting there, you're home, you made your first trip and you're home," I was saying to myself. We taxied Easy to her dispersal pan and our own ground crew was at supper. A relief crew was there to guide us in and help us out. We shut Easy down and got out to look at the damaged wing tip. It was gone. Five feet had just been blown off. Hooollyy! That was close, I thought.

"Skipper, you're still living a charmed life," Jack said. I was sure I was. Our regular ground crew was just driving up in their motor pool truck and Skeets, the head maintenance crewman asked me if there were any problems. "Skeets, I think the starboard Nav. light is out," I said. He walked around to the starboard wing tip and said, "Skipper you smart apple, you think you pulled a good one on me don't you? How the hell am I to get you a new wing?" he was surely annoyed but then I knew he would have Easy ready for flying by our next operation. In all of our missions, never once were we required to fly in any aircraft other than Easy. The ground crew would work day and night making repairs.

We took the crew bus to the interrogation room and it was there that we were told that we had lost two of our squadron's aircraft. "Who did we lose?" I asked the Chief Intelligence officer.

"It was D Dog, a new crew, just arrived here from CU the other

day. It was their first trip. All dead. The pilot flew the aircraft and then he bled to death on the end of the runway. Couldn't even shut her down," he told me. "Did you know the crew Skipper?" he asked.

"Not very well. I just met the captain this morning on sick parade," I replied.

I had to leave and get out into the air and be by myself. "You okay Skipper?" Jack asked.

"No Jack, I'm not okay. I knew Scotty and we had plans for his birthday party tomorrow. He would have been twenty one. How could I have been so daft as to make plans that far ahead?" I said. I left and walked away. I couldn't help crying. "Happy Birthday Scotty. You're home now laddie." I wept. What a wretched war this was.

THE SQUADRON LEADER

S ometimes in our life we come across an individual who stands out in our memory above all others. We remember their looks, the way they talk and other little individual characteristics. We remember how they related to their friends. My best friend, who incidentally was old enough to be my Father, was one of those.

Warrant Officer Gill Stevens was a permanent force RAF type. He was much older than almost everyone in the squadron. He was 6'2" and stood erect, with a certain air of British dignity about him. His blue eyes radiated his zest for life and also his friendliness and respect for everyone, regardless of rank or position. Gill exercised daily, keeping himself trim and healthy. His muscular appearance indicated his concern for his well being.

Gill was bald and, except for a little fringe of grey on his sideburns, there was little to indicate his age. We often joked about it but Gill would change the subject immediately. No discussion. He would joke about it by telling everyone he was just over 40. "Yeah, a long way over." we would joke.

Gill joined the RAF in India and had accumulated thousands of hours of training and operational flying. He came from a military family, his father being a retired Lt. Colonel in the British Army. Gill had grown up and schooled on army bases and was a military man through and through. He truly loved flying and it showed in his superb flying skill and his enthusiasm. Gill was actually fifty-three. He figured that he had pulled a fast one on headquarters staff in their not having discovered his true age. We thought he must have doctored his files somewhere along the line.

Gill must have had friends in high places and talked them into giving him an overseas posting to Bomber Command, 186 Squadron of Three Group. His crew were slightly on the elderly side as well but certainly not as old as mine. There were no spring chickens here.

It seemed that we were destined to become kindred spirits with

Gill being at the top end of the age category and me being at the low end. I obtained my crew because no one wanted to fly with a kid for a pilot. Gill got his crew because no one else wanted to fly with an old man for a pilot.

The 86th and 186th squadrons were located on the same base, which is where we met. We seemed to hit it off right away. I met Gill in the SNCO's Mess (Senior Non-Commissioned Officers). Like me, he was only entitled to the privileges provided in the Sergeant's Mess.

"I say youngster, rather young to be wearing those heavy wings aren't we?" he laughed as he sat down at my table.

"I'm not as young as I look Sir," I answered.

"Thanks for the compliment son but I'm only a SNCO like yourself," he smiled. Warrant Officers wore officer's uniforms so I naturally took him to be one. It never dawned on me why an officer would be in an NCO's mess. He smiled warmly at me and I liked him right away.

My crew were all commissioned officers except Roger, our tail gunner and I. Like myself, Gill's crew were all NCOs so my crew didn't have the same opportunity as I had getting to know them.

Gill immediately struck up a friendship with the grandpas in my crew. They could certainly relate to one another. On a few occasions, we took our leaves together. We were invited to Birngham to the home of Gill's rear gunner. Gill decided that I needed a father to watch over me so he just assumed that roll. I think he understood the problems I was continually facing.

I took to Gill because he was an authority figure and father image. I respected his authority as much as I did that of my bomb aimer, Jack Buvan.

For most of my flying days on the squadron, Gill was my mentor and was always there when I needed him. My crew too, felt they were required to see that I stayed clear of trouble and zealously protected me from undue pressure and sometimes abuse. I often heard Gill and Hank talking about me and how I was holding up under the strain of operations.

We couldn't understand why Gill had not received his commission as he had more service than all of us put together and

was a tremendously capable pilot. He was well liked by everyone and had a way of instilling confidence when it was difficult to create any. He guided me as he did all the other younger members of his crew like we were his personal responsibility because, in Gill's mind, we were.

He would make certain my bags were properly packed and my travel vouchers in order whenever I went on leave. I came to depend on him too much.

We were flying short trips, every day usually, to the Ruhr Valley. "Happy Valley" we called it. I could never figure out how it got its name. It was far from a happy place. Being heavily industrialized it was defended to the hilt and the bursting anti aircraft shells left a dense black cloud over the target. The smoke wouldn't hurt you, it was what was inside that was the killer. Gill told me that if you saw the smoke it was close enough. If you smelled the cordite then it was very close. If you could hear the crack and see the red flash as it exploded then you would be lucky to survive. It had hit you.

Most times we were lucky as we often heard the crack and saw the red flashes and listened to the shrapnel hitting the fuselage. Holes and tears and things like that would often appear along the wings and through the fuselage but otherwise Easy was holding together. Shrapnel could go right through an engine block.

I was having a very hard time at this point in my tour. I had lost a lot of friends and fellow crewmembers and each trip became more difficult to do. It didn't help to hear the flak pounding its way through the aircraft, sounding like hailstones on a tin roof. I was wondering when it would be Easy's turn.

I was appointed a GH leader and "Easy" was outfitted with the latest technology in radar called H2S. The pathfinders had been using it for almost a year before we got it. "GH" equipment we called it. I think the appointment came because our Navigator, F\L Jack McKay, was the best.

This new radar was the most advanced equipment yet devised for finding the target through heavy clouds or at night. Headquarters felt that Three Group would do much better if we had more accurate bombing for our daylight raids. So it was, that a few

aircraft in each squadron were outfitted with the equipment.

The method used was to have four or five aircraft form up on a GH leader. They would drop their bombs when they saw the fifth bomb leave the leader's bomb bay. This proved to be a more effective way to destroy a specific target.

The GH leaders were identified by the two yellow bands painted on their fin and rudders. All the others had to do was to find aircraft with the yellow stripes, identify him as their assigned leader and form up on him in a "V" formation.

We all wondered how I became a GH Leader and Gill didn't. Gill asked me to make sure he was assigned to my group on each raid we went on. He said he could keep an eye on me better. His crew was always assigned to my formation. He always liked the port wing position. It was like he was teasing me as he allowed his aircraft to creep closer to me. He told me he was just keeping me awake and on my toes.

Each day we watched the DROs (Daily Routine Orders) for Gill's name to appear on the promotion list then early one morning there it was. My rear gunner, Hank and Gill were to go into London for their interviews. We had stacked up 28 trips to date and the thought of a trip to London was exciting. Ray, Gill's rear gunner and I would tag along. We went into London for two days while they were being interviewed.

I thought back to my interview, remembering how devastated I was when I was turned down as I was " Too young and couldn't command respect".

Ray and I visited a nearby pub while Gill and Hank were getting their third degrees. These interviews were very important as a candidate's commission success depended entirely on the outcome. They returned smiling and excited, as both had been successful. Gill was beside himself with excitement and enthusiasm. Both men were anxious to order their uniforms. They would be measured and their uniforms ordered in Knightsbridge in London. It would take a week or so before they arrived. Until then, they would just have to wait for the day they could enter the officer's mess. I was now the only non-com in the crew.

It turned out that headquarters knew all about Gill's age and his

attempts to conceal it. They just hadn't caught up to him yet. His promotion was back dated four years and his appointment was to squadron leader. He was to receive back pay for those years. Twenty thousand pounds or eighty thousand dollars. He was ecstatic. We were very happy for Gill and joined him in his celebration. He paid, of course.

I wasn't very happy for me. I was now the only one of my crew still in the sergeant's mess. It was embarrassing and humiliating. I tried very hard not to show my feelings but my crew sensed my unhappiness. They insisted I have a hot cup of tea while they finished their drinks because I still wasn't allowed to drink.

I was feeling sorry for myself and almost forgot what the occasion meant to Gill. I should have been more caring for him and his new promotion. All those worries he had been carrying for so long were for nothing. Every one was celebrating with spirits and beer while I was getting high on tea and soda water. Gill and Easy's crew had forbidden me to drink, not even beer. I didn't like the taste anyway. Everyone seemed to have a thing about my drinking.

Hank came in and joined us, all smiles and accepting congratulations from everyone. "Tough luck Skipper, you're still getting a bum deal but your turn will come. Maybe next time," he tried reassuring me.

We returned to base and of course the members of Easy's crew were happy for Hank but knew I was hurting. "Skipper you just have to pull up your socks and get your commission. Remember you're the last NCO of this crew. Can't have that now can we?" Jack went on. How could I ever forget?

In the meantime, Gill had found a very nice lady living in Birmingham close to where the Barradels lived. That was Raymond Barradel, the family of Gill's rear gunner. They were quite wealthy, being top executive people in the Cadbury Corporation and they had opened their gorgeous palatial home to us wayward airmen. We were always invited to spend our leaves at their home and because I was the youngest they singled me out for special treatment and I enjoyed every minute of it.

Like most other people who knew us, it was quite beyond them that the captain of the aircraft should be only a sergeant, while the

entire crew was commissioned officers. Hooolllyyy! It was beyond me too. Far beyond me.

Gill's lady was lovely and we were introduced to her at the Barradel's. They invited her to visit and have dinner with us. Most times it was just we Canadians who visited each time. I still had the Browns in Mildenhall that I could always go to but Ray had asked me several times to come up and I couldn't refuse any longer. The other members of Easy's crew were with their families in the various parts of England. These times were very precious to them. Hank's commission was verified in DROs and so, with his new uniform on, we all celebrated. Then they took off for Hank's first night in the officer's mess. I had given up on ever seeing the inside of that building. It did make me feel sad and lonely that I was unable to be with my crew on these more relaxing moments.

Our next operations turned out to be very tough ones for Easy's crew. We took a hit under the port wing with shrapnel flying everywhere. A large piece came right through the port side of the cockpit and out through the canopy. A small piece of Plexiglas cut my cheek and it bled like fury. I thought for sure, looking at the mess that was developing on my gloves and on my face, that I was on death's door and that I was not long for this world. However, I seemed to be functioning okay and we flew on to the target, dropped our load and headed out before Bill the wireless operator could come forward to help me. "Well matey, this should be worth a VC or at least a cross of some sort," he kidded. "Hero medal for sure," the navigator laughed and said, "Tough luck Skipper, it's just a band-aid scratch, you'll have to wait 'til another time for the medal". I laughed although I was sure shaking.

On returning, Gill came to the hospital to make sure I was being looked after. He then took off for London to be with his lady friend who had travelled down from Birmingham so as to be near him. She had rented a small flat in Bury St. Edmunds, a small town near by. It became a gathering place for us and we enjoyed having some place to go off the base.

The Browns, who lived in Mildenhall, were my closest friends and were like family to me. I was treated like one of their kids. I rather enjoyed being with them where I could sort of let my hair

down and be a kid again. I could almost forget about the war. I hated the bars and the pubs and never went in them. I wasn't allowed anyway.

Frank was the terror of our crew. He lived to consume alcohol and in his off-hours he was inebriated beyond recognition. He would go on a drinking spree and ride his bike into bramble patches and then stagger his way back to my billet where he'd wake me up demanding I patch up his many scratches.

"Frank get the heck out of here. If you're caught in the NCO's billets, you're in trouble," I cautioned.

Late at night or early in the morning he had to tell me of his numerous female conquests in town. He loved to embarrass me but I think half his stories were exaggerated. What a liar. When he was sober he was great but that was only when we were flying and even then I could smell liquor on his breath. We came to the conclusion that this was the only way Frank was able to get through his tour.

Gill returned to base with his new uniform. He modeled it for us and told us that he was getting married in a couple of weeks. We were all invited. He was on cloud nine. I think we all were. The big event would take place on our next leave. June, Gill's lady friend had confided in me her deep concerns about Gill's last trips and that having just a few more to go made it almost unbearable. "I'll watch him, June," I promised.

The briefing board showed that Gill's "R Roger" had been assigned to another GH leader. I thought there had been a mistake so I approached the CO and drew it to his attention.

"Oh Hell, Skipper you're right. Does it make any difference? I can still change it back if you like," he said.

"I would feel better about it Sir. Gill will be wondering why the change," I replied.

"Okay son, it's done." With that he changed the names and advised the Intel Officer. The raid was to be on Gelsenkirken. The ETA on target was 1030 hrs. which meant take off at about 0700 hrs.

We had our breakfast of Spam, fried eggs and buns. This special menu was provided for all crews scheduled for Ops. Sort of like a Last Supper.

Then we were off to the dispersal areas and our aircraft. "Skip,

I'm not getting any oxygen back here," Hank advised.

"Have you tried the master valve, Hank?" I asked. He had gone over everything. This meant that after all of our previous trips we would have to transfer to the spare aircraft "D-DOG". This was a bad omen. Too many crews were lost flying in spare aircraft. The instrument mechanic walked over to the rear turret and talked to the gunner. I was just about ready to shut down the engines when Hank called again to tell me that the mechanic had found the trouble and that everything was okay. Hooolly! That was close.

We took off to our rendezvous over Redding. Here was where all the groups could sort out their GH leaders and form up accordingly. Gill formed on the port quarter just behind "F-Freddie" who was immediately on my port wing. "Z-Zebra" was on my starboard wing, while trailing him on his starboard quarter was "O-Oboe".

We set course for Germany. The weather was clear here but as we neared the Dutch coast, the clouds started to close in under us. That didn't stop the flak though. Outside the target area, I saw two Lancs blow up some miles ahead. I reported to the navigator to take the time. He would log any aircraft going down. He asked if we could identify the unfortunates. We were too far away and unless you had been looking at them before they blew, you could never tell who it was. We soon reported three more going down. Fortunately they had dropped their bombs and were through the target area. All three had suffered direct hits and were burning out of control. We watched for survivors. A wing came off another and it tumbled down through the sky. If I hadn't been so busy at the time I think I would have cried. It seemed so impossible to see a Lanc tumble from the sky and fall in so many pieces.

The sky didn't seem to be overly smoky from the mass of bursting shells yet why were so many aircraft going down? We realized we were experiencing another "Radar Predicted Flak" operation. Not the usual saturation flak, just direct hits on our aircraft. There was no evasive action for this stuff. The crew was frightened. I was petrified as I watched the maelstrom unfolding ahead of us and we still had to enter it.

It's strange, the things that run through your mind when you're

under pressure. I couldn't help thinking about Gill with his new fiance and of the happiness he was experiencing with his new commission. He was still flying as a SNCO. His commission would not be recognized until it had been published in DROs.

Gill was all ready for it. He had received his uniform with the three rings on the sleeve. He sure looked impressive as he modeled it for us. That's as far as he could go. He still couldn't wear it. The celebrations would start when we came home.

Hank's screaming voice on the I/C snapped me out of my daydreaming as I listened to him describing that Gill had taken a direct hit and was burning. I looked back over my shoulder and saw "R Roger" burning fiercely and diving towards the clouds. I banked towards his smoking aircraft with the rest of my formation following. I had to see if anyone was bailing out. The whole aircraft appeared as a flaming torch. The flames would subside somewhat as he dove but immediately he'd recover, the flames would roar up again with a vengeance. Gill continued doing this until he disappeared through the clouds. I was weeping openly. "Oh, please Lord not Gill," I prayed.

I heard Jack calling Hank to see if our formation was still with us. There was an explosion very close behind us. "Hank how are things back there? Did we pick up anything from that last burst?" Jack continued. When Hank didn't answer Jack ordered Bill to check on the rear gunner to see what was wrong with his intercom.

"Jack, Bill here, Hank's copped it. He's dead. The whole turret is a tangled mess." Hank had taken shrapnel through his neck and chest from the explosion. The turret could not be moved so that we could remove Hank's body. He bled to death and we couldn't help him.

We continued onto the target and Jack dropped our bombs guided by our new GH equipment. The rest of the formation knew that we had taken a hit.

We returned home with no further incidents and once we had cleared the target area the flak ceased. I was devastated as I tried to cope. I could hardly make myself believe that Gill was gone and losing our first crewman was more than I could stand. I cried myself home as we tried to talk each other through the shocking experience. Now I knew what it was like to lose two of your best friends.

The debriefing was a total disaster for me. I never could drink the operational rum ration so I was excused and sent to the hospital. I was given a sedative and put to bed to sleep it off. "War is Hell" as the expression goes, is the most understated description I had ever heard. It failed to describe the awfulness of our experiences.

Gill was gone and we had heard no news of what had become of his crew until after the war. Gill had stayed at the controls until the very end trying to allow his crew to get free. Three members made it out by parachute while Gill and the others perished.

Ray Barradell had booked off the operation with a very bad cold. Not his choice but Gill's. He couldn't go on the trip. This was the end for Ray. His feeling of guilt at not having been along was more than he could bear. He was pulled from operations. I was sent on a week's leave and went to the Brown's in Mildenhall. They were my overseas family.

June, Gill's fiancé, returned to Birmingham, her life shattered. Gill never had a chance to wear his uniform or join the officer's mess. His money went into his estate in India. There were no other members of his family alive and so it was turned over to the state. June got none of it as Gill had not had time to change his will. I wished I could have talked to Peggy or Ken during this terrible time of my life.

My time with the Browns was just what I needed. They really took care of me and were the best medicine in the world for they sensed my loss. They suffered along with me.

Another reason for our week's leave was that our tour had been increased from 30 trips to 35 trips. We still had six more to go. The state of our mental condition concerned the MO and decided the rest would do us good. Any respite from this terrible business was good. Gill as well would have had to make one more trip to complete his tour. Who would be next?

EASY'S TURN

Most briefings were somewhat somber affairs. Everyone was busy thinking about what was being told to us and what the target was going to be like. Many tried to hide their concerns by assuming a nonchalant attitude. Jack said they were just trying to cover up their true sense of foreboding. There were still a few others who outwardly displayed their premonitions of doom.

In my case, I think partially due to my age and lack of worldly experiences, I never felt much other than the things at hand. True, I now knew that I was vulnerable and, youth or no youth, lady luck would only ride with us so long. I was no longer the naive youngster I had been just few weeks before. The personal loss of Gill and Hank were almost more than I was capable of handling. My crew and especially Jack, my bomb aimer, were always at hand to help me sort out my feelings and concerns about the raid and tell me what sort of things we were going to encounter. I could figure most things out for myself but there were certain things said that gave other meanings to the briefings, which I could easily miss or let go over my head. In other words, I didn't read between the lines. Their insight helped me sort out a lot of things. I recall Gill telling me, "Skipper, you just fly the airplane and let them do the thinking. They won't give you a bum steer." My friend was right.

My crew guided me through 35 operational missions safely, well most times it was safely. I had it pointed out to me many times and by many experienced people that I was in over my head. I was too young to comprehend what this whole matter of operational flying was all about. I was fortunate in having a very experienced crew who could see things before they happened. But for them I would never have come this far.

All through my first days in the service I had grown to realize that being young, small and smart were three characteristics one did not wish to possess if one wanted to be accepted and make it with your peers. I can think back even further to my days on the ranch

where I was always having to prove myself. So other than the fact that I was eighteen and could fly the Lancs as well as any of the others, I found myself still having to prove myself. So much for reflections.

The briefing was for Botropp in the Ruhr Valley. It was an oil refinery that was producing aviation fuel. There were to be two bombing attacks, one after the other. Each wave would have eighty aircraft and would be bombing from eighteen thousand feet.

The sky was going to be cloudy, with 9/10ths cover. We were to have three aircraft in our formation not counting ourselves. We were to come in on the target from the South East after having made a diversionary run on another target which we would over fly. This often set the defenders of the real target off their guard and we would get in and out with few or no casualties. We knew the flak would be heavy in the Ruhr but perhaps we would be lucky enough to escape the fighters.

The trip would last 4:30 hrs. Quite fast in and out. The rendezvous went very well and Jack told me that he had spotted our aircraft forming up on us and that we could get underway. "Jack, we still have a couple of minutes to go," I told him. "Forget it Skipper, let's just get out of this mess, we can dogleg if we need to. I think we should get out of the rendezvous area as soon as possible," he advised. I saw there were literally hundreds of aircraft milling about trying to marry up with their formations. "Okay Jack, let's go," I agreed.

"Jack (Navigator) take the time of our outbound," I said, knowing he would have already done that. I just had to make some comment to relieve the tension.

"Done Skip," he replied.

We reached the Channel with our formation tight on each wing. The weather down below looked rotten with scuddy rain clouds sweeping past the windows. We were still climbing through the clouds at that time but what I had seen below in the Channel convinced me that no one would ever survive a ditching in those waters.

The flak appeared right on schedule for our Dutch coast crossing. This was one way we always knew, clouds or not, that we were crossing the coastline. The flak was always there waiting and ready to try and punch us out of the sky. They were good but not as

good as the flak crews from the Ruhr.

We were just breaking through the clouds into clear skies when Roger passed on a sighting. A Lanc was turning back. We couldn't see any damage but nevertheless something was wrong as he was losing altitude and finally disappeared into the clouds. Hmm, one down and we hadn't even started.

"Aircraft on the Port Quarter astern Skip," Roger called again. "I think it's a 109 (Me 109) and he seems to be flying parallel to us," he added. I looked around to see if there were any other formations about but couldn't see any. "Jack, are we still okay for time?" I asked. I was a little concerned as five minutes over a target area by yourself is asking for deep trouble. This much I could figure out for myself. I had seen it happen many times before.

"Skip, Nav here, we still have 20 minutes before our south leg. I hope we spot some of the others soon," he said. He assured me that we were on course but still ahead of time. Then I thought of the other Lanc and wondered where his formation was. It had to be somewhere near by.

"Enemy aircraft off the Port Quarter, prepare to dive port," the rear gunner shouted into his intercom. If I needed awakening, those words did it. The commentary started.

"ME 210 at 1000 yards and closing, prepare to dive Port," came Roger's voice. Each time this scenario unfolded my heart would start pumping faster and faster. I couldn't see what was happening other than if the attack was coming from on top and then I could glance over my shoulder and see it for myself. Fat lot of help that was. This is why the pilot had to do exactly as he was told and follow the instructions of his gunner.

"Dive! Dive! Port! Go!" I pressed the control yolk forward as much as my straps would allow and turned Easy into a steep diving turn into our attacker. With a full bomb load, Easy fell like a ton of bricks and my only concern was to not let Easy rip her wings off. We were loaded to the maximum this trip with all the HE we could carry. I remembered asking our ground crew if the bomb doors were thick enough to stop flak or a 20 mm cannon shell. I didn't wonder for too long as they pointed out that the doors were paper thin to conserve weight and wouldn't stop a fast bird. So much for the confidence one got from having your doors closed. I rotated Easy

and we rolled up the starboard side and struggled to regain altitude. Sometimes this was all that was required to break off the fighter attack. His guns were fixed and he was required to point his aircraft at you in order to strike a hit while our guns could shoot regardless of where we were going.

I looked around and asked the guys to see if they could see our formation.

"No dice Skipper," Frank replied. He had the best position to spot the other planes. I had climbed to the very upper fringe of the clouds. Another 100 feet and I would have been in them. The fighter had dived on past us into the scud.

"I've lost him Skip, don't see him anywhere," Roger yelled.

"Skip! There they are, off to Port, at about eleven o'clock," Frank confirmed the sighting. The formation had spotted us and were doing a minor dogleg to allow us to catch up and resume our position. I had just turned towards them when Frank announced that one of our formation, G George, was breaking out and diving into the clouds hotly pursued by a fighter. Then another fighter came shooting up out of the clouds just ahead of us.

"I got him Skip," Jack claimed. Jack had him in his forward gun sight and opened fire almost immediately. We could see the tracers from Jack's guns arching across the skies and shortly after Frank's guns opened up as we were drawing under the ME 210. Pieces started to fall off the target and then his tail fin came off. The aircraft went into a tight spin from which it would never recover although the pilot might bale out.

"Hoooollly," I shouted into the I/C. "Jack, you guys got him!" It wasn't often that a Lanc shot down his attacker. Attack we had and shoot the guy down we did. I was thrilled and I suppose a bit giddy. "Settle down you guys, we still haven't dropped our stuff don't forget," Jack admonished. That sobered us but the elation of having shot down our first aircraft was really overwhelming. We would certainly be heroes back home when we returned. Hmmmmm. If we returned. What a morbid thought.

The other two aircraft of our formation swung in to us and at the same time we spotted the rest of our first wave. "Skipper, they're higher than we are. We don't want to be down below them," Frank

cautioned.

"Hoollly! Jack, how come they're that much higher than us? We're at height now, what the heck is going on?" I asked.

"Skipper, we gotta go to twenty thousand feet. There's high cloud over the target area," Bill the radio operator cut in. You better start climbing now Skip," Jack advised.

Looking ahead we saw more fighters engaging our group. They were certainly higher than we were and there was a lot of activity. Fighters were buzzing around like angry hornets.

We were on our south leg and about to do a 180-degree turn to the target area. "Skipper we got 6 minutes to drop, are we okay?" Jack asked.

"We got uglies at 4 o'clock high Skip, we're going to have visitors," Roger called, the excitement showing in his voice as he got ready to give me his commentary.

"Skipper, 210 coming in 6 o'clock low, 800 yards and closing, 500 yards, prepare to dive port Dive! Dive! Go!" Roger yelled. Down we dropped, rolled to starboard and started our climb. Perhaps it wasn't enough to create the necessary firing angle between the fighter's shells and us. I heard him pass under us and as he flew under Jack's guns opened up again. He had been watching out the side and could see which way the fighter was going to pass. Frank's guns were angled forward to fire on the fighter if he climbed upwards. Tracers from the front guns followed the fighter and for a minute the fighter cockpit lit up like a Christmas Tree and then it burst into flames and the pilot baled out. Some marvelous shooting on Jack's part. His shells had hit something in the cockpit.

I couldn't believe what was happening. Two fighters and both from our front turret. Almost unheard of. "I'll take a formal congratulatory note from one and all," Jack joked in a rather formal way. I didn't say a word as I was speechless, that is until Frank called that he spotted a fighter passing under us from port to starboard.

Where the heck had he come from? "Where is he Frank?" I asked.

"Don't see him Skip."

"Anyone else see him?" I asked. No one had seen anything other than Frank. If there was one thing that really got your neck hairs

standing on end, it was knowing you had a fighter close to you some place and not knowing where he was. All of a sudden, two holes appeared in my windscreen just to the one side of my forward view and splinters flew everywhere. Then my side window disappeared and I could hear guns clattering away and Frank telling Roger that he had the guy in his sights. A moment later more shrapnel burst into the cockpit and I felt blood dripping down my cheek and my hand was bleeding. I really didn't feel much of anything but I knew I had been hit. I asked Bill to bring up the first aid kit as I had a few nicks to seal up.

"Rightly Ho Skip old son, hold on, you going to handle it okay?" he asked. Jack called to ask if he should come back but I told him I thought we were okay.

"Skipper, we got a minute to drop, are we on course?"

I told him we were right on but then asked him why there were Lancs coming into the area on all sorts of different headings. "What goes?" I yelled at him. "Got me Skipper," Jack replied. Our height heading and airspeed were okay so we should have been right on. He had the target on screen but there was a lot of flak.

"Jack, start dropping WINDOW (metallized strips of paper which, when dumped out of the aircraft, created distorted images for the German radar. It only benefited the aircraft behind)." I realized how giddy I really was when I would make such a suggestion while we were on the critical last seconds of our bomb run. "I can't Skipper, we're dropping in a couple of seconds. Port, port just a tad--Steady on now, steady--steady-- Bombs Gone!" he yelled. Just then a flak burst hit right under us. I heard the shrapnel banging off the fuselage and through the bomb bay doors, which, until a moment ago, had held 6 tons of bombs. I banked Easy and headed out. Aircraft seemed to be everywhere. I wondered why they had not gone in on the proper headings as we had done.

"Jack take the time, we either have had two chaps go or the Germans are firing up scarecrows (Anti Aircraft shells filled with rubber, cloth, oil and tar, which would simulate an aircraft blowing up)." These were sent up to unnerve us and they did. "Jack, did you get those times?" I asked. No answer. I twisted in my seat and could just make out Jack seated at his desks. "Bill, check Jack's intercom

will you?" I asked.

"Oh Jeeez Skipper! Oh No God!" I heard Johnny shout. Then the I/C went quiet. I knew without asking what had happened. I just couldn't ask. A piece of shrapnel had penetrated the floor decking and come up between Jack's legs, gone up through his chin and through his head. He lay in a pool of blood on his desk. My Australian school teacher would teach no more. I wept quietly to myself. Shells were bursting everywhere. We had been targeted by radar. Another shell burst just above Frank's turret completely demolishing it. He died immediately without knowing what had hit him. Frank had collected his last bad debt.

I was feeling nothing at this point. Shock seemed to have taken over and I was numb all through. A part of me had vanished with Frank and Jack. I wept to myself.

I turned Easy on her final leg home. We were over France and would cross over the coast almost on the border between Belgium and Denmark. Jack, our bomb aimer, called me to see if he could do anything. "Will you come and help Johnny, please?" I asked. Jack passed by me without a word and, knowing my agony, squeezed my arm. My own bleeding had stopped so physically there wasn't anything too wrong with me.

Our two casualties would just add to our already heavy losses. I guessed it had to happen sooner or later according to the odds everyone was always talking about.

"Blackadar, this is Beddar Easy, I have two casualties on board and request turn to land, over."

"Beddar Easy. Is the nature of your casualty an emergency? Over."

"No Ma'am," I answered to the lady operator.

"Easy from Blackadar, you are turn five, repeat you are turn five." I hardly knew what to do other than to settle down and concentrate on landing.

The bomb aimer was humming a tune. How could he do that at a time like this? He was still behind me and standing with Johnny and Jack. He kept humming. What was the tune? Waltzing Matilda. Oh God. That did it for me. I could hardly see the instruments for my tears.

We continued circling until we were given turn one to land.

There was nothing said by anyone. We just sat there in shock as Easy squeaked onto the runway. I don't know how I was able to see through my tears. I called for an ambulance to meet us at our dispersal pan as it would be closer than to taxi all the way over to the control tower. I let Easy roll to the end of the runway, turned off and taxied the pan. I selected the bomb doors but they wouldn't open. Too badly damaged I guessed. I shut the engines off, the ground crew was quickly blocking the wheels, and looking over the damage we had suffered. They sort of sensed that things had gone badly when we failed to open the hatch door right away.

I sat in my seat, unable to move. Bill came forward and patted me on the shoulder. He too was wiping away tears. My injuries seemed so insignificant, compared to the ultimate sacrifice Jack and Frank had made.

Roger and Bill got the hatch open and were jumping out. They were telling the ground crew of our loss. They never mentioned our successes. Our ground crews felt as badly as we did. The ambulance pulled up to the side door. I looked out my side window and saw Mr. and Mrs. Swanson standing by the perimeter buildings, knowing something was very wrong. I couldn't look out at them. I'm the one who is supposed to take charge. I'm the captain of the aircraft, the Skipper. I couldn't move.

Jack took over as always. They ushered the first aid people up to the cockpit to help me. The wound was not a very bad one. More like a slice. It cut my skin but the bleeding had stopped. I guess my face was a mess and looked a lot worse than it really was, what with the blood from my eye brow washing down into my tears. My helmet was torn as well.

I finally crawled out and was helped into the ambulance. Mrs. Swanson came running over, unable to stand by any longer. She was always worrying about me. "Skipper. I'm so sorry. You're going to be just fine," she comforted me. I shook as she put her arms around my shoulders. "We have to go Mrs. Swanson," Jack consoled her.

I was driven to the hospital and Frank and Jack were driven to the morgue. Things seemed terribly unfair. Jack rode with me and saw me stitched up in the emergency room and then given a sedative. I will always remember my first drink of rum. The

ambulance attendant gave it to Jack and instead of drinking it himself he lifted it to my lips and made me drink it. I huffed and gagged but swallowed. He winked at me. "I think you're old enough now Skipper. Good for what ails our boy," he said. His eyes were red too.

Word soon spread about Easy's kills and of our loss. It seemed that, up until now, the Kid was a good omen, a good luck charm. We had lived a relatively sheltered and safe existence and Jack had made us heroes with his two kills.

That day we lost twelve aircraft and many more had been shot up. How many of the crews were able to bale out we didn't know. Perhaps they were safe somewhere. We knew two crewmen were dead. Our Jack and Frank. We were sent on leave for a week. I went to the Browns in Mildenhall. The rest went to their homes.

Jack received a Bar to his DFC as did Jack and Frank. Bill, Johnny and Roger all received their DFCs. I got a Bar to my Medal and we were all given honourable mentions. A few days later F/L Jack Buvan was mentioned in DROs as having been awarded the DSO (Distinguished Service Order) for meritorious service of bravery. I had five more trips to go to complete my tour. Officially, the others had completed their tour seven trips ago. It was truly an act of faith that they elected to extend their tour until I was finished.

Me-210

GROWING UP

F/L Bruce Gilbert and his crew had endeavoured to replace Gill Stevens in our lives. Although Bruce and Gill were very much alike, there was no way Bruce could fill the void left by Gill's crew. Bruce and Gill had known each other back in India before the war and were the best of friends so it seemed natural for them to become buddies with "Easy's" crew.

Few crews allowed friendships to build, other than passing acquaintances. This was a shield of armour against the terrible hurt we experienced when a friend was lost. Crews came and went without ever knowing the other members in the squadron other than by the Name and Identification Letters of their aircraft. I found that whenever Gill went on leave or was away for one reason or another Bruce was delegated to keep an eye on me and help my crew keep me out of trouble for it seemed trouble of one sort or another generally located me. It was in this regard that Bruce came to me one day telling me how concerned he was. "Skip, are you okay? How are things with you after all that's happened? Why don't you take some time away from the crew and just have some time to yourself?" he enquired.

"I'm okay Sir. The MO said I was experiencing minor shock symptoms and it would pass. He suggested I do the same thing, that I get away from the war for awhile," I replied. "I haven't a clue where I'd go to get away from everything, unless I went to Mildenhall and I hate to burden them when I'm as miserable as I am. I can't even stand myself," I said. I think I'll just stick around here."

"The hell you will, chappie, you're going to go to Mildenhall and visit your friends there," he said. "They're young and you relate well with them. I think that's exactly where you should go," Bruce advised.

"Come on Bruce they're just kids and besides they have their own troubles, what with rationing and all," I said.

"Well listen to who's talking about just kids. Aren't we growing up in a hurry?" he kidded.

"Yes Sir, I am. Maybe I'll just take off for a few days to Birmingham or Bury or some place like that," I replied.

"I don't think it's good for you to be alone Skip. You'll start feeling sorry for yourself," he said. "Well son, I have to leave, I have a very important date tonight, think it over though. I'll see you in the morning," he said and was gone.

I was really moved by Bruce's concern over my well being. Since Gill had gone, Bruce seemed to take over in his place. He watched me like a hawk. I would often see him and Jack, our bomb aimer, talking together. By their glances every so often in my direction, I presumed they were talking about me and they would hush up when I came near.

I didn't know who our new crew members would be. We'd find out when we returned. It was hard for all of us to realize that Frank and Jack would not be returning. How could anyone take their places? No one would do the job as well as they did. Our new replacements would have a difficult time filling their places.

I was in the NCO's mess watching a long drawn out chess game, which I had started three days before and someone else had picked up. "Phone call for Junior." I heard the mess sergeant call. "Phone call for Junior," he called again. I knew he was calling me but I wasn't in the mood for their usual teasing so I chose to ignore his joking. It seemed that everyone enjoyed trying to get under my skin.

If I answered, everyone would shout, "Now how in the hell did Skipper know the call was for him?" I usually went along with the funning but tonight I wasn't in the mood even though they were just trying to cheer me up. "Tele' for Skipper, come on junior, answer the bloody phone will you?" shouted the impatient bar man. He knew I was there and just wasn't answering.

"Okay I'm coming, I'm coming," I replied.

"Hello, this is Sergeant Scott speaking," I answered.

"Skipper, this is Matt," the boyish voice said.

"Hi Matt, it's good to hear your voice again. What's up?" I asked.

"Skipper, we want you to come up on your next leave. Do you suppose you would like that? We really want to see you. We haven't heard from you for ages, or at least it seems that way. Please say you'll come Skip, Please?" Matthew pleaded.

I immediately pictured him in his living room with everyone standing around while he talked. "Matt, I start leave tomorrow, would you want me that soon?" I asked. I was also thinking about Bruce's words to "Get away."

There was silence for a second and I could hear them chatting in the background. "Skipper, please come right away, tonight if you can, we'll meet you at the bus. There's a bus at 11 o'clock that you can catch if you get with it. I know it's late but we are most anxious to have you here so we will have much more time to visit and all that," he said.

"Really old chap, we do want you to come, right?" Matt's father had come on the line. An answer to a prayer I thought. Just what I needed and without any more hesitation I replied, "Thank you Mr. Brown, I'm really glad you called me and I'll be on the late bus," I said. "Ta" was the only reply on the other end.

It didn't take me long to change into my civvies, pack my small bag and dash to the transport office to bum a ride into Bury St. Edmonds where I'd catch my bus. The bus was almost empty and I enjoyed the quiet all to myself. I had lots of time to think about my situation and to reflect on all that occurred over the last few weeks. I sat and stared out the window into the dark. In spite of the fact I was looking forward to visiting the Browns again, I felt terribly empty. Something had gone out of my life. For the first time since starting Ops, I started to think about what was happening on the ground during one of my raids. During an Op I rarely had time to think about the destruction I was wreaking nor the hundreds of lives I might be taking. Now it was haunting me. What was I doing here? Then I remember the enemy fighters surging over the coast into the park in Bournemouth and killing all those women and children but even that memory didn't help much.

The loss of my friends was finally sinking in. What was the meaning of it all? What a tragic waste. I wanted to weep.

Until now, I don't think it fully registered that it could happen to me. It was always the others who lost crewmembers. The thought that it might be our turn to die was frightening. I didn't think I would be very good company for the Browns.

The bus pulled into Mildenhall and the depot was crowded with

passengers waiting to get on. Everything was blacked out so it was hard to see anyone. I got my bag and stepped off the bus into the arms of Mr. and Mrs. Brown. It was almost like coming home. The kids were there and welcomed me like a returning brother. That was how they felt and it was how I felt. It was exactly what I needed.

Matthew and Keith were all over me, hugging and shaking hands. I was overcome with the especially warm welcome. Mrs. Brown noticed the look on my face and she saw the tear in my eye and gave me a hug. "Well Skipper you're in good hands now, we're happy you have come to be with us," she said as she hustled us away to the car.

"I have some gas coupons for you Mr. Brown. Maybe that will help pay for your fuel bill," I said.

"Much appreciated Skipper. I know you have no use for them so I will accept them with much gratitude. My word, there is a whole three months or even more here," he said.

I told him I had scoffed them off one of our ground crew.

It was one o'clock in the morning when we arrived at the Brown's and after some hot chocolate and biscuits, we were ushered off to bed. Matt and I always shared his bed when I came. Mrs. Brown came up to check on us. "Just tucking you in is all," she laughed. She sat down on the edge of the bed. "Skipper, we heard about your loss and also of your injuries and we want you to know we share your feelings," she said. "We are so proud of you and your efforts on our behalf. We want to share the joy and, of course, your sadness," she soothed in her very gentle voice.

"Thank you very much Mrs. Brown. I appreciate this time with you all very much," I answered, trying to hold back the tears.

She left so Matt and I could talk.

Matt wanted to know what it was like flying Ops. and was I frightened? How could I begin to tell him? He looked at my stitched eyebrow and wrist.

"How did you hear about our trip, Matt?" I asked. "Well, Mr. Merrystone, who lives next door, brought home some DROs from the base where he works and we saw the casualty lists along with the awards. Your name was on both and because he had met you at our house he thought we would like to know," he said."Then a

friend of yours called to tell us that you were about to go on leave and that he thought we could be of some help. Cheer you up sort of thing," he said. "We will Skip, you're like my brother, you know?" Matthew confided. There was a tear in his eye.

We talked for a little while and then I drifted off into a sound sleep, the first in over a week.

We were up early each morning, not wanting to waste any time of my leave. The weather was bright, warm and sunny and we spent most of the day riding our bikes through the countryside and fishing and swimming in the pond.

As hard as it was to do, everyone kept the conversation away from the war. They asked about the ranch and about Ken and wanted to know if I ever heard from Ken over here. I really enjoyed that because it gave me a chance to talk about my family and about the wonderful life I had growing up on the ranch.

I was slowly getting back to normal again and was actually putting on some weight. I was also growing a bit taller though Matt was still almost three inches taller than I was and he was only 15.

Matt, Keith and I went out biking in Mildenhall and just about pedalled ourselves to death. I was exhausted but I felt good. I got to know the countryside pretty well and we would visit with some of the country folk. The weekend came to a close and the boys had to go off to school.

"Skipper, I have a smashing idea. Why don't you come to school with us today?" Keith suggested. He was the mischief in the family and was laughing as he explained his plan. They were excited at the prospects of another day of fun. "We'll just say that you're a visitor from Canada and staying with us for awhile," he laughed as he envisioned the reaction of his classmates.

"Keith's right Skip and why not? It would be such a lark and it wouldn't hurt anyone. You would get a chance to see what our school system is like," Matt added.

"Skipper, why not go along? I'm sure there would be no problem if you went with them," Mrs. Brown said.

"We won't tell them who you really are unless someone finds out," Matt said.

"This will be such fun," Keith said. Everyone was getting into

the feel of the thing and I finally agreed that I would go with them.

"Skipper, you just slip into one of Keith's school uniforms. You already fit them better than he does," Matt laughed.

"Matt, you're just jealous cause Skipper wouldn't wear any of yours," Keith quipped in return.

It was settled and I got dressed in Keith's blue blazer with a crest on the pocket, white shirt, navy tie, grey pants and black shoes. I came back downstairs with Keith laughing and joking alongside. Mrs. Brown looked at us both and declared, "I can hardly tell you two apart, my goodness just look at you." I looked at myself in the mirror alongside Keith and I hardly recognized myself. This was going to be fun.

We left for school and I was about to learn something about the British educational system. We had decided that I should go into Keith's class rather than Matt's so I wouldn't stand out too much because of my size.

I was introduced to the teacher and students as a relative of the Brown's and nothing more was said. I just sat and did what the others did. We even had a game of soccer at break period. I was asked to tell the class about Canada and about ranching in particular. This went over so well that they brought in two more classes, including Matt's, to join in the questioning. Gone were my thoughts of the war and operations.

I was enjoying being a kid again. It was well worth the experience just to throw my cares out of the window and totally engross myself in the school activities. I had a hard time keeping Keith from spilling the beans as to who I really was.

The day went just fine and we finished with an invitation to come back the next day or as often as I wished. No one tumbled to our deception and I was back in class for the balance of the week.

Thursday evening, while we were just finishing supper, an American Airforce staff car drew up in front of the house. A Captain knocked on the door and asked if they had a young man staying here from the RAF, a sergeant Scott.

"Skipper," Keith called, "I think this Officer wants to talk to you." "Skipper, yes that's his name," the officer said.

I came to the door, wondering what this was all about. "Yes

Sir," I said.

"You're Skipper Scott?" the officer asked, looking me up and down. "Sergeant, the Commanding Officer would like you to visit him tomorrow morning, if that's convenient," he said.

I was just about to say, "No, I have school," when I caught myself and told him I would be happy to come. "Can you tell me what it is about?" I asked.

"Well, Sergeant, you're sort of a hero on our base. I wasn't there at the time but we've sure heard about you." He went on, "Forgive me but I have a hard time believing I am not talking to a school boy. You certainly hide your age well."

"Thank you Sir," I smiled.

"We'll send a car for you at nine, if that's okay. You sure are one surprise, I'll tell you," he added as he left.

Everyone was anxious to know what was happening and why the Airforce had come to visit. "I don't know how they came to know I was here," I said.

"I'll bet it was Mr. Merrystone," Keith said.

"See Skipper, you're a hero here," Mrs. Brown chuckled.

The next morning I dressed in Keith's school uniform. I didn't want to put on an ordinary sergeant's uniform when I was visiting the big cheese of the Airforce and besides I hadn't brought any dress clothes.

I was feeling nervous and a little jittery at the thought of this visit and wondered what was taking place. Why did they want to see me? I was nervous as I waited for the staff car.

The car drove up exactly on time and the driver asked me twice if I was Sergeant Scott. We enjoyed seeing the surprised look on people's faces when they learned who I was and the driver was no exception. Matt pictured it as a little conspiracy on our part.

Mrs. Brown laughed at the driver's discomfort. She knew that he was wondering if he had come to right house and if I was really the passenger, he was to pick up. We would certainly have a chuckle about it later on. I wasn't all that sure that he had the right passenger as well. I didn't know what was going on at all but thought it would be nice to visit the base again and renew some old acquaintances. I felt I would rather be enjoying my holiday than doing anything else. We arrived at the base gate and the driver had to show credentials and

explain who wanted to see the passenger. A phone call and another scratch of the head and we were passed through.

We arrived at the headquarters building and I was ushered in to the CO's office. I think the CO was rather taken aback by my attire. "God Skipper you look younger than the last time I saw you and God knows you looked like a baby then. It's hard to believe you're nineteen," he laughed.

I explained to him why I had chosen to come dressed in the school clothes I had borrowed from Keith. He laughed and agreed that I perhaps would feel better this way. "Not so intimidating huh, Son? We heard you were here visiting and we wanted to meet you again and perhaps show you in person just how much you impressed us," he said. I have taken the liberty of having a few of the officers you met while you were here over to have a drink so you can get re-acquainted. We have lost several of the men who were here at that time, I am sure you understand," he apologized.

"I had the opportunity to read your airforce DROs where you and your crew were mentioned. I want to extend our sympathies for your loss and our heartiest congratulations on an award you justly deserve. Your friends and your family must be very proud of you," he added.

"Thank you Sir," I replied. I still wasn't very comfortable sitting in his huge office. Just then a knock on the door announced the arrival of several officers whom I recognized from my stay at the base several months before. The CO introduced me to the new officers. They had asked to be included in the welcoming group. It was very flattering.

It was great to renew old acquaintances and rehash the events that took place. They wanted to know about my last few trips leading up to our loss.

"Skipper, how is it that you're just a boy flying operations with the RAF?" one of the new officers asked.

"Don't answer that Skipper, we've already told these guys that the RAF is not robbing the cradle, you just wear well," the CO said, chuckling.

We continued talking about the German Fighter tactics and the new improved radar controlled anti-aircraft guns. I told them my

experience with it and they seemed very interested, especially when we discussed our H2S.

"Skipper, we want you to join us later in the mess. We have a little something for you, which we'll give you at that time. In the meantime, I would like these guys to show you our new B17G. It's going to replace our old "Fs". By then it will be time for lunch," the CO said. His clerk hastened us out of the office.

We walked over to the nearest hangar where I got the grand tour of their latest addition. It was quite impressive but still no Lancaster. I was surprised to see an H2S scanner poking out of the bottom of the aircraft. "I think you guys have been pulling my leg a little, making out you weren't aware of the H2S we were using," I said jokingly. They laughed. It was time to walk over to the Mess. While we were walking past the control tower, a voice from a bull horn rang out, "Skipper, get your little arse over here, on the double!" Everyone started to laugh.

"Go ahead Skip, we'll wait for you," my escort announced.

"Skipper, you little twerp, how the heck are you?" Lt. Bill Downey gave me such a smack on the back that I nearly fell flat on my face. He had been on duty in the tower the day I shot up his office while I was after the ME 210. "How are you Willie? You don't look a day older than when I saw you last," I replied after I got my breath back.

"Well, I sure as heck am. Look at all my gray hair. You sure look good youngster," he laughed. "I really wanted to talk to you alone and tell you how proud we are of what you've been doing," he said. "We heard through the grapevine that you got a couple of medals, plus your crew have three fighters to their credit." He went on, "Skipper, do you know why you're here?"

"No Willie, not really. I guess to visit and to meet some old friends," I replied.

"Like hell, maybe I'm not supposed to tell you, but I don't want you to be shocked to death as I know how modest you are. You're getting a medal from the brass. The boss put in for it and you're getting it today. It was just luck that you were here on your leave and that we heard about it. They would have done it through the RAF if you hadn't been here," Willie told me.

"Willie, I don't want any medal. What the heck is it for anyway?" I asked, starting to feel uncomfortable.

"You know what for kid and we honour our heroes," he said.

I have never felt so out of place in all my life. The mess was full and I was ushered over to the Commanding Officer's table where all the station brass were sitting. I knew exactly what the rest of the mess must have been thinking when I walked in. "Is this the guy we're supposed to be honouring?"

Oh well, I had no choice but I was some embarrassed. I was very uncomfortable as I sat eating and chatting with the officers closest to me but I wasn't very hungry. I was too nervous now that I knew what was going on.

There were some good natured jabs at the RAF and I was a little slow on my rebuttals. They were just trying to keep me on my toes they laughed.

Good Grief! I happened to glance over the tables and there, sitting with several other officers, were the Browns, every one of them. They had been invited to be the guests of the Airforce and to witness my getting the medal.

The CO called for silence and the presentation took place. I was presented with the Air Medal. It was awarded and authorized by the US Secretary of Defense for meritorious service. Hooolly!

I was speechless and had a difficult time coming up with an acceptance speech. I was flattered and embarrassed at the same time. The Browns came over to congratulate me and to take me home. I made my farewells with a promise to return.

We went home and all the talk was about this special day in our lives. They told me how the CO had approached them, told them what was happening and invited them to attend. The kids were allowed to miss school. They were very happy for me.

We went biking again and swam in the pool, then returned home for supper. I was exhausted; the events of the day were tiring. I had been on edge the whole day.

The Browns had really helped me get my feet back on the ground. They were all so kind to me. I could now finish my tour.

EASY'S LAST FLIGHT

Have you ever prayed for a day to come and then when it did you prayed for it to go away? Well, this is exactly how I was feeling. We had flown our last few flights with relative ease and not even a flak hole. I know thoughts had been racing through our minds, that this was the lull before the storm, the prelude to our final demise. Jack, in particular, was feeling the almost unbearable tension as we flew our last trips. He, Bill and Johnny were now about to fly their 43rd operation and all because of me.

They had decided that they would extend their tour so that they could be with me to help finish mine. I had no right to expect or even allow them to make this unselfish act of friendship and camaraderie. After all, they had completed their tour when they reached 35 operations.

When I rejoined them, they had already flown eight operations. They were seasoned warriors. They had been safe, they had done their duty, their wives and families had made their sacrifices and were entitled to their men coming home safely. They chose otherwise. I know the matter had been discussed amongst them and they unanimously decided to see me though my tour. For this they would be credited with an additional tour. This was a special consideration under the circumstances.

Our last few flights had all been to the Ruhr Valley and our missions had taken us very close to our own ground forces, which were surging ahead to the borders of Germany. The flak appeared to be just as heavy and extremely accurate, being as they were now quite adept at interpreting their radar screens.

On a few occasions we were required to fly two operations on the same day. An example of this was our mission to Duisburg. We just sat on the ground long enough to bomb-up, refuel, eat lunch and depart again. We were running short of aircraft and these trips were intended to soften up the Valley's industrial centres prior to our forces breaking through to the Rhine River.

We were bombing from lower altitudes, like twelve thousand feet and sometimes as low as five thousand feet. We could sometimes see people in the streets. Low level flying was always exciting because it gave you a sense of speed, which you could never experience at eighteen thousand feet. The thoughts which kept nagging me, all through those last flights, was how terribly sad I felt that our Navigator, Jack McKay; our Mid-upper Gunner, Frank Malorey and our Rear Gunner, Hank Scott were not going to be with us on this last trip of "E for Easy". Of the seven original members, only four were going to be with her on her last flight.

Our groundcrew informed us that Easy was being retired as well. She had completed her tour. She would be heading for the Maintenance Unit for dismantling. "E-Easy" NG146 was scrapped on May 7th 1945. Her old fuselage just couldn't take any more patching. She had survived one crash landing and her fuselage looked like a pincushion because of all the patches. If Easy could talk I wondered if She would tell us that She was feeling like we were excited yet terrified.

All crews agonized over their last trip. They worried, fretted and almost refused to fly it. How often had we heard of other crews not returning from their last flight? Either your first or your last they used to say.

I was ready and was being encouraged by my crew. "Piece of cake, Skipper," Jack said. "Just another Op, what's the big deal." I knew that it was certainly not just another Op and it was a big deal.

It was understood, like an unwritten law, no crew ever made plans to celebrate or tell other crews of their plans for when they finished. A silly superstition but no one was about to test its validity.

Easy's crew was playing it pretty casual and made no mention to anyone that this was their last. We were quite confident that no one, other than the Adjutant, really knew we were flying the last one.

We sauntered nonchalantly into the briefing room and took our seats, trying to act normal, when all the time we were inwardly dying. "Gentlemen and Junior, the target for this morning is---. Wait for it you chaps. No, it is not Cologne but you're close, your target is Bonn. You will be home by noon and I expect you all to clobber the hell out of this place as it may be the last operation on this city in the war," the CO

said. Everyone cheered and the tension had been broken.

The Intelligence Officer gave his spiel about the importance of hitting the refinery and the marshalling yards. "We don't want any more supplies getting to their front line than we can help," he chuckled. "I understand from the Met people, who you'll hear from in a jiffy, that you are in clear sunny sky there and back, now isn't that different?" he went on. "Your bombing height will be 9,000 feet so you'll be able to smell the kerosene fumes." Everyone was now loosening up and enjoying the briefing. I almost forgot what trip this was. The Met man went through his spiel and then turned the briefing over to the CO.

"Chaps, the flak will be heavy, as you no doubt realize, but we think the fighter cover should be almost non-existent. All their birds are busy trying to protect Hitler in Berlin. Poor chap is terribly frightened of Mr. Stalin who, at this moment, is making plans for re-furnishing the Reich's Headquarters."

We all laughed and the room was certainly a lot different than when we had first entered. Even I was starting to feel that things were going to be all right. Jack looked at me and gave me a wink. "See, what did I tell you Skipper, we got it made," he said. I secretly wished that he hadn't said that.

"We are sending all of the aircraft that we have serviceable which is ten of you. We're planning for a sixty aircraft mission but we can't tell until 0 hour exactly how many will be ready. Easy will lead the GH formation so that puts you on target before the others get finished breakfast," the CO joked. "Jack, I want you to keep an eye on our boy today, just so that he doesn't get carried away and attack from nine hundred feet rather than nine thousand," the CO quipped. Jack looked at me and put his hand on my shoulder. Everyone knew what the CO meant, as he was always giving me a time. I was wondering if he was alluding to this as being our last trip. Nothing more was said in this regard so I assumed that he had meant nothing by his remark. I guess he knew, like everyone else, that my crew watched over me like a mother bird.

When the briefing was complete and we had been assigned the aircraft in our formation we left the room, feeling quite a lot better than when we had come in. I guess it was because of the light

hearted way in which it had been conducted. Perhaps we were going to make it after all.

Phil Jones, our Navigator, (taking over from Jack) was quite good at guiding us to and from the target area and he never got us lost. I recalled that Jack had got us lost once. That was the time I was required to wear the uncoveted award of the "Most Derogatory Order of the Irremovable Finger". It was a humorous award presented to the crew on the squadron who had committed the most stupid blunder of all. I had to wear it until someone committed a blunder suitable enough to take it from me. Our M.D.O. of the I.F. was awarded because Jack couldn't find our position no matter how what he did and I was lost as well. It was one of the thirteen night raids we had been on and we were TRULY LOST. I didn't know where I was nor did my Navigator. Our only clue was that we must be heading out over the North Sea but way off course. Through the clouds we got glimpses of water but never any land. F/L Jack Buvan, the bomb aimer, suggested we issue a "MAY DAY" call and get them to take a bearing on us. These, of course, only as a last resort.

"MAY DAY, MAY DAY, this is Beddar Easy requesting a position bearing. MAY DAY, MAY DAY." Bill spoke again into our radio. "Beddar Easy, requesting a position bearing," he went on.

"Beddar Easy, this is Blackadar Control, you are approximately 5 miles from base, turn on course 060 degrees, we are at present in slight cloud cover but the field is clear. I say, Really Junior, what is it you are about?" came the control.

"Oh Jack, what the hell have we done?" I asked.

"Coo Blimey, wouldn't that Lark you now?" Bill, our radio operator, said. "Well, you chaps should know to trust old Jack, huh?" our Navigator retorted.

"Beddar Easy, request permission to land," I radioed the tower.

"I say, MAY DAY Junior, indeed!" came the tower. "You are turn one to land."

"Ah, come on guys,"I replied. "Easy on final and thank you chaps."

There was no question that we had won the award fairly and squarely and how embarrassing. I was only glad that I had not been an Officer at this time as Bill, Frank, Johnny and the two Jacks had to take all the needling in the Officer's Mess. There was just Hank

and I to take it from the other Sergeants. Oh well, the trouble was that it was published in the Rondell Magazine, a RAF publication circulated to all airmen. How embarrassing! Funny that I would think about this occasion when I was preparing for my last trip.

We rode the crew transport out to the aircraft and, of course, our Ground Crew knew about our last flight and they purposefully stayed away from any conversation about this being our last. Mrs. Swanson came over to me while I was doing my walk around and gave me a big hug--she knew also. "Come home safely Skipper, we need you back here you know," she said. She was trying to keep me from seeing the tear in her eye. I hoped she didn't see mine. When we were all aboard and about to close the door, one of the ground crew passed through a letter from all of them to all of Easy's crew. The letter was to be read over the I/C when we had dropped our bombs and were on our way home.

How does a person explain how he feels at a time like this? After having started these engines so many times and after the usual run ups and checks, I was doing it for the last time in my beloved "Easy". I was gentle in how I was handling the throttles to move Easy into our take-off run. I secured my lucky scarf around my neck and said a silent prayer. "Please God, please give me the skills to bring Easy and her precious crew safely home again."

I released the brakes, throttled Easy onto the runway and opened up full power for our last takeoff and, like the lady that She was, Easy lifted off and climbed away to our rendezvous point. I had no qualms at all about this take off and it never occurred to me that we might have an engine failure or a blow out. I just knew that we were going to make it.

We picked up our formation and headed to Bonn. The flak was very heavy and quite accurate and we were losing aircraft but I was the first over the target area with my formation and not one piece of shrapnel hit us. Almost like Easy was not going to allow us to get this far and then toss us to the "Hereafter".

We dropped our bombs and turned for our coast-bound leg and home. It was only on our way out that we learned of the large number of aircraft that had been shot down. We could see our fighter escort overhead but there was no need of them today. There

was not a fighter in sight with a cross on it. We crossed the coastline to a lighter than usual welcome of Ack Ack fire since the heavy guns had been moved away or captured.

I opened the letter from the ground crew and read. "To Skipper and crew. This is your final operation on behalf of your country. We are so proud to have been assigned to Easy and to have helped in our own small way to keep her flying and to help return most of you home, safely again. We regret that Easy is also being retired but then what would Easy be without Skipper and his crew of "Flying Gentlemen"? We are losing our very dear friends and believe us when we say that we flew every mission with you in spirit if not in body. Your pain and anguish were our pain and anguish. Your happiness and joy were ours as well. You are reading this letter knowing that you are safe and are now ready to go home to your loved ones. God Bless you and may He go with you as he surely has so far." Signed by all the ground crew members of Easy. There wasn't a word spoken as I read it. I knew that I was blubbering into the mike.

"Backadar Control, this is E for Easy. Request turn to land over," I announced.

"Beddar Easy, this is Blackadar Control. You are turn two to land, do you have any special requirements?" the tower asked.

Now what the heck did they mean by "Special Requirements". I had never heard them ask that before.

"Skipper!" Jack spoke up. "Ask them if we can do a low pass over the tower."

"Blackadar Control, this is Beddar Easy, request permission to do a low pass over your position. Farewell and all that sort of thing," I said.

"Beddar Easy, permission for one low pass. Congratulations Easy. Well done. You are still turn 2," Control radioed. "Take it gently Junior." "Roger Blackadar," I replied. This was to be our victory fly past and I banked EASY towards the tower from our final approach and dropped her down to, I think, about one hundred feet, not much more, and we swept past the tower. We could see all their faces staring out the control windows. Unknown to me, Jack had unwrapped a bundle of Window and shoved it out the Window chute. It blossomed right in front of the Control Tower and for some

hundreds of yards thereafter.

From Jack, "I say, did you ever see anything so glorious in your Whole Life?

"Blackadar Control, Easy on downwind, request clearance to crosswind and Final, over." I asked.

"Easy, from Blackadar, you are in deep trouble little man." The voice spelled out the word. What had I done now? I settled Easy onto the runway and coasted to a stop, before the first intersection, and turned off. Jack, what does Control mean, "I'm in deep crap"? I asked.

"Bloody straights can't take a joke, a little bit of humorous antic, so to speak," he said.

"Jack, what are you talking about?" I asked.

Roger, our Rear Gunner, knew and replied for Jack. "Skipper, did you know that our infamous Flight Lieutenant dropped a bundle of Window on the control tower?"

"Good grief Jack! Why did you have to go and do that for?" I asked.

We taxied to our home perimeter pad and shut Easy down for the last time. Each of us just sat there and in his own way said a prayer of thank you. So many others had not returned. The ground crew was banging on the main door to get in. Roger was first out and climbed down. He assured the Ground Bods that we were all okay and he thanked them for their letter. We all climbed down the ladder and hugged and patted each other on the back. I stood outside then slowly walked over to where I had last seen Mrs. Swanson waiting by the workshed. She gave me a big hug and we both cried. She was such a dear lady as was all her family. I assured her that I would be over to see them before I left then took my departure on the crew truck to de-briefing.

The CO was present at our debriefing and informed us that we had indeed completed our tour of operations and also told me that my three original crewmembers had been awarded an additional tour. We were also congratulated on our success in spite of all their concerns. We had defied all reason and completed our tour.

The CO said, "Well young man, we are very proud of you and your crew and must say you are a credit to your parents and to the RCAF from whom we borrowed you. We were ready to send you all

home tomorrow, however, there is a little matter requiring your personal attention. Before you leave the base, you will pick up every piece of Window laying in this airdrome. Is that understood Junior?" he asked.

"I understand Sir." I cowered behind Jack, as I usually did under such circumstances.

Everyone laughed again but knew that the CO was dead serious. It took us three days to pick up the strips of paper but we did have a lot of help. The ground crew and the Swansons and their neighbours were picking it up from their fields and several other crews came to help. Jack had told his wife that he was back and safe and was going to threaten a few women before he returned home. I know she just laughed at him.

We had a celebration at the local pub to which our ground crew and the Swansons were invited. Before I left to go to the Browns in Milldenhall, Jack took me aside and we talked about what we had done. "Skipper Laddie, I am going to miss you like I would my own son. Please write and keep in touch, it has been a pleasure knowing you." He put his arm around my shoulder as I tried to hold back the tears. I left shortly after for Scotland and home.

I was saying goodbye to the real Captain of the Easy Crew. It was he who had guided and directed us to this point. "Thank you Jack, for your patience and understanding with this little kid," I said.

Jack left the next day for his family in Devonshire. Flying Officer Johnny Carr was next to say goodbye. "Ta for now Skipper, best of everything and thank you. I'm here today only because of you," he said. Flight Lieutenant Bill Barker was next and we just hugged but he reminded me that he still sort of held me responsible for the incident of the "Elsan Can" but that's another story best forgotten.

The rest of the crew were to be assigned to the Replacement Centre for re-assignment and completion of their tours. I found leaving these friends as hard as it was leaving my home on the ranch when I left to return to Winnipeg. I was not in very good shape but I was older and I had grown and I was no longer a little kid. I was still a flight sergeant even though my commission was to be published while I was on leave in Mildenhall. I never got to enter the Officer's Mess with my own crew.

THE NORTH

PREFACE

"The North" is a collection of stories depicting the life and hardships faced by the Bush Pilots and the Cree residents who lived there. No telling can truly do justice to the actual experiences of being there.

The majestic beauty of the North country, is only marred by often tragic death which lurks endlessly day and night year around. It is a life that can be only shared by those who live and work there.

TABLE OF CONTENTS

pg.

HOME

My trip across the Atlantic was relatively uneventful, unless you call evading U Boats throughout the night uneventful. I was on the Queen Elizabeth, and had boarded her in Gurrock Scotland. We were heading for New York in the U.S.A.

I always enjoyed the sea, and would have made the sea my career, if the Navy had accepted my application. Many times I thanked my lucky stars I had been rejected, when I looked down into the English Channel, and watched the freighters with their destroyer escorts battling monstrous seas. It must have been treacherous trying to stand on those slippery decks while chopping ice away from frozen superstructures. There were submarines lurking everywhere. I was glad to be flying above it all, at least with any luck I'd be home at night. Sometimes there just wasn't enough luck to go around. Perhaps it all worked out for the best.

The train ride across Canada seemed different from the one I'd been on a year and a half ago. Maybe it was me. I know I was seeing things from an entirely new perspective. Certainly different from when I was seventeen, and heading for the war.

The countryside looked bleak and cold, but then it was only February and there were still lots of winter ahead. Every railroad station was swarming with family members, flapping their arms and stamping their feet to keep warm, waiting to welcome their loved ones, or in some cases bidding them farewell.

My father and uncle were at the train station to meet me.

"It's very good to see you again my boy. You certainly have filled out and you look very dashing in your uniform," he said wiping his eyes with his handkerchief. I had never seen my father in tears before, and it was a very moving experience.

"Your mother will certainly be impressed Skipper at the way you have grown and how mature you look. Nothing like military life to straighten one out, I always say," my uncle said, throwing in his two bits worth. I think I finally realized, that I was not the only one who had gone through some agonizing times since I had been away.

I managed to control myself, and we drove home. I was not the same little kid that left from this station, what seemed like many years ago on the first leg of my Airforce career.

I had two weeks leave coming, and then I'd get a posting some place. I was hoping it would be out West. I finally received my commission after I had completed my tour of Operations. Pilot Officer Douglas Scott. Well at least I came home wearing an officer's uniform, this would make my mother very happy. She would have me on display soon enough.

Everyone was very nice to me and for once I was being treated like an adult. Many of our family friends expressed surprise that I was no longer "Little Skipper." I had grown since leaving home and that helped.

"I am going to give you a coming home party Skipper. Just a few of your old friends in to welcome you home. Wouldn't you like that?" mother asked, knowing full well I had no friends and how much I hated parties.

All my complaining only brought unhappiness to our home so I decided that I would try to adjust and not fight the system. I knew how I felt when I left for overseas, but my estranged feelings were even more pronounced. I was not the same boy who had left a year ago, and everyone was beginning to realize that fact.

The party was exactly as I thought it would be. My, so-called friends, and I use the term loosely, had not enlisted and were well along with their university education. They were sons of my mother's friends and I found I had absolutely nothing in common with them.

"What was it like Skipper? It must have been absolutely horrible for you being so young and vulnerable," they asked trying to make conversation. This annoyed me and I couldn't wait for the party to end. I wanted everyone to go home. It was awful. I realized I had a very large chip on my shoulder almost defying these guys to knock it off. I was jealous of them. Here they were well along their planned careers while I was still junior and had no plans at all. I felt I was right back where I had started, and that my experiences over the past years had no relevancy in my life. It didn't seem to count for much amongst these people. I thought I might go back to the ranch and work there for awhile, until I made up my mind as to what I was going to do. I knew I'd be out of the Airforce sooner or later, as the war in the East was also winding down.

Ken had suggested on several occasions that I should use my brains, and not wind up like him. What good was a war experienced CowPoke, who couldn't do anything else but repair damaged War tanks and bulldog steers.

Everyone on the ranch wanted me to come and I toyed with the idea for some time. I needed to be away from my folks and to be with those who really understood me and loved me. I couldn't help thinking back to the times I thought I would never see any of them again.

I managed to behave but family relationships had not changed. Billy my young brother was gone so apart from him, I didn't feel I had too much of a bond holding our family together. Mother had grown much older but her values had not changed much, at least not that I could see. She was still climbing the social ladder.

Our first meeting was a very moving one, influenced by the loss of my brother I think. My Aunt Velna confided in me, that Mother was overcome with grief, when she had received the telegram about my being missing. This news almost on the heels of Billy's death.

I visited Billy's grave, and wept. Mostly because I felt guilty hardly knowing him, thanks to mother and father. I would liked to have known him when he was in his teens, and growing up.

I talked to Peggy and she told me of Ken's return to a huge heroes welcome and of his getting reacquainted with his wife Ellen. He had left for overseas before his son was born. Peggy told me that most of my friends from Millarville and Turner Valley had joined up and several had not returned including my good friend Lynn Spence. That upset me. I wondered what my ranch family would be like when I saw them again.

When I finally got hold of Ken we decided that he and I would pool our finances and buy more cattle. He had received his military discharge and was anxious for us to get together.

I had been home a week and a half, when my posting came through. I was being posted to Calgary. I wondered how I could be so lucky. Everyone, throughout my whole life, had been telling me how lucky I was, and I certainly had to agree with them. My luck was still holding. I was being posted to No 3 S.F.T.S. (Service Flying Training School) in Calgary, as Flying Control Officer. I was also getting a move up the promotion ladder, to Flying Officer. I was to

leave right away and would be compensated for my shortened leave later. I couldn't have been happier. Mother knew why I was happy, and that bothered her.

"I suppose you are overjoyed at being able to leave home again and join your ranch pals," she offered sarcastically.

Things had been slowly improving at home and it was just about time for me to leave for Calgary, when my mother insisted I have a full physical check up before I went away. Uncle called me and asked me to come into his office, he wanted to give me a thorough check up before I went to Calgary. He explained that many of the young men, who had been in battle conditions, were returning with serious psychological problems. Reliving their traumatic ordeals over and over again. I had experienced a few nightmares myself but didn't think I was war shocked. I didn't have any twitches or anything like that. " So these are a few of your war momentous. I heard you were bringing back with you, " he said examining my shrapnel scars.

"You are a hero at home Skipper, regardless of how you feel. Your father never stopped bragging about your war experiences. Almost like he was reliving some of them himself," uncle said. " They missed you terribly, especially when Billy passed away."

"Uncle? Were you with Billy when he died? Even though we really never knew each other, I wondered if he ever talked about me," I asked finding a huge lump forming in my throat.

"Skipper. You were all he ever talked about. How his big brother was flying Lancaster Bombers overseas, and about your winning your medals. Billy loved you Skipper and carried a picture in his wallet to show everyone. Every nurse and doctor in his ward knew about his brother. He was such a brave little boy laying in that terrible iron lung knowing he would never get out of it. He wanted to see you before he died. I'm sorry if I am making you uncomfortable Skipper, but you see you weren't the only one who was sad in your home." I couldn't stop the tears from flowing. This was the first time I had cried since leaving England.

I arrived in Calgary, and prepared to take over my duties as C.F.C.O. (Chief Flying Control Officer) of Calgary and three other satellite aerodromes. Strictly an office job.

The officer I was replacing had died along with several

high-ranking staff from the airbase. They crashed when their Avro Anson, hit a thunderhead cloud, and tore the tail off the aircraft. All their parachutes had been carelessly dumped in the tail section. None of the officers had seen overseas duty, thank goodness. That would have been terrible, to have completed a tour of operations, then to die by a careless mistake. Like going through the war, then killing yourself, by slipping on a banana peal.

I was assigned a young flying officer, to act as a messenger boy and to fly me around to all the bases, and wherever else I wanted to go. He was classified as a Service Pilot (Taxi Driver). Robert was twenty three and in a couple of months I would be twenty.

"Skipper it just isn't fair. Here I am spending the entire war as a taxi driver while a little kid like you flies your tour of operations and is back home with a chest full of medals and tons of experience," he complained.

Robert taxied me around like I was a group captain. I liked him and we got along well. He was continually asking about what it was like. I really didn't want to talk about it too much, but I could understand his curiosity.

"Come on Skipper lets get a drink. I'm buying," Bob would say. I was still not in the habit of drinking anything stronger than a soda or a glass of milk.

I explained the rules I had to abide by while on squadron. He laughed as though it was the funniest thing in the world. "Robert, I was only a sergeant, and didn't get my promotion until I was leaving England. I never had a drink with my crew throughout the entire tour," I complained nostalgically.

One bright and sunny afternoon, we took a Cessna Crane, (Twin Engine five place aircraft), to the ranch. We made a very low pass over my Aunt Peggy's house then landed on Ken's lower pasture. No one was living on the old place, and it had the only good field close to Peggy's. I remembered we had a couple of barnstormers land there once. The field was stubble as the hay crop had been taken off.

"I knew it was you, you little monkey. I been just waiting for you to pull something like this, that's why I sent Johnny over to meet you, I knew you'd be walking," Peggy laughed when we first met.

Our reunion was a very tearful one and I was truly was home.

I was happy to be back on familiar ground after so long. I could hardly believe how Johnny and Mark had grown. They were even more surprised to see I was no longer a midget. They were still taller than I was.

I agreed to come back on my first leave, and stay with grandma and grandpa. The room they had added on for me before I left to go back to Winnipeg, was still there and waiting for me. Two days later I was back.

Oley was working on an oil refinery tank farm about 4 miles away, and came home most nights, so I would be able to see him as well.

My arrival at grandma and grandpas was an exciting occasion. They were very happy to see me.

Grandpa had a tear in his eye as he confided they had feared they might never see me again, especially after they received news I was missing.

"Peggy reassured all of us that we would all see you again and not to be so worried," he said. Peggy was sure that I would be back. She said she had a feeling deep inside her heart.

I rode everyday, and I am sure I put on some weight. I was even 5'10' inches tall.

"Well finally our boy has grown up," grandpa said. "Skipper you sure have grown, I wouldn't have known you if I had met you on the street," he kidded. I reminded him of the pictures I had sent him to prove I had added some height.

I even got to go swimming again, but this time, I hid all my clothes. I wasn't going to take any chances on Peggy getting to them.

I made several," Emergency landings" on the lower pasture that Spring, and I enjoying myself once again remembering old times long passed.

Summer was starting to show, and I was interviewed for permanent status in the Airforce. I expressed my desire to get out, and applied to be discharged. I had heard that the airlines were taking airforce pilots for training, so I thought the earlier I got out the better. I was promoted again, because of the office I held, to flight lieutenant. I thought this was typical of the way the military did everything. Here I was about to leave the services, and I am promoted. After all these years. I finally get all my promotions

within a period of a few months. Where were all these promotions when I really wanted them? I could have joined my crew and spent more time with them in their officer's mess. The only thing my promotions did, was inflate my ego and get me a higher discharge settlement. That would help my pay when I left. " Don't let that promotion go to your head Skipper Sir, I can still tan your little arse officer or not," Ken warned. I was home all right, it seemed some things never change.

I travelled to Toronto for an interview, with Trans-Canada Airlines. They were very nice, and for once, made no mention of my youth. They informed me bomber pilots were not exactly what they were looking for. What they wanted were pilots from transport command. They were looking for pilots who had flown large twin and four engined transport aircraft across the country and on transatlantic flights. Hmmmph. That didn't seem fair. What a let down this was. I was also told that we were engrained with too many, "devil may care habits." They felt we would have a hard time breaking them.

My flying time was transferred to the Department of Transport, and I was issued a commercial license. Now if only I could get a job flying. I heard that the Abitibi Pulp and Paper Company, in Pine Falls Manitoba, wanted a pilot for their little four place Stinson 108C. Referred to as a Stinson Station Wagon because of its wooden panelling inside.

I got checked out on the float-equipped aircraft, on the Red River in Winnipeg, and was hired. My job was to fly timber cruisers and engineers to various logging camps along Lake Winnipeg. I flew the balance of the summer and fall, at least I got some valuable float experience. I didn't like the work very much, and the black flies nearly drove me crazy. Try taking off with a full load of passengers, and each one smacking at black flies that gorged themselves on our bodies. They were everywhere. I darned near lost it on one occasion. This was too much for me. I couldn't stand those flies, and the number of flying hours I was getting wasn't worth it.

I got paid by my flying hours, and not on a salary. I decided to leave this prestigious position. I knew pilots were plentiful and finding someone to take my place would not create a problem for Abitibi. It was September 1945, and I wanted to get something more

challenging to do and get away from the flies.

WISAGACHUK

ᐘ ᔅ ᒡ ᒡ ᐸ

I heard that the Hudson's Bay Aviation Division was hiring pilots, so I spoke to my father and asked him to put in a good word for me, which he did. It turned out that I was too young and inexperienced for the job. I was, however, referred to M&C Aviation in Prince Albert Saskatchewan. I was told there was a part-time opening, I would have to get myself up to PA. I was also contacted by the Hudson's Bay Fur Trade and asked if I would like to work part time at their Lac La Ronge trading post as a clerk until a full time flying opportunity came along. I figured this would be a good way for me to get to Prince Albert without costing me a thing. I'd also be in a position to get my interview with M&C.

I was hired and sent to PA where I was transported to Lac La Ronge on a freight truck. The road northward was only usable in the winter while the ground was frozen hard.

I was met by the Trading Post Factor, Bill MacNamy and was shown where I would be working and where I would live.

"Well laddie this will be quite a change from what you're used to, but if you work hard and forget about the city, you'll enjoy yourself," Bill said with a Scotch accent you could cut with a knife. He had a round ruddy complexion with red hair and clear blue sparkling eyes.

"You'll be billeted with the misses and me," Bill said. I liked him right away.

I had left Prince Albert so quickly that I hadn't had my interview with M&C. I wrote and told them I was in La Ronge and would be available for an interview anytime. The company had a base there and their planes were in and out all the time.

Most of their pilots were ex-RCAF types and we got along well together. There was Chief Pilot Lefty McLeod, Art Atkinson, Clark Reddy, George Greening and me, just to mention a few.

They delivered my letter directly to their boss who flew up one day and talked to me for a few minutes. He then hired me for

part-time employment until a full time opening became available. Over the next several weeks the chief pilot checked me out on the company planes.

The part-time arrangement was good for both the Hudson's Bay and M&C. A qualified commercial float pilot, available on a moments notice, and a store employee capable of running things while the post manager was away buying fur. The Post manager had been a little sceptical about hiring a part time clerk, especially one who could leave to go flying at any moment. Bill agreed to give it a try and see how things went. I would be paid only for the time I worked and would have to pay board for the time I was not working for the Bay. Did I mention that Bill had come directly from Scotland to join the Company?

This arrangement worked very well and M&C and the Hudson's Bay Company were quite happy. The airline paid me for the actual flying I did, and I flew a fair bit. I also learned the fur trade business and was even learning how to speak Cree the native language.

M&C had two Stinson Station Wagons, one of which was permanently based in La Ronge. I flew this much of the time. They also had two Norseman, four Wacos, one Fox Moth and two Avro Ansons on skis for use in the wintertime.

The Wacos were 5 place bi-planes. They reminded me of little flying models that required twisting the propellers to wind the elastic bands. They were much underpowered, using the old radial Jacobs L4MB engines. When you were loaded, you really needed a lot of space in order to get off and sometimes they just wouldn't lift at all. I think it was because most of the time we were overloaded. Sometimes we had to unload some of our cargo or passengers, especially in hot weather. The boss was never happy about that and threatened us with our jobs. Even though I had a job apart from aviation, I never wanted to be be fired. The Saskatchewan Government expropriated M&C Aviation and incorporated it into their existing Air Ambulance Service. They already had a Stinson and a Norseman in their fleet and bought two more Norsemen and two Wacos. This would make them the largest carrier in North Western Canada. The government agreed to continue the existing arrangement I had with M&C. I would fly in emergencies and when otherwise required.

During this time I was speaking Cree quite well and was even buying raw fur for the store. The Post manager was convinced that the arrangement we had with the airways was a good one and beneficial to both. Our staff consisted of two part time Cree and myself. My flying time was growing rapidly and I was getting some great experience. I could never have afforded to buy this kind of training. Bill often flew with me when I had room as he enjoyed these flights very much.

La Ronge had a population of 200 White and Cree. This would fluctuate, depending on the time of year. Wintertime saw the Cree away trapping and fishing. They would return in the spring with their furs and replenish their supplies. They would stay for a week or two, then take off for their fishing grounds and summer camps.

In La Ronge there was also a Mission Residential School operated by the Anglican Church. The school had an enrolment of about 60 children, ranging in age from 6 to 15 years. These were children of native families who trapped and fished all year round for their livelihood. I was very critical of this program. It seemed ridiculous to take these children away from their parents as it deprived them of learning the native skills that would help them and their families. When the children were released from the school they would return home and immediately start asking where their white sheets and pillowcases were. Where was their knife fork and spoon? Where were their beds? No indoor toilets? They were not happy. Mom and Dad were not happy. The school graduates were absolutely useless to their parents. They couldn't hunt, trap nor fish. They were not capable of helping the family at all. One father told me his kids were good for nothing.

The children eventually took off for the towns and cities, for the "good life". They ultimately wound up on welfare and as beggars and alcoholics. The white man didn't want them either. How tragic. Perhaps the churches meant well but there could have been a better way to teach them their native skills as well as the whiteman's.

We also had a small Anglican Church pastored by a native Indian and his wife. His wife was white and did all the work. They served the community of both white and Cree.

The community was made up of the postmistress, her husband, three children; the Government Fish Plant manager, his wife, no

children and the plant head engineer, his wife and no children. Then there was Chris Swenson and his native wife and three children, all grown. Swenson owned and operated a fur-trading store in the village. Then there was Bill MacNamy and his wife with no children. Bill was my boss and ran the HBC trading post. There was the Department of Natural Resources agent, his wife and two small children and the Airways agent his wife and no children. There was also a couple of other white men who made their living hunting and trapping and repairing outboard motors. There were four ladies and the head administrator of the Residential School. Then there was the Government Nurse, Liz Thompson, her husband and two boys. We also had a little hospital, which was overseen by the nurse. She was provided with a nice home where she and her family lived. Her boys went to a boarding school in Prince Albert. The nurse ministered to all the natives and whites alike, doing a quite creditable job. Then there was the RCMP detachment. There was a corporal in charge and one constable. They lived in government lodgings. Both were married, but no children. This made up the village of Lac La Ronge.

It was because of the residential school that I received my Indian name Wesagachuk. Each Christmas time, Bill the Bay Post Manager, played the part of Santa Claus for the mission school. The program was for all the children of the village, whites included. Gifts and candies were provided for each child. I don't think the native children knew who Santa was but they soon identified him with their great spirit, "Wesagachuk", because he gave them gifts.

Bill convinced me, that as a new comer, I should take part and what better way than to take his place in the Santa Claus costume. I couldn't find a way out of taking his place, after all he was my boss. I actually enjoyed the program and the gift giving. It was quite an experience. I was really moved by the reaction of the children to the gifts. The older kids knew it was me in the Santa's outfit and from that time on I was referred to as Wesagachuk. An honour, to say the least. The name stuck with me for as long as I remained in the North.

FALSE ALARM

The local nurse, Elizabeth Thompson (Liz) was, on occasion, required to fly with the Airways into some of the most remote areas in the northern part of the province. She would do inspections of government run outposts and would inoculate the children for infectious disease. She would also be required to fly on Mercy Flights. We called them Mercy flights because we were usually required to rescue someone or act as an air ambulance in the case of severely ill or injured people. Whoever happened to be available in La Ronge at the time the call came in was the one delegated to fly the nurse.

I recall this beautiful spring morning when the agent came up to the Hudson's Bay Trading Post. I was working with the Post Manager at the time.

"Come on Skipper, you and Liz have to fly to South End, on Reindeer Lake. There is a small native village on the South shore of the lake, where a couple of white people operate a trading post. The government has an agent operating the post and radio and carrying out other government business. It's an emergency evacuation I think," the agent informed us.

I met Liz Thompson at the dock where she was waiting with her little bag of medical tricks. "Morning there Junior, how're you today?" she shouted.

"Fine Liz, nice day for a trip, hope it isn't too serious," I said.

"Well, some native girl was portaging on a difficult rocky area and she slipped and rolled down the rocks," she explained.

"Break a leg or something? "

"Yah, or something. She was eight months pregnant and the post manager thinks she is losing the baby," she went on.

The agent shoved us off from the dock and I started CF SAO. The Norseman quickly started drifting toward the centre channel. There is an island that runs parallel to the shore and acts as protection from the winds that came in from the east. Dog Island they called it. The natives tethered their dogs there in the winter when they came in from their trapping trips.

We were quickly airborne and headed North. Nurse Thompson rode in the right seat whenever she could as she loved to handle the controls, which I would flip over to her side. She did pretty well too.

An hour later, we set down on Reindeer Lake and floated to the dock. We were quickly ushered to the store where the lady, her husband and two children were waiting. Liz pulled out her stethoscope to listen to both the lady's heart and to the heart of the unborn infant.

"Well, at least she has no broken bones but goodness did she get bruised, poor thing," she said. "Skipper, we may have to get her to Prince Albert, if what I think is right," she said.

"What's the score?"

"I think she's lost the baby, I can't get a heart beat at all," she looked concerned.

"Put these on Skip and see if you can find a heart beat." Many other noises came from the earpieces of the stethoscope but no heart beat. I shook my head.

"We're going to have to take your wife into Prince Albert," Liz informed the husband who immediately advised his children that their mother was going to be away for awhile. He would have to send his wife off alone as he had to look after the children.

We loaded the patient into the plane and I gave instructions to the agent to contact La Ronge that we were going to have to refuel. He should also alert Prince Albert that we would be requiring assistance, as we would be landing in darkness. The forecast was a good one showing PA to be in CAVU conditions (Ceiling and Visibility Unlimited). In conditions like these, it would be easy to see the North Saskatchewan River where we would land in PA.

We landed in La Ronge and hastily refuelled. Liz Thompson told the agent to radio ahead that the woman's condition was not good and that there was a good chance she might not survive. She was running a very high fever.

The local radio station in Prince Albert announced over the radio that a Mercy Flight was under way and some cars would be needed to line the river road, with their head lights on, in order to give us a reference guide for the river landing.

The moon was so bright, I didn't need the additional lighting along the river, but they did help in determining my altitude above

the water. We landed without incident and taxied to the dock. Newspaper reporters and curious people were gathered at the dockside and there was a great deal of excitement and commotion. There was also an ambulance waiting along with the Department of Indian Affairs doctor. A preliminary check with his stethoscope also suggested we had been right. The patient was transported to the hospital and Liz and I departed for the Royal Hotel, to wait for the doctor's diagnosis.

We were sitting in the restaurant of the hotel eating doughnuts and drinking coffee. One of the reporters from the radio station had joined us when the doctor walked in. He looked at me and then at Liz and shook his head. He sat down and ordered a cup of coffee. Doc just sat and stared at us without saying a word. The look on his face suggested the worst had occurred and the patient had been lost. Then he smiled and kept shaking his head looking at each of us in turn. "Well Doc, don't keep us in suspense, how is our patient?" Liz asked.

"Your patient and her new son I am happy to say, are doing remarkably well, considering the ordeal you put them through," he replied.

"Ordeal WE put them through? We saved their lives didn't we?" I ventured. I had a feeling that we had not heard the entire story.

"Skipper my boy, it is a good thing that you have a flying job because as a diagnostician you would starve to death," Doc chuckled. I knew then that my intuition was correct and we had somehow goofed.

"You too, Nurse Nightengown, you too get the golden bed pan," he said chuckling.

"Doc, both of us checked for a heart beat of the baby and there was none. None at all," I ventured.

"Well, how would you expect to hear a heart beat through all that shit?" Doc replied.

"Did either of you heroes stop to think that perhaps the lady in question had not had a bowel movement for over a week? She was plugged up tighter than a cow's arse in fly time," he laughed.

"You flew over four hundred miles at great expense, to say nothing of the risk, for a woman who was suffering from no more than a severe case of constipation. Ugh! You two are really

something," the doctor continued to enjoy himself at our expense. The newsman from the radio station was laughing so hard he was nearly falling off his chair.

"Oh boy, are we going to have a ball with this one, Skippy baby, you are sure some hero," he laughed and departed to make his editorial for the late news. Liz and I both had a sleepless night and without going to the restaurant for breakfast we tried to sneak back to the docks without being seen. Unfortunately, we were not to get off so easily. The first people we encountered were natives from La Ronge.

"Wacheee Wesagachuk," they greeted. They started to laugh and make obscene gestures, suggesting I didn't know the difference between a baby and a big turd. Even the women had some remarks to make. It seemed like Liz and I were bound to walk a gauntlet spread out especially for the "heroes of South End". Hoooolly! How I wanted to be out of here.

"Well, what are you grinning about?" I asked Liz.

"Actually Skipper, this really is the funniest thing I have ever heard," she laughed. I told her I failed to see the humour in it and how was I going to explain this fiasco to management?

We arrived at the dock and SAO was ready to go, thank goodness no delays would be encountered. We had three passengers to go to La Ronge. That at least was some good news. Getting my flight plan cleared was another matter. The agent was listening to the local radio station when he heard the broadcaster telling about the great mercy flight conducted in the middle of the night. The flight was carried out with great cunning and skill by two of the North's well known personalities.

"Come on Liz, time we got out of here," I said.

"What's wrong Skipper old son, you got a bee in your Hmmm Bum?" the agent said, laughing fit to be tied. This was humiliating and embarrassing to say the least.

"Oh, by the way Skip, your patient had a baby boy early this morning. They're calling him the "Little Shit". Hoo Haa," he laughed.

I started SAO and we taxied out into mid stream. I was fuming but sort of chuckling a bit too. It was rather comical if it hadn't been so serious. I knew that the worst was still to come when we landed at home.

The reception in La Ronge was as I expected. Wesagachuk blew it this time. Lots of laughter greeted us. The Prince Albert newspaper carried the story. Our war hero had flown another BOMBING mission. Hmmm. Liz Thompson's two boys John and Donald were waiting at the dock grinning from ear to ear.

"Wipe those silly grins off your faces," she spat.

Bill, the post manager, was all sympathy between uncontrollable bouts of laughter.

"Ah come on Bill, I've had enough of this crap," I said. With that he almost destroyed himself with more laughter.

"Ha Ha, crap. That's a good one laddie. Ha! That's sure a good one. Ach well, better luck next time huh?" he laughed. How was I ever going to redeem myself?

PETER

◁.7 ⌒ ⌣⌃⌒
Small Boy in Cree

Quite often the Bay post manager, Bill McNamy, would fly with me just for the ride, particularly if it was an ambulance mercy flight and I needed help. He was very helpful as an interpreter as he spoke Cree like a native.

It was a dull overcast day and he and I were flying at about one thousand feet over Snake Lake, a short distance from La Ronge, when Bill noticed a hole in the ice close to shore. Bill spotted tracks in the snow leading up to the hole and exclaimed, "Skipper that hole in the ice is not normal, there's something happening down there. Circle back lower will you?"

There were three people laying by the shore, not moving or waving. They had obviously broken through the ice. How they were able to pull themselves out was a mystery to us. I didn't see any toboggan or dogs or any other equipment laying around. They must have gone under the ice. These people would soon freeze to death if we didn't get to them quickly.

We landed the Waco CF-FGK about 100 yards from the shore as I was leery of the ice conditions. Bill got out and ran ashore, staying close to the headland and away from the soft ice. I shut the aircraft down and quickly grabbed my sleeping robe, the emergency blanket and the engine cover and ran over to where Bill was working on the victims.

"Skipper, go get the emergency kit. It doesn't look good here at all," he exclaimed. The temperature was about -20 degrees fahrenheit and the young people were about to die from exposure.

"God Skipper, these children are freezing to death," Bill shouted. We built a fire and put the engine tarpaulin close to the fire so they could lay on it.

It was almost impossible to get the kids out of their frozen clothing, but Bill said if we didn't, they were surely goners. They were like boards and there appeared to be no life in them at all. We virtually had to chop their clothes off them. We laid them out on the

tarps and covered them with the bedrolls. Bill brought up some water to make tea and I got that underway on the fire.

"I doubt we're going to be able to save them," Bill said.

"Look at their colour and those clothes were frozen hard to their skins."

The older boy and a girl would be in their mid-teens maybe fifteen or sixteen. The third child was a white boy, maybe ten years old.

"Massage the skin lightly and don't put too much pressure on them. I'll get some tea into them, we'll see if that helps. I don't think there is any way we're going to save them." There were no signs of life in any of them. Only the little one had his eyes open but Bill said he was seeing nothing, just staring straight up. Bill took off his own parka and wrapped it around the young girl. Their hands and feet were in terrible condition. Actually hard to the touch.

"Skipper, get La Ronge on the radio and tell them we need a larger plane in here right away. There's no way we can carry them and we have to evacuate them right now," Bill ordered. I ran to the plane and got the La Ronge operator. "You'll have a plane in about half an hour. We'll intercept Lefty at Birch Rapids. You know who the kids are?" the DNR (Department of Natural Resources) operator asked.

"No Ned, they're unconscious."

It seemed like only a minute had passed when we heard Lefty on his approach. He had spotted the Waco sitting on the Lake.

We wrapped the children in Lefty's bedrolls and carried them to his plane. He had Norseman CF-SAO. It was large enough to allow us to lay them flat on the floor.

"Bill, you're going to have to come with me and help with these kids," Lefty advised.

"Skipper, you get that outfit of your's started before I leave, just in case you need help," Lefty ordered.

The Waco started after a few turns and I left her idling while I cleaned up the fire and the gear we had left. There was nothing that belonged to the young people. Their equipment and supplies had gone down through the hole. It was only a minute or so before Lefty passed over me on his way to La Ronge.

It was starting to get dark before I got airborne and headed home. La Ronge was only 20 minutes away but I didn't want to be making any night landings. I landed and started putting the aircraft

to bed, draining the oil and taking it into the workshop where it would be kept warm overnight. I covered the engine with canvas covers and made sure the skis were clear and wouldn't freeze down.

When I had finished, the agent informed me that the older boy had died and the others were barely holding their own.

Bill met me as I was walking up to the hospital and said we had done the best we could but there wasn't much hope for the girl.

"They must have been there for quite a while Bill," I said. He told me they were still unconscious but the little boy seemed to have the best chance.

Liz Thompson was working very hard to save their lives but it seemed like she was waging a losing battle. When I walked into the hospital she came out of the treatment room, shaking her head.

"Why couldn't you have been about half an hour earlier?" she asked. I wondered that too.

I entered the room and I could have wept as I looked down at this poor little kid. His chest was moving up and down in a regular motion but that seemed to be all that showed there was still life there.

"Liz, who's the white youngster?" I puzzled. His face was discoloured from the freezing as were his hands and feet.

"I don't know Skipper. I haven't seen him around here before. He may lose one or maybe both his legs. What kind of a life would he have then?" Liz questioned. I wondered where he had come from and whose child he was. What chance would the boy have?

"Skipper, if you're going to stand around here, you can get to work. Keep massaging his legs and his feet, just gently right from his hips down to his feet. From the top to the bottom. Don Thompson, Liz's husband, was eye dropping warm water into the boys' mouth and it seemed to be going down. Liz Thompson gave the boy an enema of very warm coffee.

"Skipper, massage his stomach and don't push too hard, "We were pouring hot fluids into both ends. The tea was laced with sugar and whisky as a stimulant. She was still working on his arms and chest while I continued massaging his stomach.

I was certainly feeling sympathy for the little guy laying there close to death. Seeing him barely breathing brought a lump to my throat. I prayed he would make it.

"Keep massaging his tummy Skipper." Liz instructed. We all

worked on the boy until our hands and arms were numb. I was learning something new and I hoped it was going to work.

The boy's feet were no longer stiff and colour was starting to appear. John, Liz's oldest son, came in and stood watching, asking his mother if there was something he could do. He told us the boy was Peter Bird. I asked John if Peter lived in La Ronge and if he knew where his parents might be. I wondered how long it would be before the moccasin telegraph would get word to them.

Peter startled us all, by giving a low moan, then a blood curdling scream as the pain of his thawing took hold. He passed out again. It wasn't too long before He came around again and started to move. He tried to turn over, all the time crying and moaning from the terrible pain.

"Let him roll over if he wants to. Help him if you can. He needs to move his muscles," Liz ordered.

He opened his eyes, looked at me through his tears and just stared. "Watcheee Napeo. Peter, astam abbsis napeo, astom mulosson absis napeo (Hello boy. Peter, come on little boy, come on good little boy)." I said in Cree. A small smile crossed his face and he tried to raise up on his elbow and the nurse told us to help him. His face was now showing colour.

"Where is my sister?" he asked, in almost perfect English.

"She's not here Peter. You just rest now and don't talk. Lay back and rest," Liz instructed.

"I think Peter is going to make it just fine. I believe that with some good therapy he'll keep both legs," she said. Peter Bird was going to live and due mainly to Liz Thompson and, what the doctor later called her unorthodox treatment.

The doctor arrived from PA, examined Peter thoroughly and declared that He was going to survive and all in one piece thanks to Nurse Thompson and those of us who worked on him.. Therapy would be required but he would be back to normal again. The doctor claimed it was nothing short of a miracle that Peter had survived and was in such good condition.

John Thompson sat with Peter all that night talking to him and assuring him that he was going to get well again. He also told Peter that his sister had not been as lucky as he had been. Peter just lay staring at the ceiling when John told him about the rescue and how

he came to be here.

Dr. Bessett was so impressed with Liz that he wrote a letter of commendation to the Department of Indian Affairs on her behalf. I was told there had been some questions from time to time about her nursing ability. I, for one, had no reason to doubt her skills as I knew from my own experience that she attended to my problems satisfactorily.

The Mounties (RCMP) advised us that Peter and his sister lived on Nutt Point at the extreme east side of Lac La Ronge. Their parents, Sarah Bird and Eric Jones had lived there along with their young daughter when Peter was born. They lived in a log house built by Sarah's father many years before as a winter trapping outpost.

Peter's father was a Welsh mining engineer who spent his time prospecting for gold ore deposits in the rich Nistoyak River Basin. He had dreamed of striking it rich one day. Sarah Bird had gone to the outpost to keep house for the engineer. Peter's sister was three years old at the time.

Eric Jones was much older than Sarah and made her do most of the hard work around the place. When she wasn't teaching the children she was cutting stove wood, carrying water and even hunting on occasion. Eric insisted the children learn to read and write English right from the start and would not allow them to speak Cree.

Sarah was a product of the Indian Residential School so was familiar with the white man's ways and customs. She cooked, sewed, and taught the children. She also taught the children to speak Cree when their father wasn't around.

Eric was a very hard man and would not hesitate to abuse his housekeeper, if he felt so inclined. The older he got, the more inclined he became.

He went out on the lake one late fall day and never came back. No one ever heard or saw anything of Eric Jones again but they found his freighter canoe overturned on the lake several weeks later.

Sarah was without money and tried to live off the land by hunting and trapping but her own health was getting worse with terrible bouts of coughing and eventually Tuberculosis got the better of her. A passing trapper dropped in to the cabin and brought the family to La Ronge. Sarah's sister, Elsie Bird, took the family in until they could get welfare. Sarah had relinquished her rights to treaty

money when she took off with Jones. She was without any means of support. Peter, we learned, was actually 12 years old but small for his age. He didn't look like his mother with her native features and colour. He was white with light brown hair and blue eyes, not a good situation to be in being of a Cree mother. He was labelled a bastard and a half-breed. He didn't know what that meant but knew it was not a good thing to be. His English was almost perfect because his mother had taught him well and he learned quickly. It was his native language that required some work.

No one spoke English in Elsie's home although she had been in the residential school like her sister. Elsie's 16 year old son had been living at home with his mother. He was Peter's cousin. He had perished on the hunting trip, and Peter's Sister Cora, passed away shortly after arriving in La Ronge.

It seems Elsie Bird had heard of a large number of deer roaming around the Snake Lake area and the young people had been ordered by Elsie to hunt them and bring some meat home for the winter.

They loaded the toboggan with a few meagre supplies and departed for Snake Lake. Their two-dog team had no trouble pulling the load over the smooth ice, and as they were approaching the opposite shore they broke through.

Peter's sister and cousin had perished from the freezing cold but Peter was to live and with that terrible memory forever.

Peter's mother had been sent to a TB Sanatorium in Edmonton where her condition was deteriorating and she was not expected to live. His aunt had had enough of her sister's children and was trying to find other homes for them. Elsie Bird was determined to blame Peter for her son's death. Twelve year old Peter was the only survivor so he was on the receiving end of her wrath. Peter was alone and I knew how he felt.

He was flown to Prince Albert and kept in hospital for almost two weeks where he took therapy on his legs and arms. I went to see him as often as I could and we were becoming good friends. I couldn't help feeling a bond developing between us. I had spoken to Bill and his wife about how I felt responsible for Peter.

"Skipper, you're too young to be saddled with the responsibility of a youngster. What on earth will you do with him?" Bill lectured. I had made up my mind. If Peter were willing, I would become his

legal guardian. Jean, Bill's wife, thought my feelings for the boy were overshadowing my better judgement.

They agreed to allow Peter to stay with me. The Indian Affairs Department wanted little to do with it as they already had more cases than they could handle. They suggested Peter be sent back to his aunt until they could make other arrangements. After all, she was still receiving his welfare checks. This was a poor arrangement and I knew it wouldn't work.

I agreed to pay room and board for Peter at the post residence. Bill questioned me further.

"Skipper, what the hell you plan on doing with him? He's a bastard you know and you're going to be stuck with him for sure. Why you're still a kid yourself," Bill said.

Both Jean and Liz came to my rescue with a suggestion that, if I could afford it, why not send Peter into PA to school with John and Donald, Liz's two boys? It was a great idea that would solve many problems and start Peter's education.

Peter turned thirteen on December 12th and we gave him the first birthday party he had ever had. Bill and Jean invited Liz, Don, and their two boys. Peter was overwhelmed and happy with his new life.

Christmas came and I flew most every day hauling liquor and heavy mail loads. The trading post was busy too and Bill asked me to spend as much time as I could squeeze in clerking behind the counter. It seemed like money was flowing like water as checks for fur and fish were being handed about like Christmas cards. I flew my last trip Christmas Eve and the plane was loaded to the hilt with mail and liquor.

I ran into a heavy snow squall just north of Montreal Lake with still a half-hour to go. It was snowing so heavy now that I could hardly make out the winter road laying like a winding white ribbon just below. I had been told to never take your eyes off your ground contact or you were doomed. Your eyes can't locate it again. You're in a "whiteout" condition. No horizon.

I was flying at about 100 feet and following that road like I was driving on it. What if I crashed? I wouldn't be happy giving my life for a planeload of booze. I knew everyone was waiting for this last shipment before the holidays. What would Peter do if I couldn't make it in. It would be very disappointing for everyone if I couldn't

deliver all these Christmas goodies? At long last I saw the bridge that crosses over the Montreal river. It flows into the south end of La Ronge. Right ahead I could see Dog Island and I knew I was home. I touched down onto the snow-covered bay leaving great whirls of bellowing snow behind.

It was snowing so heavily that I couldn't see the shoreline or the buildings until I was only 100 feet away. I finally found the transport depot, taxied over to it, and shut the airplane down. I think every man and his dog was waiting for his Christmas Cheer. The postmistress took her bags of mail while the depot agent gave out the parcels, calling out the various names as I handed them to him. I looked around for Peter and spotted him standing alone off behind the crowd. I realized the anguish he must have been going through waiting for me. The storm was getting worse.

Native people do not show emotion in the same manner as white people. They are more reserved and reluctant to show their feelings. Not so with Peter. He walked slowly over to me and with tears running down his cheeks held out his arms. "I didn't think you were going to get in Skipper," he said. "Who would look after me? Where could I go?" he questioned, the tears clouding his blue eyes. We just stood together watching the unloading. I wondered how he was able to shed his thirteen years of tradition and behaviour in so short a time.

I had not as yet revealed Peter's existence to my parents. We didn't write too often and there was no need for them to know. I mailed a Christmas card as I usually did but no presents were exchanged. I did wonder how they would take the news if and when I told them.

Peter and I were invited to spend Christmas Day with Bill and his wife. There was just the two of them. It was an exciting time, especially having Peter with us. His recovery had been remarkable and his legs were almost back to normal.

Once again I was asked by the school administrator to be Santa Claus for the annual Christmas concert. The entire village would turn out for the festivities and the gifts that were handed out. I would put on the traditional red costume and beard and hand out the presents. I was very tired and rather reluctant to participate but Bill finally convinced me that I had a duty to perform. After all, it had been his responsibility until now. "You'll enjoy it Skipper." Bill

assured me.

"Skipper, you look like Wesagachuk," Peter said. I knew who Wesagachuk was. The natives had given me that nickname last Christmas. He is the Great Spirit who watches over all people and gives gifts to help them.

"Well, I sure as heck don't feel like Wesagachuk. I'm scared and I wish this was over," I complained.

Everything changed when Peter said, "Skipper, you are Wesagachuk to me." I continued to struggle with my beard. Then he started to laugh.

"What's so funny?" I asked.

"Your stomach isn't supposed to be way up there. It's supposed to be down here," he said, pointing to my stomach. With that he pulled down on my pillow stuffing and shoved it into the front of my baggy pants. "Now you look like a fat Wesagachuk," he laughed.

The concert went off without a hitch and I held the little girls and boys on my knee and handed out the gifts prepared by the native band leaders and the church. I don't think these kids had any idea what was going on as far as Santa Claus was concerned but one thing was evident; they knew who Wesagachuk was. It looked like I would have my nickname for a long time to come.

The more time Peter and I spent together, the closer we became. I couldn't go anywhere without him coming along. He would still visit his friends and sometimes spend a night. His aunt wanted nothing to do with him. The amazing thing that struck all of us was the way Peter was handling himself and speaking English all the time. Very seldom did he speak Cree and never in front of me.

I flew several more trips in the Waco and was able to take Peter with me. It was still the Christmas Holidays as far as school was concerned. I recall us flying into Black Bear Island Lake where Jean Foster had his home. He called it his home but it was more like a travel lodge having something like 14 rooms. Everyone who ever flew in the North Country knew of Jean and his hospitality and would try to plan their stop overs there.

Jean was married to a native woman and had two children. David a boy about Peter's age and eight year old Agnes. Jean, like Eric Jones, Peter's father, insisted his children speak English but were allowed to speak Cree as well as their mother. Peter and David

knew each other so had a good time visiting. Jean's wife was very happy that I was looking after Peter. She had known his mother and was sure she would be happy for him. It seemed everyone had heard of the rescue on Snake Lake and figured Bill and I to be heroes. They felt it was meant to be that I should have Peter.

TO SCHOOL

The Christmas holidays were over and it was time for Peter and I to finalize his plans for school. We had discussed his going to Prince Albert to boarding school but now the time had come and he was frightened. Peter would be leaving La Ronge and would be on his own in the big city. I worried about him and how he would adjust to his new life. So far things had gone well between us. There were quite a few tears shed and I think I was feeling as bad as Peter. He never complained, just sobbed to himself, as we prepared to leave to go to the school. At least he knew the two Thompson boys who were going with him. I could certainly relate to how he was feeling as I'd been there too.

The church boarding school in Prince Albert was operated by the Anglican Church and was highly recommended. The children wore uniforms so as to eliminate any class or social differences between the children. The school was noted for its high standards of performance and discipline. The children would learn to take their place in any social environment. It was a wonderful school and I felt lucky to be able to have Peter join in mid-term. I think Liz Thompson had a great deal to do with that.

Children were accepted from all religious persuasions even though it was operated by the Anglican church .

With mixed emotions I left Peter in the hands of the headmaster and to whatever fate had in store for him.

Time went by quickly and Spring was in the air. Peter continued to adapt to his new surroundings. He was accepted easily into the school ranks. He was a handsome youngster with blue eyes, light brown hair and white flashing teeth. He was small for his age and I could certainly relate to, and sympathize with him in this regard. I knew all about being small.

Peter looked very smart and every bit the scholar in his new school uniform. I remembered my mother insisting that my brother and I dress for dinner in exactly the same outfit as the school uniform. Blue blazer, grey pants and white shirt. They had a school crest on the breast pocket. Peter had never worn a tie or suit jacket

before but it didn't seem to bother him .

Knowing the Thompson boys and knowing I would see him every so often made his life a little more bearable and not so lonely. Many of the other children coming from remote areas in the north would not see their parents until holiday time.

Most week-ends we would be together and I would take him and the two Thompson boys downtown for dinner.

Whenever I came to the school he almost flew into my arms he was so happy to see me. The head master told me that Peter had literally taken off. He was an excellent student and with his reading improving, he was making top marks in everything.

"The boy is trying so hard to please you Skipper. Actually he is quite amazing. I must confess we had some misgivings about taking the youngster since he had very little previous schooling and then starting him right off with English speaking children. We certainly don't have such feelings now. We have a few discipline problems in the school, but never Peter. This boy is an example to all the other students in his class. He works so hard and he is so polite. He is certainly a charmer." the headmaster explained. Peter was certainly fitting in.

The next months found me doing little flying and a lot of fur trading and clerking. The Hudson's Bay Company, on Bill's recommendation, offered me a full time job as post manager of the store at Stanley Missions. It amounted to triple my present wages. The additional money would sure help with Peter's expenses. The big problem, as I saw it, was giving up my flying. I would have to quit the Airways job.

A few days later, the Saskatchewan Government came to me with an offer of a flying job. They had decided to open a fish receiving station at a small outpost at Birch Rapids on the Churchill River. The post was quite beautiful in its location and there was to be an aircraft (Norseman) stationed there to serve both the Government Trading Division and also the Northern communities. They asked me if I wanted the job of running the post and flying the fish. I discussed the situation with Bill and he suggested I take the job. I could still keep my flying job and have a home for Peter during the Summer. Both Bill and his wife were convinced it was the best choice for both Peter and I.

I accepted the government position and was installed in my new location with some fanfare. There were many native families gathered for our official opening. I was post manager as well as resident pilot. This was the only such post in the Government Trading Company. Fresh fish would be brought by the fishermen to Birch Rapids where I would weigh, buy and then ice the fish for transport to the Fish Plant in La Ronge. I would store the fish in an ice house if I couldn't make a load. I traded the fish for store vouchers. They could get all their supplies from our store. The venture was a huge success.

I would often be away from the post on other flying duties due to the fact I was the most available pilot. I flew many government officials and their staff. I would usually make it home every day and find several families waiting. Time doesn't mean too much to the native people nor to most everyone who lives in the North.

I hired an old friend from La Ronge who wanted to come to Birch Rapids to keep house for me. Her name was Kakago, the Cree name for Raven. She was in her late early sixties and was meticulously clean and kept the living quarters of the post spotless. She lived in a tent along the water's edge but prepared and ate her meals with me. My laundry was always done. She sometimes worked in the store, interpreting for me when I was having trouble.

Each day my Cree was getting better. Even Peter wasn't laughing at the way I spoke his language any more. Kakago would be a great help when Peter came home for the holidays. I was counting the days until he was finished school and I could bring him home. I wondered how Kakago would view the change in Peter. She knew him in La Ronge.

OVERLOADED

I was unloading tubs of fresh fish at the plant in La Ronge when I received orders to fly into a small lake South West of Bear Island. I was to pick up and transport two men to another lake eighty miles North. I could get that done and be back to base before sunset. The lake was a very small one but I knew I could get in easily enough. It was the getting out that bothered me. It all depended on the load I would have and the winds at the time of take off.

When I arrived there was a small dock with two men standing and waving at me. They were beside what looked like tons of supplies. Along with what was stacked on the dock they informed me that there were two dogs and two 45-gallon drums to load as well. Hooooolyy! I'd never get out of this place without making two trips.

"You guys should be waiting until freeze up to take all this stuff out," I suggested. They didn't laugh, all they wanted was to get out of there today. Pronto. I tried to tell them that there was no way we were going to take all their supplies in one trip. I'd never get off I told them. I informed them they were going to have to pay for two trips.

"We were told you could handle it all on the one trip. Hell, we ain't paying for two trips." I said there was no way and they should sort out what could stay and what I would take. I would get as much on as I could then give it a try.

I wanted to leave one of the two 45 gallon drums but they said they required that fuel on this trip for sure. They loaded the drums up front right behind my seat. Then they proceeded to load the rest of the cargo. I knew better than to ask them to leave the dogs and besides they didn't weigh all that much. One of the natives saw me looking at the dogs and said, "Dogs come too?"

"Okay, but I think the way we're going one of you guys are going to have to stay behind."

"Bull shit Wesagachuk, we're almost loaded," one other said. They sure liked to use that expression a lot. I guess it best expressed their view of the white man too. I knew what that bull stuff was. It was what I was going to find myself in if I couldn't get this crate to lift off.

I loaded the aircraft until there was only room for the two passengers. I was going to have to leave some traps and a couple of boxes of lead weights. The tailends of the floats were under water. Hooolly! As if my being overloaded wasn't enough the wind was dying. It had been blowing right down the lake all the time we were loading but now it had changed. What little there was a crosswind.

One method we used in this kind of situation was to get as close to the longest end of the lake then barrel down to the other end making as many waves as you could. With all the weight I was carrying, I was sure making some big ones. I taxied to the farthest end of the lake, opened the throttle, and prayed for enough speed to break onto the step. I turned into wind, pulled the rudders up, dropped 10 degrees more flaps and with luck I'd have enough speed to lift off. If I managed to get onto the step I could hop over the little strip of land that divided the lake I was on from a larger one beside it, I could always settle down onto the other lake. There were a few bushes and luckily no trees.

The dogs were barking which made concentration impossible. I was afraid that they'd get loose and come forward. I had hauled dogs before and even had a dog fight in the cabin once. I aged twenty years in five minutes. The outside temperature wasn't too hot which would help the take-off.

I opened throttle and it's amazing how fast you cover the length of the lake but I was still not on the step. I made the right choice, shut it down and decided to take another try at it.

"Wesagachuk chicken shit." one of my passengers admonished. That was all I needed, some dumb cluck criticizing me. Funny how quickly these people learn the appropriate English words when they have to. Otherwise they "muchkegway" English. Don't understand a word you're saying.

I made the choice. Off we go again and this time I knew I was going to make it. I was hoping that my good luck batting average was still holding up and I had made the correct decision. I guess it wasn't so bad. We got up on the step and were slowly gaining speed. It was agonizingly slow but I felt we would get off. I could lower more flap, hoist her over the little finger of land and plop down on the other lake if I had to. CF-SAN was churning up a storm with water flying everywhere when I passed the point of no return and I

was committed. Almost at the same moment I knew I was in trouble as I could just feel her straining to get airborne. I wasn't going to be able to stop in time nor would the flaps help. She just wasn't going to lift off. PILOT ERROR. I shut her down and tried to turn as she dropped off the step but as hard as I dug her heels in she could not stop and we hit the shore and rode nicely up on it, leaving both floats and their various struts and wires on the shore's edge. The aircraft gently came to rest on some scrub bushes. The prop of course was bent all to heck but otherwise it didn't look too bad. If I had been going any faster the fuselage would have continued on into the next lake.

"I told you guys we were too heavy and that we wouldn't get off." I said.

"You're the Madagan Ogimaw (Airplane Boss)," one sarcastically observed. Sure, NOW I'm the boss of the plane.

My radio brought instant cussing the like of which I have not heard since leaving the ranch. I remembered how Ken would cuss our balky horses. I think he even invented words for the occasion. Hooooly!.

"Where the hell you leave your brains kid, how the hell we supposed to get that sucker out of there?" Mr. Kenward, the boss, asked. He never inquired as to our health and safety. Well, he must have come up with a plan because the radio came back that they were sending Art Atkinson and Red McKenzie, the engineer, to get me airborne again.

Art and Red landed on the larger lake and were able to nose up onto the shore only thirty feet from where our aircraft was resting. They brought repair parts and a new prop.

We off-loaded onto Art's aircraft and he took off with my passengers, leaving part of the load and Red and me. We would have to figure out how we would get the aircraft on her floats again. I had heard that Red was a genius when it came to salvaging aircraft and he was certainly proving it now.

We hoisted the aircraft up on a single tripod and laid poles underneath to support the fuselage. Red turned out to be as good with an axe as any B.C. logger. We were getting the floats untangled when Art returned with two more native helpers. With the additional help we got the aircraft back on her floats and in the water. Four hours later we were ready to start up. Red worked on the engine

checking it over.

"She's all ready Skipper, wind her up and let's get out of here," he said, looking very exhausted. The damage had turned out to be minimal considering the weight I had been carrying.

I didn't get the terrible tongue-lashing I was expecting over my error in judgement. I pointed out they would have ordered me to get everything on the aircraft so I would make one trip. They agreed but perhaps I should have waited until the wind got up. Well it never did in the three days we were there. I still took off with no wind.

I had promised to be with Peter for the weekend but my misfortune in the bushes changed those plans. Peter had heard the news over the local radio station and had become very quiet and sullen, staying pretty much to himself. The headmaster had become quite concerned about him. The news advising that I was okay and was returning with the plane in a few days quickly restored him to his usually happy self again.

The recovery operation cost the Government Airline quite a bit of time and money, not only from the crash and repairs, but also from the loss of several hundred pounds of fresh fish that had been waiting for me at Birch Rapids.

It wasn't only my boss that was high.

CAT TRAINS

It had been snowing heavily for the past week and we were beginning to wonder when it would ever let up. Even the dog teams were finding it difficult to follow the trails. The Bay Trading Post had snow up to the front windows. Bill had several natives clearing an area in front of the store so the dog teams would have some place to rest. The cleared snow soon built up to five and six fofoot piles. So far this Winter we hadn't had too many extremely cold days like -25 or -30 degrees and now with this snow coming so early, we were wondering what kind of ice was being made under the heavy blanket.

One of our many fears lay hidden under the innocent blanket of snow. Water.

The weight of the snow on the newly formed ice caused it to crack and the water escaped onto the surface of the ice but still under the snow covering. Any unsuspecting traveller or aircraft settling down onto this dangerous surface would find themselves horribly frozen in. Frozen in as firmly as the ice under them. Slush ice. It could usually be seen easily from the air as a dull grey but on a bright sunny day the pilot was unable to see the difference in colour.

Most of the hauling to the Northern posts was done by Cat Trains during the Winter months. It was by far the most economical way to get bulky freight items to remote locations. The trains consisted of three and sometimes four large freight sleighs pulled by a caterpillar tractor.

The sleighs consisted of a large platform measuring 8 feet by 20 feet. They had no sides and all the loads were tied to the platforms under heavy canvas covers. These platforms are mounted on large heavy sleigh runners with steel sheathing that protected the wooden runners from splintering when riding over rocks. The runners were mounted on bunks, which were eight by eight heavy timbers on which the platforms rested. The runners were fastened together by huge cross chains which, when the front sleigh turned one way, would cause the back sleigh to turn the other thereby allowing the sleigh to turn in very short distances.

At the rear of the train was a caboose, which contained the food supplies for the trip and an airtight tin heater where the Cat Skinners could come and warm up. There was a table and a double bunk where they could sleep when off duty. The Cat Skinners were usually natives trained to operate the Cats.

If they were travelling over very rough terrain there would be two Cats in the train. One would be equipped with a bulldozer blade on the front end and a winch with many yards of steel cable on the back. This Cat was used to clear portages over land when the train had to leave the lake and proceed to another one by going overland. These portages were usually very short but unless they were levelled there was a chance that the entire load would topple off and hours would be lost having to reload, often in temperatures of 45 and 50 below zero. It was quite dangerous and very hard work. Many limbs and fingers were lost to the terrible cold.

We were alerted to keep an eye out for these trains and to note their progress. Break downs were frequent, and the trains would signal us to land. We would be given messages as to what repair parts were to be brought to them. Sometimes we would bring an injured crewmember out.

The trains were operated by Frances Brothers Transportation Co. and by the Saskatchewan Transportation Authority. There were usually four or five crewmembers and these fellows worked hard and under the worst conditions you can imagine.

I recall flying over to check on a train one day and I noticed the train strung out on the lake and about 50 yards in front of the first sleigh was a hole in the ice. There was no tractor on the front end. It had broken through.

When the operators suspected the ice to be unsafe they'd hook a long cable from the tractor to the tongue on the front of the sleigh. This would distribute the weight better. So, with the tractor strung out in front of the train, they would continue carefully over the dangerous areas. Sometimes even this was too much and, as in this case, the tractor would break through the ice and lay on the bottom, tethered by its umbilical cord of steel.

The operators would then have to use the other tractor to haul poles from the nearest land and then construct a tripod over the hole. By using the tractor winch and a pulley they would slowly raise the

sunken tractor to the surface where a platform would be constructed under it. They would then winch the salvaged tractor to more solid ice and begin the long repair. If the operator had time before the tractor went under, he stopped the engine, thus saving it from damaged pistons when water was ingested.

I landed and it was decided that they would require another Cat and more crew. I radioed the situation and another Cat was dispatched along with a crew of men, as well as repair parts and another caboose. I was happy to be a flyer. The crews were grossly underpaid for the tough work they did and for the risks they took. The young natives were quite young often no more than fifteen or sixteen. I thought, "There but for the Lord's good graces goes Peter."

These chaps were just about done in. Still they smiled and joked about what had happened. They never worried about anything. "What will be, will be," was their motto. I told them it would be about three days for the other Cat to arrive and that seemed to be just fine and they were going to continue the salvage operation just the same.

I saw several more wrecks like this during my time in the North and heard stories about having to reload toppled sleighs as many as four times in a night. Crossing portages was very dangerous because if the loads shifted to one side or the other, the runners would start to cut deeper on the heavy side and the sleigh would eventually topple over. Everything would have to be reloaded. Imagine doing that several times a night in forty below zero temperatures and when you're so tired you can't keep your eyes open. I remember a caboose catching fire and leaving the crew without food, warmth or shelter. Three of the crew froze to death, huddled around the Cat engine. They had run short of fuel due to the fire.

BIRCH RAPIDS

School was out and I went to get Peter and the two Thompson boys. As we were leaving, the head master asked me to step into his office. My interview with the headmaster was excellent, and one of the proudest moments I could remember. Not only had Peter adapted well to school life but also he had taken top honours in his class. And if this had not been enough, he received the two scholarships he had applied for.

On the first evaluation tests he had taken to determine where he should be started, it was decided he was a grade six level. One third of the way through the term, Peter was moved into grade seven to see how he could manage. He managed very well and took to school like a duck to water. He loved everything he was doing and couldn't seem to get enough. He studied hard and was always clambering for more homework. They couldn't satisfy his keen desire for more knowledge. His teachers claimed he was a delight to have in the various classes. The headmaster was very positive and encouraging. Perhaps the great bond that was developing between Peter and I was due to my identifying so closely with my own life and schooling. To think that a boy who had not had any formal education to this point had not only caught up to where he should normally have been but had even surpassed it. They were passing Peter into grade eight. And all this after only six months. No wonder they were all so pleased with him. The Thompson boys were very happy for Peter, even though they had not done nearly as well. They were good friends and helped him adjust to school life. That meant a lot to Peter and I.

I took all three boys out for a celebration dinner. We would leave the next day for La Ronge and Birch Rapids. I wondered how Peter would feel about moving back into his home element. Would he want to, or even be able to, make a choice between the two lifestyles?

Liz and Don Thompson were at the dock to meet John and Donald Jr. It was always a joyful occasion getting the boys home from school. We loaded some supplies and took off for Birch Rapids and Peter's new home.

When we arrived there were several families camped by the post waiting for us. They were full of questions for Peter about what it was like living with the Whites and if he liked it in the big city. Their questions were in Cree but Peter answered in English so I would understand as well.

Between Kakago, Peter and I we kept a very tidy and clean home. We bathed off our dock amongst the canoes and the plane. Most of the time I kept the plane tied to the dock, unless there was a strong wind, then I would anchor it to a buoy a short distance away.

This was our first experience at living together and I found myself drawing analogies between my life with Ken on the ranch and Peter's life with me here in Birch Rapids. Perhaps I was being too sympathetic to Peter's situation. Maybe I was letting my feelings for the boy block out reality. As Bill and his wife put it, "I was letting my heart, rather than common sense, rule our situation." I hoped this wasn't happening. I tried hard not to spoil him but I couldn't help but feel he deserved some special treatment for his marvellous efforts at school. He had certain responsibilities at the post and I expected them done. He made the beds and washed the kitchen floor. He kept the floor in the store clean as well. He never once complained or asked for favours.

Peter and I agreed that there was no choice between his and my cooking so we took turns at destroying good food. Where was Kakago when we needed her?

He had an insatiable appetite for books and reading material and read everything he could get his hands on. He could remember as well as I could when I was his age. Another photographic mind.

The big difference between Peter and I when I was his age was my trying for acceptance and caring. For someone to love me. Peter, on the other hand, knew from the very beginning he was both accepted and loved.

That summer turned out to be the best summer I had spent in a long time. It would probably have been even better had it not been for the black flies and mosquitos, which were there in great numbers. I was bitten so badly and so often that eventually I built up immunity to them. They do still not bother me. They never did bother Peter. When we discussed why I was getting bitten and he wasn't, he laughingly replied, "Maybe you should take a bath Skipper."

He got so that he could tend the store while I was flying and wound up doing most of the books and paperwork. The fish were coming in hot and heavy and we'd often work into the early hours of the morning packing fish. We were so far North that we worked in daylight throughout the twenty-four hours. Sometimes we'd even lose track of time and eat our breakfast at the time we would normally be eating dinner. It bothered me sometimes but never seemed to upset Peter.

The summer fishing turned out to be more than expected. Our fish purchases were the largest on record and the store did a whopping business. I was so busy flying the fish out that Peter had to run the store almost entirely by himself. He even filled out the order forms for more supplies. I was just too busy.

Peter and I had been collecting the odd stray dog deserted by the Indians travelling South. The fish came in handy for dog food. We had eight dogs by the end of the summer. These we sold back to the trappers on their way North in the fall.

I couldn't imagine what I would have done had I not had Peter with me. He was such good company and a joy to have around. With the amount of flying I was doing, the Government decided to send Red McKenzie up, to do a hundred hour check on the plane, rather than my flying out to Prince Albert to have it done. I had explained that I didn't want to be away from the post for the time it would take to do the inspection. They readily agreed to send Red to us.

He spent three days with us and during that time I certainly had my eyes opened to the ways of the Cree. Peter reluctantly left the room while Red told stories of his infamous life amongst the Natives. He bragged at how many children he had up here. Peter agreed because he knew some of them. Red was certainly some character. I got so that I would put nothing past him, believe only half of what he told us and completely disregard the other half. Red wanted to do a couple of test flights to check some instruments, so we flew them at night.

Peter flew with us and was all questions about the various instruments and what they did and even how they worked. I swung the wheel over to his side in the right seat and let him fly the aircraft.

"Holy shit cakes," Red hollered, "the kid's a natural." Peter was all grins. The infamous Red McKenzie had called him a natural.

"Skippy my boy, you'd best teach that boy of yours to fly, I'm tellin' you he's got the touch, and you know it," he said.

On the night before Red was to fly back to La Ronge, he quizzed Peter on the instrument panel and took him through the pre-flight check for start up. "I'll be go to hell! Napio here, knows how the flight panel works better than most guys that are flying for us," Red exclaimed. "How come you remember all that stuff so quick Peter?" Red asked.

"I just remember things I see or am told about," he said modestly. "Red, thank you for spending so much time with me on the aircraft stuff that was just the best," Peter said.

Red flew out with me to La Ronge the next morning and all he could talk about was Peter's keen memory and his definite interest in airplanes. I was really proud of him too. "Skipper, if you can rescue another kid with as much brain matter as Peter, just do it for me and I'll pay you," Red laughed as he walked up the dock. I thought about the number of children Red had already.

The Airways agent walked down to the dock and informed me I was taking the Nurse to Stanley on my trip. I would drop her off on my way back to Birch Rapids. She was bringing her son John with her and would visit a few of the native families who lived near the Mission. It was usually her custom to hire a young native to take her around in a canoe, as most of the places could not be reached any other way. She was happy to be able to pay her son to take her on her rounds and John was a good canoe handler.

"How's our boy getting along up there Skipper?" she asked.

"Just fine Liz, he's a great help and good company," I replied. "He runs the store by himself most of the time," I said.

"You've become very fond of him haven't you Skip?" she asked.

"Fond is hardly the word Liz, the boy is part of my life now. I don't think I could do without him. Not just that he works so hard for me but because I love him like he were mine, " I replied.

"You know that boy worships you and there is nothing he wouldn't do for you," she said.

"Yeah! all he ever talks about in school, is how his Dad was the best bush pilot in the North and that he could do anything," John Thompson cut in. "It was the kids in our class who started calling you Peter's Dad. We had to write an essay on our fathers and what

they did. We talked about what we would write about and everyone told Peter that he had an easy one to write about with his Dad being a bush pilot. His essay was the best in the class.One day Peter asked me if I thought you'd be annoyed when you found out about the kids calling you his Dad. It really bothered him. He said he wanted to have a Dad too, and besides it sounded better calling you Dad rather than by your first name," Johnny concluded.

"He hasn't said anything about it yet John. Maybe he's afraid I won't like it," I replied.

"Well he certainly excelled in his schooling. I'll bet that made you proud to be his father," Liz added.

I dropped them at Stanley and then headed north east to Birch Rapids. Clouds were building up pretty good and it looked like I was going to be in for some heavy rain before I got home. It was pouring when I set down on our Bay and there was a good chop developing on the water. I was surprised that Peter wasn't at the dock to take my lines when I docked. Now where in the heck could he be? Surely he heard me land. He was always on the dock to meet me.

I tied up but thought better of leaving the plane at the dock and looked around for the canoe so I could take the line over to the buoy. No canoe. Hoooollyy! Now I was getting worried. Peter must be out with the canoe somewhere, and we're in for a big blow. Funny thing though, I hadn't seen any canoes on the lake and that bothered me even more. All sorts of terrible things started to run through my mind as I ran up the stairs to the store. I looked around inside and found a note written by Peter.

"Dear Dad,

Jonas McKenzie came to the store wanting a 30.30 rifle. He and his Grandfather had been hunting and had tipped their canoe. All their supplies were lost. It took him two days to walk around the lake. They're at the north end by Nemeben Creek. It was too far for his Grandfather to walk. There is also a bear near their camp. I decided I should take Jonas and some supplies and bring the old man back . I took lots of gas, so should have enough. Don't worry."

"Love Peter."

The wind was building and I wondered why I hadn't seen Peter on the lake. He must have been following the shore when he saw the

bad weather coming up. That was smart. I thought back to Peter's letter. "Peter, please be careful, I can't lose you," I agonized to myself. What a boy. He had made out a complete list of everything he took and even included our first aid kit and a 30.30 Winchester rifle along with ammunition. He seemed to have thought of everything.

I went out onto the porch to see if I could hear anything. The plane was smashing against the dock too hard for me to let it stay there. I slipped out of my clothes and dove in taking the towline with me. In bad weather we would slip the towline through the ring on the buoy and then bring it back to the dock. I would then fasten it to the starboard float cleat and undo the plane's lashings. The plane would be free to be pulled over to the buoy. This worked like a charm, although I found the pull was almost too much for me. The plane was heavy and wanted to start sailing with the heavy wind blowing. Finally I got it over to the buoy and secured. It would be safe there but still no Peter.

I knew Peter would have more sense than try to make it back in this storm. He was pretty good with the outboard and the canoe but not experienced enough to handle something like this. I couldn't get Peter's letter out of my mind. "Dear Dad." I silently prayed he was safe.

The clouds were very black making it almost like night and I started the lighting plant so as to get some light on the dock as well as the store. I was dead tired and crawled into my bunk but I couldn't sleep.

I had built double bunks in the small bedroom provided in the store to give us more room. Peter demanded he have the top bunk so as to be able to toss various objects down on me. I hoped he was warm and was taking care of himself. I fell asleep.

The storm raged on for the next day and a half and I was absolutely beside myself. No Peter, no canoe, and the weather was too bad to even think of taking the plane to look for him.

Finally the storm let up and dissolved into a bright sunny afternoon. I brought the plane off the buoy and tied her against the dock. I couldn't wait any longer, I had to find my boy.

I taxied into the wind, hopped her up onto the step and kept her there, driving along the shore line. No sign of the boat there so I lifted off and flew over to Nimeben Creek. No boat, so I circled around searching every clearing I could find looking for smoke or

other signs. Surely he would hear me and make his way to a clearing or to the shoreline. I decided to set down and taxied into the mouth of the Creek. I found signs of campers but no canoe. There had been a fire but it was cold. I walked along the Creek for a way, looking for any signs. Nothing, but as I got a little further along, I spotted bear tracks. Hoooollyy! "PETER!" I called. "Peter for heaven's sake where are you?" I was getting desperate. I had a hard time seeing for the tears in my eyes. I came across a place on the shoreline where the canoe had been pulled up. Then some tracks leading back towards the lake. These were Peter's runners making those tracks and they were heading along the shore. I got back in the plane and taxied cloe to the shore, following the tracks. I had gone almost three miles around the shore, partly on the step and partly just taxiing, when I spotted some smoke coming from some trees along the shore ahead. I knew a fire had just been started because it was making heavy white smoke. This had to be Peter.

I headed for the smoke and coasted up to the shore. Peter had heard me coming and was putting his fire out. He came running out of the bushes and secured the front of the float to some shrubs. He had several scratches on his hands and face but otherwise seemed to be all right. "Am I ever glad to see you safe and sound." I said. I was having a hard time controlling the lump in my throat as I hugged him.

"Dad, they took the canoe and all the supplies and just left me here." There were tears in his eyes as we hugged. "They took everything even though there was a bear nosing around our camp, they just left me," He sobbed.

"Come on Peter, you're safe and that's all that counts. Let's go home."

"I knew you would come." He was looking at me with those sparkling blue eyes of his.

"Peter I'm very proud of you," I told him. We climbed aboard and took off for home, flying low over the water to make little spumes of water from our vortex.

"Makes things look like we're travelling 1000 miles an hour," Peter laughed. It was good to be home again. We ate supper, washed up and within minutes we were both sound asleep.

The next morning we flew up to Stanley with fish nets for the Bay post. Peter spotted our canoe and motor along the post dock. It took only a few moments for him to tell some of the local natives about

Jonas and his grandfather. When the local natives heard what had happened, they were furious and quickly had the culprits in custody, wanting to know what I wanted done with them. What was I to do with an old man and a young boy? Jonas told us that his grandfather was kind'a gone in the head and had made him take the canoe and go with him. I gather from his story it was a terrible trip. The old man had wanted to shoot the bear so he could brag about it to all his old cronies. Unless he was going to shoot the bear in the mouth that 30:30 wouldn't have hurt the bear from 20 yards. Jonas told us the old man had promised to pay for the supplies and the canoe when they got to Stanley.

"I'll never go with that old man ever again, he is loose in his head," Jonas said.

Everything seemed to be in good repair so we strapped the canoe to the struts and loaded the motor and gas tank inside. Liz Thompson had been waiting for us and had heard the whole story. Johnny couldn't stop asking Peter every detail of his trip.

We landed the Thompsons at La Ronge. "You should report that to the Mounties," Liz said.

"And what would they do to the old man? I'll just let it be and Peter'll pay for the supplies," I kidded.

"Dad. I don't have any money," he replied, in all seriousness.

We loaded up the supplies for the return trip to Birch Rapids. All was quiet and serene for a change. No fishermen and no traders. Peace for a little while. Well almost. Kakago had returned and was in the store with supper on the table.

We would sleep whenever we got the chance because the fishermen could come at any time, day or night, and want to sell their fish and replenish their supplies. Peter was very good at helping them select the quantities and kinds of supplies they needed. He wouldn't sell them anything they didn't need. The people trusted him completely and he never took advantage of their trust.

When I was into Black Bear Island Lake delivering some supplies, David Foster asked if he could come and spend a few days with Peter. I agreed. Was Peter ever surprised when David got out of the plane. "Hi David, what are you doing here, your Mother and Father get tired of feeding you?" Peter laughed. He was in the midst of filling a large supply order for some families enroute to another lake.

The native travellers were finding it much easier to buy their supplies from the Birch Post, rather than bring it all the way by canoe from La Ronge. They liked doing business with Peter. Our sales were breaking records. Each load of fish I took to La Ronge saw me returning with a full load of replacement supplies.

The boys worked very hard, hauling all the boxes from the dock up the eighty feet to the store. Never once did I hear a word of complaint from either of them. They were both strong for their size and would tackle boxes that were much too heavy for them. They were getting tired and so was I. It reminded me of the days on the ranch when I would be so exhausted after a day of haying that Ken would have to put me to bed. Well, so it was with Peter and David. I had just finished moving the plane away from the dock and was climbing back up the stairs to the store when I found them sound asleep on some wooden crates. I carried them up to their bed without either of them waking up. I don't think they knew how they got to bed and they never said anything about it in the morning.

"You guys have got to lose some weight, I can't carry you any more."

RED McKENZIE, ENGINEER

It was still snowing lightly when Red and I took off for Deschambault Lake. We required a bulldozer to clear away the heavy drifts on the lake in front of the town. Dog Island, a long island laying in front of the townsite, provided protection from the strong winds blowing in across the lake. I counted 40 dogs on the island one time. It was a good thing they were all tied up and couldn't get to each other or there would have been a massacre for sure.

Their main diet was frozen fish. They seemed to thrive on it from the look of them. The natives didn't consider their dogs as being anything of value so often neglected them badly. If a dog wandered off while the family was crossing a portage, they just left him. Wolves or porcupines would make quick work of an Indian dog.

The airways agent came up to the store and asked me to fly a load of supplies to a small group of natives who were making their way to La Ronge. It had been pre-arranged that we meet them on their trip south. There was an aircraft working out of Deschambault Lake requiring some repairs so I took Red McKenzie with me. He was very good at his job but had a way of getting himself, and those who associated with him, in trouble.

Red was no spring chicken and had lived in the North most of his life. He spoke Cree very well. In fact, so well you would think he was Cree. He was a bachelor but said he didn't have to be married, he had children spread all through the North Country.

I remember walking into the Stanley Bay Post one day and the store was full of customers. I hadn't been in La Ronge very long so was unaware of the general 'goings on' in the northern villages. Standing around the candy barrel were four children ranging in age, I thought, from six to twelve years of age. The kids were as white as I was. One guy had hair as red as could be, another was blonde. I didn't know there were any white families living here.

I started talking to them in English. They all laughed and hid their faces, thinking I was some funny guy. I wondered what the joke was. The post agent came to my rescue. He told me the kids were Metis

children and didn't speak much English. "But they're as white as I am," I exclaimed. "Oh sure they are. They got white daddies. The Red headed one is Red McKenzie's. Those two fair kids are Frances Brothers Transport offspring and that little guy is a Bay product from a clerk we used to have here. Hoooolly! I couldn't believe my ears. "Well youngster, you better get used to this as you'll find them everywhere you go. You just better watch yourself boy or else you'll leave a few of your own around," he laughed.

"You ask Red someday and he'll tell you all about it," he said. I wasn't so sure I wanted to hear any more, let alone hear it from the manufacturer himself.

Our take off was rough but in spite of the snow the visibility was pretty fair. Red was a talker and his mouth never stopped. "What's a young kid like you doing way up here in God's Country?" he asked. I gave him part of my history and how I came to be here. "You like working for Billy boy? He's sure one tough character," he went on. "I got mad at him one time 'cause I thought he had gypped me on some furs I sold him. Well, that Scottish sucker picked me up and turned me upside down and tossed me out on my ear, and I don't back down from no one either," he said. "Billy never gypped anyone out of anything, in fact, I guess he gives better prices on furs than anyone," he then volunteered. I told him I liked Bill and, even though I was new here, I had come to know him pretty well. Bill still flew a lot when I had room. "Yeah, Bill loves to fly whenever he gets the chance. He's one of the best radio operators up here too," Red claimed. All the Bay posts were in touch with one another via Ham Radio.

Red continued to tell me of all his female conquests. He informed me that he would sure look after me. "Ha, you're in for one big surprise youngster, you still being a virgin and all," he said. Good grief! Was it that obvious? I was wondering what I had to say to him to make him quit.

"I guess you don't have to prove it to me Red, I've seen one of your kids already," I said, laughing at the thought of this old geezer and his so called conquests.

"Yeah well, that's Sammy." he stated proudly. "These women up here think it's an honour to have a White man's kid so they're after your tail the minute they get a chance. " I've just been trying to make them honourable," he laughed. "You have to beat 'em off with a

snowshoe sometimes," He just roared with that one.

I liked flying "CF-SAN", she was almost the oldest Norseman in the fleet but once you got used to her she would obey. Fall asleep or become too sloppy and she would soon make you realize she wouldn't be taken for granted.

The snow had stopped but the sky was still cloudy and the air was as smooth as silk. Red spotted our landing area and I flew low over the spot to make sure the snow wasn't too deep for us to land. "Keep over to the left and put her down just where the snow has blown off." he said. It looked good to me so I made my approach, I could see the camp where we were to deliver our load. The wind was in the right direction for me to land parallel to the shore so we wouldn't have too far to taxi. When there was deep snow I wanted to stay clear, never knowing what was underneath. I was coming in quite fast but a long way upwind from the camp so I figured I would have her stopped pretty close. Red cranked the flaps down, we touched and bounced once, and she settled down to stay. We slid along and came to a stop.

The families were there to greet us and of course Red had to have his say with all the news and to make eyes at the married women. I must say, they were making them right back at Red. Good Grief, and their husbands standing right there. They just laughed. Red would say something vulgar and the ladies would just hang their heads and smile innocently, twittering between themselves. I was only just learning to understand the language but I knew Red was talking about me. Hoooolly! I wanted out of here.

We had everything unloaded and SAN started. We said our goodbyes and took off, heading to the village, where we would stay overnight. We would then continue up to North End Reindeer Lake. I had noticed a heavy build up of dark clouds but it wasn't until we got about 20 miles out that we ran into a heavy snow squall. I decided that we should turn south, away from the storm. More cloud and more snow, what the heck was I going to do? The darned weather forecast hadn't painted this bad a picture.

"Skipper, we better head back to Deschambault and spend the night there until this stuff blows over. No need to take chances, huh?" Red advised.

"Maybe you want to instrument us some place," Red quipped. I tried radioing the Village DNR post but no answer. I had no choice

but to return and follow Red's suggestion. After all, he knew this area and had a lot more experience than I did.

We were welcomed once again and after removing the battery and draining all the oil out of SAN, we covered her up with our engine cover and left her to the elements. Red did most of the work and I noticed he took no chances with anything, he was very thorough. When we left to walk back to the shore, I felt SAN was well looked after.

The oil and the battery were carried to shore on one of the toboggans. Red and I were assigned a spot in the main tent amidst a great deal of laughter and kibitzing by the women of the group. The tent had large space heaters, where we could keep the oil and battery warm. They were very hospitable and made us welcome. Too welcome, I thought. Little kids were everywhere and poking into our things. We both had Arctic Three Star sleeping bags, which were supposed to be the best in the world for Northern areas.

I had to have Red interpret some things they said but other than that I think I was learning the language very well. I sat watching the kids fool around, playing games, while Red was in deep discussion with the men about furs, trapping, fishing and whatever else. We drank vast amounts of tea laced with pounds of sugar. This was the only way to drink tea," I was advised.

After we had eaten I had heard Red and the women talking about me and I was more than a little apprehensive about spending a night here, but so far so good.

It was snowing very hard and I knew we would have a job cleaning off SAN in the morning, if it ever stopped. We ate dried bear meat and fresh cooked bannock. I couldn't stomach the bear grease they used for butter so ate my bannock dry but with syrup to help moisten it. Then we had more tea.

As it gets dark so early the families retire quite early. There were four tents in the area where the families slept. We were in the largest one. It was warm and they had two or three coal oil lanterns to light the tents with. Our tent got very warm and I was forced to take off my parka and my top sweater or I'd suffocate. The smell was something else but I was getting used to it. Being we were the visitors, it seemed that everyone gathered in the big tent to talk and laugh. The place smelled worse than anything I had ever

experienced before. The babies howled and stunk of urine. Hoooollly!. Well, I guess it was better than freezing to death.

I had to go outside to relieve myself and was busy doing so when two young girls came racing over to where I was standing, trying to embarrass me. Hoooolly! I laid out my bedroll and was getting comfortable when Red came over telling me that the old man wanted me to be happy. He was offering me his wife or his daughters, whichever I chose, to keep me warm. They were drinking potato champagne which the Natives make as a tonic against the cold.

The daughters were little children and the old lady was Old. HHHOOOIlly! I decided to reply to the girls myself and I told them, in my best Cree, "I was always ready to share." That was a disaster. I still wasn't ready for Cree on my own yet. That wasn't what I wanted to tell them at all. "Red, tell them I am just happy to be here and to be their guest but no thank you for the ladies," I said.

"Skipper, you can't turn them down and bring embarrassment upon the family," Red said. A young boy came over to Red and whispered something to him. "The kid says his sister would be nice to you and that you would make her very happy if she could make you happy too."

"Red, for goodness sake stop all this stuff will you? Tell them I'm too young or I got a disease or something? Tell them anything but get them off of me," I pleaded. Red told them something and the kids started laughing, flapping their arms and pointing to me like I was something from another world. I took it to mean that I was chicken, and I was.

Red took it upon himself to act on my behalf and the old lady crawled into his sleeping blanket. I just couldn't comprehend such goings on and I turned my back on them while the rest of the kids just kept egging them on. How disgusting. The father just sat smoking his pipe and chuckled to himself. This was no place for a young innocent boy like myself and I wondered how long I would remain that way in this strange and beautiful country. It must have been a change in the moon because there was terrible things going on between the children as well and the other adults, I just could not believe my ears. Finally things settled down and they slept, thank goodness. Good Grief, what an experience. I was afraid to go to sleep only half dozed.

When we got up the snow had stopped and the sky was clear with the stars still shining. The fire was still very warm and a couple of pieces of wood brought it back to full life. I listened to Red kidding the girls as we ate bannock and drank tea. What a character he was. "Okay Skippy boy, let's get the oil into her. It'll be sunup in an hour and we should be on our way," he said. The Indians hauled the battery and the oil down to SAN and we got the glow pots going under the engine cover. Red did all the work and I could hear him swearing, as he had a flare up with one of the pots. They burn quite hot and will often flare up and singe your eyelashes. Terrible things but there was nothing else. We went back to the tents and drank some more tea while the women made, what presumed to be, suggestive remarks about my person. Boy, had I come close I thought.

"Red, are all native families like this one?" I asked.

"Well old son, I guess you would say it all depends on who they're hosting, yah know what I mean," he smirked. I knew what he meant.

SAN started easily with all the warm oil in her innards and the battery warmed. One always had to careful that you didn't get over anxious in your start up and over prime. Then you would stand a good chance of an engine fire. Anyway old Red was standing nearby with our fire extinguisher.

We said our good byes and thanked them amidst waves and shouts while the young boys flapped their arms like wings. Chicken Wings. "Well, that's another one," Red laughed as SAN lifted off. We arrived at North End with very little fuel left. Checking in at the agent's office, we were told that we had a mercy flight, there was an elderly white trapper who required air ambulance service. It was very cold and the ice crystals made ground visibility terrible. It was hard to see ice hummocks and cracks, that sort of thing. The trapper lived with his wife and a couple of grown children on the edge of the river just where it flowed into the lake. The general rule of thumb on situations where you were required to land near or on rivers was, "don't do it". There was always the chance of thin ice due to river currents keeping the ice from forming very deep. The other problems we were facing, in this particular case, was the ground visibility was poor due to the ice crystals and it was very cloudy with a low overast of dark, snow-laden clouds. Not a very good forecast for success. The agent had allowed me to take Red with me as he thought I might

require help in moving the old man.

When we were preparing to land at the river I said, "Keep a look out Red, this doesn't look like the best landing place to me."

"It's okay Skip, just keep to the west of the river and come in towards it," he advised.

"Looks like there's lots of snow too. I wonder how deep it is? Doesn't it look kinda grey to you?" I asked.

"Nope, it's just the clouds making it so dull, what with all this fog," he said.

We couldn't stay up here forever so I banked the aircraft around, looking for any sign of slush ice, and started my approach. Red cranked down some flap as I was coming in hot. The touch down was rough and fast and we were coasting along, when all of a sudden we started to decelerate too quickly. Water was spraying up from the skis.

"Holy shit, Skip we're in the slush," Red screamed. He needn't have told me that. I knew! and yelled at him to crank up the flaps as I poured on full throttle. SAN was responding too slowly. Oh God no, not a "freeze-in". Slowly we started to pick up speed and soon the tail was up but we were heading for the mouth of the river and open water. I didn't think we were going to make it and was afraid we would go through the ice. I could see open patches of water and I knew for sure we were going to go through. I remembered an old trick Lefty Williams told me about. Use aileron just as we do on floats, lifting first one ski and then the other, reducing ever so slightly the drag but maybe enough to give you a couple of knots more. There was still quite a bit of water splashing up but we were gaining speed, going faster and faster we went until I thought she was ready, one more rock and then up. "Red, when I tell you, give me full flap," I yelled at him. He was immediately on the flap handle. The open water was just ahead and we were doomed to go into it. Well, it was do or die and I sure didn't want to die. I rolled her left then right and then yelled. "Now Red!" Red cranked hard and SAN lifted off just a few feet from the open water.

"Oh you big, beautiful beast!" I yelled at the top of my voice.

As I circled the lake looking for a safer spot to land our passengers started waving us towards the other side of the bay from where we had touched down. I made one pass and Red confirmed that it looked good and we double-checked it when we saw one of

the people run out into the centre where we were to land. There was no water showing up in his footsteps. They were ready and waiting when we stopped. My heart was still beating so hard I could hardly get my breath. What a terrifying experience and I shuddered to think what would have happened if we had got stuck in the slush or, even worse, went into the water. We'd be frozen in until doomsday. I had been told that it was almost impossible to chop a plane free. The aircraft had to broken out of the ice and then lifted up on poles while every piece of ice was chopped off the skis. Anything left on them would create enough resistance to prevent take off. Well, I had yet to go through that ordeal and I swore I would never take Red's advice again because it as, after all, my decision. He may have been great with his women but as far as reading ice went, he was a poor performer. How did he survive this long? And I don't mean just his flying career!

THE TAXIS

I returned Peter and the two Thompson boys to school after they had spent the weekend with me. We enjoyed our time together tobogganing, skiing, eating and all those other exciting activities. It would last us all until the next time. Watching them running up the sidewalk to school was always difficult for me. Already I missed them.

I remembered when Peter first started school and the tearful time we went through. In comparison, this was a joyful time. As we left, I was thinking of the plans we had made for Christmas holidays with my parents.

The boys waved goodbye and I got in the cab and left. I always enjoyed my time with Peter and it was tough leaving him. I wondered what it would be like if I ever had to give him up, realizing then how Ken must have felt, when he knew I would be leaving the ranch to return to my parents. Now at long last I could reason why he had not wanted to get too close to me. He knew that the parting time would come.

I remember worrying that Peter would find it too hard to return to school after the great summer we had. It may have been a bit sad but there were no tears. He was actually happy to get back to school and his friends. He loved school and these week-ends we had together made it a lot easier on both of us.

The taxi took me back to the airport dock where CF SAN waited, already loaded with a full load of doors and windows for Jean Foster. I noticed on my manifest that I would be taking an RCMP Officer as well. The agent closed the rear cargo door and gave me the "All Clear" sign. Goodbye Peter, see you soon. "What's eating you Skipper? You sound like you're talking to yourself," the Mountie said.

Constable Montgomery had been stationed at La Ronge for some time but this was the first time he had ever flown with me. Most passengers liked to sit in the right seat in the cockpit if there was room. We were fully loaded when we took off.

"You don't do much flying like some of the other guys do." I said. "Well Skipper, I'm sort of on special duty in the drug and alcohol

division and have been assigned to the La Ronge detachment. You know, to get a feel of what's happening up there." he said. I knew there was an alcohol problem with the natives. No one knew how they were getting their booze. Some of the natives told me the bootleggers were taking their entire winter's fur catch in trade for a few bottles of watered down liquor. The police hadn't been able to catch them or determine how it was coming in. We discussed the problem and then he started talking about my infamous mercy flight, bringing out a pregnant native woman. That's when I decided there should be no more talk.

"Don't be so touchy Skipper, it could have happened to anyone but it was even better that it was you providing everyone with a good laugh, you being Wesagachuk and all," he joked.

"How's that Indian kid you're looking after getting along? I hear he is one smart one. I guess he is the one in ten thousand that's got some brains and knows how to use them huh?" he said.

"Peter is very bright Gil, and he's making the most out of getting an education," I bragged.

"Yah. Well watch him Skipper, they're all the same. You can't turn your back on any of them, you know," he went on. "He may look like a whitey but he ain't. They're takers every one of them. I wouldn't be surprised that some of them are behind the bootlegging," he said.

I was glad when we landed and he left for the post. If he wasn't biased against the natives I don't know who was.

I worked a lot for Bill that fall and winter was coming quickly. The lakes were starting to freeze quite hard along the shore and if the temperature continued to drop it wouldn't be long before we would be able to land anywhere. We could always land in the Bay between the mainland and Dog Island long before the actual lake froze over. We knew that if La Ronge was starting to freeze over then the further North we went the more ice there would be. Winter was here and that meant the winter road would be passable for trucks and cars. With the vehicles would come the booze traders. If only the Mounties could get more staff and get to work on stopping them.

Bill McNamy told me Corporal Gil Montgomery had been in trouble at another post. He had been transferred here to get straightened out, where the staff could keep a close eye on him. Bill

didn't like him and didn't mind telling anyone. He and I sat talking in his office when Joe Anderson, a native trapper, came in. He was drunk or very close to it. He gave us a story about how he had lost all of his last catch of fur. Some whities traded booze for his fur catch. "How much was the fur worth Joe?" Bill asked.

Joe, speaking in slow drawling Cree, told us he thought about eleven hundred dollars.

"Why the hell would you trade all your fur for booze? How much booze did you buy?" Bill asked.

"I don't know, never counted the bottles," Joe slurred.

"Bottles!" Bill yelled at him. "Bottles! There should have been cases, dozens of cases. Are you out of your mind? How are you going to pay your bill here? What will you do for food? What about your family? What are you going to do for supplies to go back with?" he asked. Bill was getting red in the face, he was so furious.

"I don't know," was all Joe was able to say.

"Come back when you're sober Joe," Bill told him. Everyone in the store could hear Bill's shouting. They pretended they hadn't heard a thing when we walked out into the store. They had all experienced the same kind of deception from the bootleggers.

"Swen tells me that he thinks the taxis are bringing it from PA in special compartments under their frames," Bill said quietly." He told the Mounties all about what he had heard and they told him they would keep an eye out for them." Bill went on. "The taxis have to make their money in the winter as that's the only time they can bring their booze in." The freight trucks kept the snow packed down on the highway making it possible for the cars to use it.

Driving an automobile over those frozen trails in the middle of winter was very dangerous work. A break down meant almost certain death by freezing. The cars carrying the booze wouldn't enter into the townsite but would park in brush alongside the Montreal River bridge entering town. Here the trading would take place. Word would get to the natives that a car was coming. They should get their furs packaged and ready for trading. The smugglers would even take frozen fish in trade for whisky.

"You know Skip, I can't figure out why the Mounties haven't got a better ear as to what's going on and then they could catch these guys," Bill said.

"Well, I heard the problem is to find out just when they are coming. The Indians aren't going to tell us, that's for sure," I remarked. "If this keeps up these poor people are going to be absolutely penniless and their families will go hungry. I hear the mission has five families that they're keeping now," Bill said.

"Trouble really stems from the fact the Attorney General's Department had told the Mounties to go easy on the revenuers,"

"Bill That's a terrible disgrace if it's true," I said.

It was a particularly cold night and the temperature had dropped to -40 degrees when Nurse Thompson came over to the post residence and told Bill that she had just received two frozen bodies, Amos Charles and Jonas Ratt. They had died from exposure down by the bridge. Both men had been drunk because their belongings were still there, as were the empty bottles of booze they had been drinking. She wanted me to take a letter directly to the RCMP in Prince Albert and not go through the Department of Natural Resources agent. "Just take it on your next trip Skipper, tell them it's from me and that it's important they read it now," Liz explained.

"Can you tell us what it's about?" I asked.

"Better you and Bill just stay out of it. The less you know the better, at this point," she said. "How long had those two been there?" I asked."Well, I'd say at least three days and did you know they were flat broke with not a penny between them?" she said.

"Well, Jonas had just received my payment for his Fisher pelts and that must have been about 700 dollars. His wife and kids are staying with the Andersons. Cora is Jonas's Aunt you know," Bill said. "I have to go Skipper, please get that letter in for sure and when you see the boys, say hello and love," Liz said, as she bundled up against the freezing weather. It wasn't very far to the hospital and the night was clear, but bitterly cold. You could hear someone walking on the road for almost a mile the sound carried so far when it was cold like this.

"Well Skipper, what do you think that was all about?" Bill asked.

"Search me, but it must be something to do with Jonas and Amos," I replied.

The oil from the plane was kept on the cook stove in the Agencies' storage building. This way it could easily be poured into the engine first thing in the morning. Sometimes when it was really cold we would use five or six Blow Pots (kerosene heating pots)

under the canvas of the engine. We had to do some preheating before putting the oil in. If we didn't the oil would gel up the minute it touched the engine block. The engine would never turn over if that happened, nor could you drain the oil again. Here it was easy to do but try doing it out on an ice pack some place where the wind was blowing 15 or 20 knots, and the pots wouldn't light. Each time you got under the canvas to get them going you would singe your eyelashes or even worse. I often told myself that this would be the last time I would spend a rotten winter doing this sort of thing. My fingers would get so stiff from the cold I couldn't feel the fuel tap on the carburettors, to drain them. Ugh! Hooooolly. It was never this cold on the ranch - never.

I had to make a short trip to Snake Lake and pick up Ernie Fisher. He owned and operated a small trading post there and had to get to Prince Albert. There were three other passengers including the Indian Agent for the La Ronge Region. The aircraft was due a 100 hr. inspection so it meant I would be staying over. I wanted to see Peter and liked to drop in to surprise him. He would get so excited.

With the plane looked after and Nurse Thompson's letter delivered, I went to the office to find out what was on my work orders. "Skipper, we want you to go to Wallaston as soon as you can. Take CF-FAR (Norseman). You have a load of survey equipment and geologists to go," the agent said. "You want to see Peter first?" he asked.

"How long will I be gone?" I asked.

"You'll be back day after tomorrow and then you can have the weekend here," he said.

"Okay Chuck, that sounds great to me. I'll be back in an hour and then get away by eleven." That should put me into Wallaston Lake about three thirty in the afternoon and by then it would be getting dark.

I borrowed the agent's truck and drove into PA and went to the school. It was always exciting to see Peter. I walked up the sidewalk to the entrance, to find Peter racing down the stairs to meet me.

"Dad, Dad, what are you doing here? I'm glad to see you, I missed you. You didn't tell me you were coming, I was just passing by the upstairs window and I saw the Company truck outside. I knew it had to be you so I ran down," he said, getting his breath. I got a monster hug and we walked to the office.

"Could I have a few minutes with Peter?" I asked.

"Surely. I'll let his teacher know where he is," the secretary said.

Peter looked around to see if there were others within ear shot of our conversation, then secretively whispered.

"I was in the cafe on Central Avenue the other day with Johnny, and I overheard three men talking. It was about some whisky going to La Ronge. They didn't think we knew what they were saying. One was that special Constable from the Candle Lake area. He seems to know all about what was going on and the others just listened. I think they're hauling whisky to Montreal Lake. I didn't recognize any of the others so they can't be from La Ronge. But it was La Ronge they were talking about. They said something like, "Victoria had paid for the trip and the shipment. She expects to get paid as soon as the trip is finished next Tuesday. Do you think that's important?" he whispered.

"Peter, how in the world were you able to remember everything they said?" I asked.

"Come on Dad, you know I have a good memory if I want to," he laughed.

"May I ask what you were doing down town at the Grand Cafe?" I scolded.

"Just looking at the girls like you used to do, "he laughed.

"You smart alec, you better watch out and no women for you yet," I quipped.

"Just joking with you Dad," he chuckled.

"Hi Skipper," the school principal came in and also said hello to Peter. "You want to hear how this youngster of yours is doing?" he asked.

"More lies Mr. VanderHoft?" I joked. Peter looked wide-eyed at me.

"I am always interested if it's a good report you're going to give me," I replied.

"I don't suppose you have all day but in a nut shell he is the school's top student. I have taken the liberty, through the school directors of course, to recommend Peter for two of our four scholarships. Can you believe that?" he glowed. Peter stared up into my eyes for a reaction. I know he saw how proud I was of him.

"I was saving that news for a surprise Dad," he said.

"I think you had better officially adopt this boy, Skipper, everyone thinks he's yours anyway," the headmaster laughed.

"Peter would probably have other ideas," I joked. Peter never said a word, he just looked at me. He had a way of staring right through you when he was deep in thought.

"Well, I really don't need to be adopted 'cause I have a Dad already. You. Right Dad?" He said, moving up beside me. I choked.

I was impressed with the great progress Peter was making and how satisfied I was with the school.

"I'll be back Friday Peter, around four in the afternoon, and we can have the weekend together. I have to go now but I'll see you Friday." I got another big hug and then I had to go. As I went out the door he just stood there, staring after me. As much as I was excited to see him, I was always terribly lonely when I had to leave him there. Two scholarships indeed.

Armed with the information Peter had given me, I went to the RCMP offices and reported that I had something on the bootleggers that were feeding booze to the Indians at La Ronge. The sergeant at the desk ushered me into an office, closing the door behind us.

"Okay Skipper, where in the hell did you get your information from?" he asked.

"I was just visiting Peter and he told me he overheard the three natives talking in the Grand Cafe and that one of them was the Special Constable from Candle Lake," I said.

"Now how in the hell would he know who the Special was?" he asked.

"Peter lived up in La Ronge until just recently and I guess he got to know nearly everyone. He knows what he's talking about and he never gets things wrong," I went on.

"You keep this information to yourself and tell the boy to keep his mouth shut about this whole thing. Just don't let him get involved in any way. You hear me Skipper? This is serious stuff, if he's right".

Peter and I enjoyed a great week-end together in PA but like all things that are wonderful they seem too short and it was time for him to return to school Sunday evening. I returned to my hotel room wondering what was happening regarding the booze shipment to La Ronge. Well, I was to find out early Monday morning when I entered the office of the Airways. There were three RCMP officers waiting

to go to La Ronge but the flight was to be delayed so that the arrival in La Ronge would be just before dark. I asked what was going on and was told that it was just some routine police work. We had never seen so many policemen going to La Ronge at one time and wondered if this had anything to do with Peter's tip off.

"Skipper, you take SAO and go to Waskeseau to bring old Doc Bissette out. He's been in there on some local native affairs," the agent instructed me. I was wondering who would be taking the police brigade up North. I arrived back in PA but SAN was gone and so was the brigade. I stayed overnight but didn't call Peter. Better he not be disturbed now that he was settled in after the weekend. The next morning I picked up a newspaper and there on the headlines was the big story about the brigades huge bootlegger bust in La Ronge.

Apparently the police were waiting by the bridge when the first of three cars arrived, loaded with liquor and watered down liquor at that. Also waiting at the bridge was the La Ronge Constable, Montgomery; the Special Constable from Candle Lake and three other natives. The Brigade from PA hid in the shadows of the bridge. They had already spotted the other policeman there. When the first car arrived there was a greeting by the waiting policeman from Candle Lake and it was like a meeting of old friends. The driver crawled under the car and started unloading cases that fit under the frame.

The second car arrived and the same procedure took place. When the third car was unloaded, the last two cars departed and then there was a pay off of some sort. Soon a truck from La Ronge drove in and parked beside the taxi. First one native arrived with a pack of fur on his back, then others arrived driving sleighs dogs pulling loads of furs and even fish. The trading started in earnest and at the height of trading and much merriment, the Brigade made their appearance. The Indians were sent home empty handed of booze except they still had their fur and fish. The others were rounded up and arrested. The two cars that were sent back to PA were picked up as they returned to the city. A newspaper reporter was there to get the news as it was taking place. He had been flown in privately the day before and was just waiting for the events to occur .

The newspaper went on to say that the police had received this

vital tip from a young boy whose identity they were not at liberty to divulge, other than he was from out of town and was attending school in PA. A great debt of gratitude was to be extended to this astute youngster in helping to nab the largest bootlegging network in the Province.

"Skipper, I have been meaning to ask you about that bootlegging bust the other day," Bill said.

"You don't have to answer but was that Peter they were talking about?" he looked around, trying to be secretive about his question.

"Why would you think it was Peter?" I asked.

"Well, I heard that the tip off had to have come from an Indian or someone who spoke Cree because in the investigation the police say that it was from a slipped conversation between the Special Constable and some other natives."

"Nice try Bill but why would you zero in on Peter, just because he speaks Cree?"

"Well, the other reason is the main one. You haven't denied one word of what I've been saying," he laughed. His Scottish accent was really brrrring along at this point. He then dropped the subject, knowing I was feeling a little uncomfortable. He was reading me pretty good and I was about to tell Bill about Peter's encounter, when in walked Nurse Thompson.

"Well, how's my favourite patient today," she said.

"You sick or something Skipper?" Bill asked.

"No, it's just Liz's attempt at some sick humour at my expense," I said, looking daggers at her. My problem was not for general knowledge but let her have her moment.

"Liz, did you have anything to do with the bust the other day? What was in that letter?" he kept enquiring.

"I told the commissioner that unless they got serious about the bootlegging and what was happening up here to the people, I was sending a telegram to the High Commissioner for Indian Affairs, supported with tons of evidence that he would be most interested in having," she said.

"I could be fired for doing what I did, but didn't want to involve either of you two," she replied.

"Liz, you sure did the right thing because it seems they got the big boys," I said.

"I know one thing, they wouldn't have acted unless they had a time and a place and that's what they got from Peter," she said.

"Ah Ha," Bill said, "I knew it, I knew it was Peter." Things slowly returned to normal and the Christmas Season was once again upon us.

I was doing a little more flying and Bill had to work harder in the store. I picked up Peter and the Thompson boys, who I was told, had been packed for weeks, happy to be going home. Peter especially, was beside himself. We were going to go to Winnipeg and spend Christmas with my parents and give them a chance to meet Peter. This was going to be a very traumatic experience for both of us. Meeting my parents and all their friends would be terrifying to anyone. I know they were all very anxious to meet Skipper's ward, as they called him. The whole idea was my parent's. I certainly wasn't thinking of spending Christmas with them. I had thought of going to the ranch but decided my parents should get to know Peter and to pass their judgement. It had been hard writing and telling them of Peter in the first place, especially when they wrote back telling me how I had ruined my life.

We were staying at Norman Ervine's home until we left for PA and then Winnipeg.

"Dad, can I go to the Christmas dance tonight?" Peter asked, giving me his straight through me stare. I haven't been to one since I was just a small kid then."

"And what are you now?" I kidded.

"I have to go to see Bill but you can go and I'll drop in after I'm done. Okay?" I suggested. Norman's wife was Cree and her name was Wetebegatic, meaning Dirty Forehead, I guess because her forehead was very dark. She fawned over Peter like he was her own. When he left for the dance he looked just like any other native teenager. He wore black denim pants and a heavy Cowichan sweater. On his feet were moosehide moccasins with the typical moccasin rubbers worn over top. What was she trying to do to him? Well one thing was for sure, Peter was certainly dressed for the party.

Bill and I walked down to the dance hall where we found the place jammed to the doors and the smoke and smell were enough to drive you outside within a minute or two. That's why I sort of delayed my going until the last minute. There were great goings on

and the whole hall seemed to be clapping and encouraging some dancers in the middle of the floor. The natives have a foot dance similar to an Irish Step Dance. It's very complicated and requires lots of practice. Then I heard, --- "Mollasin Peter, Mollasin! (Good Peter, Good!). I pushed through the watchers and there was Peter and one other youngster, both trying to outdo the other's stepdancing. I didn't know Peter could dance, let alone do it so well. Hoooolly. I couldn't believe my eyes as I watched him. He was playing out, I could tell.

"Skipper, who taught Peter to dance like that?" Bill exclaimed. "Wow, can that kid go." The music was getting faster and the boys were dancing harder. I knew that this used to be a competition at all the dances. Several young people would start the dance, trying to eliminate each other. Two or three would be left trying to outlast the others in order to determine a victor. The boys were sweating gallons. No wonder the place stunk so bad. I was surprised that I didn't smell any liquor or find anyone intoxicated, as was usually the case.

I couldn't help but feel proud of the boy but felt he was out of place here, not at home at all. There he was, egging on his opponent, trying to beat him if he could. Then the music stopped and everyone crowded around and cheered the winner. Peter had won and I must admit he was one great little dancer. I wondered where he had learned it and learned it so well. We lost sight of him and searched around to see where he had gone. He was sitting on a bench by the door, when we found him. "Dad, were you here a minute ago?" he asked.

"You mean when you were dancing up a storm on the floor?" I kidded him.

"Peter that was the best I have ever seen on this floor," Bill congratulated. "Where did you ever learn to dance like that?" he asked.

"I learned from my mother and by watching other kids when I was small," he said.

The fiddler and guitar player were hard at it again and we couldn't stand the stuffy place any longer.

"I have to get some fresh air," I choked, and got up to go out.

"Dad wait, I'm coming too," and the three of us left.

"You can stay Peter, if you like."

"No, I'm coming with you," he said.

Bill McNamy said goodnight and headed to the Post. We walked the opposite direction to Norman's house without saying anything.

The night was so clear and the moon was so bright that it seemed a shame to break the spell. Our footsteps echoed into the night as we walked along.

"Dad, I don't belong here any more," Peter said with a slight trembling in his voice. I knew what he was thinking.

"What makes you say that Peter?"

"I don't think like these people any more, don't look like them, and don't feel right dressed like this. I Could hardly stand the heat in the hall, it almost made me sick," he said. "Am I wrong feeling like I do? I feel right when I'm with you and when I'm at school but feel like I'm betraying someone. Like I'm being unfaithful sort of," he went on. "I didn't care that I told on those guys the other day, it didn't bother me at all 'cause I'm not really Cree. Nobody wants me around and I could never come back and live here. Old Wetebegatic talks nothing but Cree to me and she tells me not to forget my Mother and where I came from. I know she gets cross when I answer her in English but I'm not Cree any more Dad, I'm not."

I didn't answer because I really didn't know what to tell him. I know he was asking me to help him sort out his feelings but I couldn't sort out my own, let alone Peters.

"I don't belong here any more," he said.

We crawled into bed and lay there with our own thoughts for awhile, with the moon shining in our window. Peter quietly said, "Dad, what would happen to me if you decided you didn't want me any more and the Cree didn't want me? I was shocked that he would think of such a thing. I was sensing first hand how the Indian children from the Mission School must be feeling. They were not accepted back with their parents because they were too used to the whiteman's ways. The whiteman turned him away because he was native. How does a young child feel when they are turned away with no one to care about what happens to them, or to love them?

"Peter, I could never give you away. You have made me so proud of you and you've worked so hard to improve yourself." I tried to keep my voice from breaking. I can remember my asking the same question of Ken when I was Peter's age. Now it was back haunting me again, only the rolls were reversed.

" Will your parents feel the same way about me when we meet?" Peter asked.

"Of course they will, now let's get some sleep."
    "Goodnight Dad."
    "Night Peter."

THE SCOTTS

Peter and I anxiously awaited the boarding call for our train. I hated standing around waiting for things to happen and Peter had a hard time controlling his excitement. We both had thoughts of what lay ahead when we would meet my parents. Christmas was supposed to be the happiest time of the year and I was hoping it would turn out that way. My folks were looking forward to seeing me after such a long time and, of course, to meet Peter.

The train trip was the most exciting experience of Peter's life and we caused quite a stir when Peter continued to call me Dad. I had certainly grown taller over the years and boasted a whopping 5'10" but I didn't look old enough to be Peter's father, more like his older brother. I was 23 and Peter looked like a twelve-year-old even though he had just turned 14. He was small for his age, just like I had been.

The first incident occurred when we entered the dining car and Peter, of course, was all eyes. Everything was new to him. "Dad, let's sit at this table." Peter said, loudly enough for everyone to hear. "Can I sit by the window Dad, please?" Peter asked. I noticed the looks we were getting and I must admit I was enjoying every minute of the occasion. Tongues were really wagging as people tried to figure what we were about.

We ate an enormous dinner and Peter's eyes bugged right out of his head when the waiter brought us the dessert wagon. I was thinking, if these people who he didn't know were shocked, what were my parents and their friends going to think. I had no problem with Peter calling me Dad, as a matter of fact I had grown quite used to it. Peter thought it was the normal thing to do. I wondered if I should get Peter to back off at least until our visit was over. How could I ask him to quit calling me Dad while we were visiting my parents? What was wrong with him calling me Dad? How was I going to explain my reasoning to Peter when, for the past year, we had been existing as father and son? Everyone in La Ronge had come to accept the fact but then we were not in La Ronge any longer.

We were heading to a big city where no one knew us at all, except my parents and those relatives anxious to meet us.

The train trip was exciting and during the trip Peter was endearing himself to all our fellow passengers. He was certainly enjoying himself as he answered their many questions about he and his dad and where they lived and what they did. "My Dad's a bush pilot and he flies up in the North where we live," he would tell them, smiling with pride. "We're going to Winnipeg to spend Christmas with my Dad's parents," he would say.

I felt I was an outgoing person and tried to be friendly but I hated people who were only interested in being friends in order to snoop into your affairs. Peter was innocent and just accepted everyone as being truly interested in him.

"My, you are certainly a very young looking father, but it is plain to see the resemblance," one elderly lady ventured. "Do I detect a slight accent?" she asked. "You both seem to have a little bit of one don't you think?" she went on. I almost choked on that one and I looked to see where Peter was. He was doing just fine, eating candy that had been offered by a young couple and their children.

An incident took place while we were relaxing and enjoying ourselves. There seemed to be a commotion taking place at the end of our car. The conductor was yelling, apparently having trouble explaining to some people why they couldn't come into our car. Passengers were all turned towards the disturbance and the shouting was getting louder. I think I heard the familiar Cree dialect at the same time Peter did and before I could say anything he was down to the end of the car like a flash. A native family were wanting to get into the car and the conductor was insisting they had no business here. Finally I heard Peter's voice speaking quietly to them in Cree and telling them that they were not to be in this car as it was for sleeping car passengers only. They were to be in another car for day passengers. Their tickets said so. Every one of the passengers in our car just looked open mouthed at Peter and the intruders as they slowly retreated to another car. Peter continued to console them as he guided them to eats in their own car. They were probably as surprised to hear Peter talking to them as everyone else. They smiled at Peter, happy to have had someone who could talk to them in their own tongue. The conductor just scratched his head and thanked

Peter for intervening.

"How come you speak their language?" he asked Peter.

"My Dad and I live up North in their country," he said, coming back to sit with me.

The lady who had been talking to me just couldn't contain herself any longer and came bustling over to start asking her questions all over again and complimenting Peter on being such a clever boy in being able to learn their language and speaking to them like he did. Peter just sat looking out the window, and blushing.

"They are our friends," he said. "Dad, I think I know how they felt not being able to talk to anyone."

My parents along with my Aunt and Uncle were at the station to meet us. I hadn't expected such a welcoming committee. There were the usual hugs and shaking of hands and then I introduced Peter to my mother. I noticed that she had not taken her eyes off Peter from the moment she set eyes on us. Peter was waiting for a cue from me as to what to do and when he didn't get one he held out his hand to her.

"I'm pleased to meet you Ma'am" he offered. She shook his hand, never taking her eyes off him. Peter looked her straight in the eye and never blinked as my mother seemed to be trying to stare him down. I hoped things were going to be all right. My Aunt came over to him and gave him a big hug and Peter returned the greeting.

"Welcome to our city Peter, it's so nice to finally get to meet you," she said.

"Thank you. It's nice to meet you too," Peter replied quietly. As we stood exchanging pleasantries several passengers who had been with us in our car came past and said goodbye and how nice it was to have met us both.

"You must be very proud of your grandson," my little old lady friend said to my mother. Oooops, we weren't ready for this yet. When would we be ready, I wondered. I decided I would just let it go by and wait for the right time to talk about it. Mother continued to look interested and we left. I honestly don't think she knew how she was going to act or receive either of us. It was difficult for both of us. We were really strangers in a way. One thing for sure Peter was sure laying it on and no one could have helped but be impressed.

The greetings were over and we were all ushered to the front door of the station, where our car was waiting. Peter, for once, was

quiet, looking out the window and answering the odd question put to him by my parents. "You're a handsome young man," my father ventured.

"Thank you Mr. Scott," he replied. Well, at least there was a good impression on one member of the family. Only twenty more to go.

I knew Peter would be thunder struck when he first saw my parent's home and he was. We were greeted at the door by Nancy our maid, who used to look after me and my brother. She had been there a long time.

"Welcome home Skipper, and this must be Peter," she said, ushering us in and taking our coats. "Why don't you two go up to your rooms and rest a bit before supper? You must be very tired from your trip. Trains are always so dirty and tiresome," my mother said. Peter's mouth just stood open and I reminded him to close it lest he catch flies. He laughed. We were shown to our rooms and Peter had one of the guest rooms right next to mine. "Dad, I can't believe this place is real," Peter exclaimed.

I helped him unpack and we laid out some casual clothes for him to wear. I went into his bathroom and ran a tub for him to take a bath. "Get in the tub Peter and I'll be back shortly," I instructed. When I finally came back to Peter's room, he was all dressed and sparkling in some of the new clothes we had bought in Prince Albert before we left. I was proud of him.

Supper was most interesting. Hooollyy! I wondered if we would ever get through it but the boy was up to the challenges my mother seemed to be laying before him. He used the proper utensils and remained quiet unless spoken to. His table manners were impeccable and he was making a good impression. Mother was observing every move Peter made, perhaps trying to find a flaw.

We spent the whole time answering questions about our plans and what it was like living up amongst the native people. Nancy, our maid, made certain Peter got two pieces of an enormous chocolate cake which I am sure my mother had arranged especially for me. She knew it was my favourite.

The house, I must admit, looked very festive with all the various decorations for Christmas. It was indeed set up for happy times and I hoped that we would enjoy it. We all went into the living room where the tree was set up. It looked to be one of the largest I had ever seen. I knew my Mother must be hurting at this time of the year

because of the loss of Billy but she had gone all out for our visit.

Peter was absolutely awe struck and sat staring into the fireplace and at the huge tree. He was a long way from home and I wondered what he was thinking. "Skipper? We have been invited to Uncle Fred's tomorrow night for supper and they're having a few of our friends over as well, sort of a getting reacquainted party," she said. I thanked her but I also remembered the last party she had thrown for me when I walked out. "You know everyone is anxious to see you again and, of course, to meet Peter," she went on.

"I would really just like for us to have this time to ourselves.

You know, just the family," I said.

"I understand but just humour me for this one time, please?" she asked. What else could I do but agree?

My father, who normally says very little, was sitting on the chesterfield showing Peter a book on animals and was intrigued by Peter's knowledge of the wild ones from the North. "You're certainly up on your animals Peter," he said, putting the book away.

Peter and I sat talking in his room until late. Because he was so full of questions I hardly knew where to start. He wanted to know all about what it was like growing up here. I told him I had gone West when I was ten and then returned four years later. Most of the time when I was little like him, I was on the ranch. He already knew that.

"Dad, do you think they like me?" he asked.

"Of course they like you, why wouldn't they. You've certainly made a good impression on them all. I can hardly believe it is you,"

I kidded.

"Ah Dad, you know what I mean," I did know what he meant and I told him I thought he had won the first round but the tough ones were still to come.

I didn't tell him to stop calling me Dad. I couldn't. That would be wrong. What would he think? He seemed to know what he was supposed to do and was trying so hard.

At breakfast the next morning, which is always a rather formal sort of event, we were all sitting down when Peter noticed a Christmas package in front of his place at the table.

"Well Peter, we thought that as it was so close to Christmas that you should be allowed to open one of your gifts. Go ahead and open it," mother said. Peter looked at me as if asking me if it was okay. He

was so excited and Nancy hovered over him like a mother hen while he opened his gift. I remember she used to do that for me, to render any assistance if I was getting into trouble. The box looked like one that would hold a pen and pencil. Peter opened it and let out one whoop, I thought he had lost it for sure. It was a beautiful wristwatch, I am sure, crafted just for him. Mother did things like that. Peter put it on his wrist with Nancy helping him. He held out his hand to admire it and then without a word got up and put his arms around my mother and gave her a big kiss on the cheek.

"Oh thank you, thank you, I really don't deserve anything as nice as this," he said.

"Well Peter," my mother said, after collecting herself from the shock of Peter's show of gratitude, "we think you do. We have seen your report card from school and we certainly do think you deserve it," she gushed. I could hardly believe my ears. I never got such accolades when I received straight A's in school. Peter went over to my father and offered his hand. Father stood up, put his arms around Peter's shoulders, and hugged him. Good Grief, I mean Hooooolyy! What was happening here? Here were my parents acting like they really cared. I had a lump in my throat the size of a tennis ball. I just sat there speechless. Nancy was watching me and I knew we were thinking the same thing. It must be, that after all these years, after they had almost lost their family, that they were realizing how important we were to them.

"Dad, did you ever see such a beautiful watch in your whole life?" Peter said, as he showed me his wrist. Ooops, watch it Peter, I thought. My mother let it pass, as did my father. Nancy caught it though and looked at me a little surprised. She told me later that it wasn't a surprise, she should have expected it but it was the look mother had on her face.

I knew we were going to have a talk and I was just hoping it wouldn't ruin all the good times we were having so far. I knew, mother of old though. Peter and Nancy went to the local market to shop and my mother and I talked. As a matter of fact, I did most of the talking and she just listened.

"Do you know the commitment you are making and what it will do to your life?" she asked. I told her I knew all right. I told her I needed Peter as much as he needed me and how much he meant to

me. I assured her I would see him on his way into life, then I would find the right woman and marry and have children of my own. I had sent her newspaper clippings, in my Christmas card, about the rescue event where Bill and I had saved Peter from death and how I had taken him as my ward. This she seemed to accept, in fact she offered to finance Peter through his schooling. She was very impressed with him and the way he seemed to fit in. "What are you going to tell your uncle Fred and your Auntie tonight?" she asked.

"Just the truth mother. They can accept it or not, I don't care," She just looked at me. I think she was hoping I wasn't going to leave the party like last time.

Mother took Peter shopping in the large Bay Department store and of course this was all overwhelming to Peter. He was so full of everything words failed him. They purchased an entire new wardrobe for him, including a suit.

When they returned Mother was a wreck but I have never seen her look so happy.

"You will never believe all the things we did and what happened to us," She couldn't get the events out fast enough. She told how Peter and she were walking past the Santa Claus visiting area where two little native children were in line to talk to Santa. They watched the goings on and Santa was having a hard time understanding the children. The parents were standing in line looking upset and confused, trying to make Santa understand. The ushers wanted to get the children moving out of the line but Peter was watching all this and took me over with him. He spoke to the children in Cree. They told him what they wanted for Christmas and he translated for Santa. He also told them Santa's message to them. They were all smiles and were laughing at something Peter had said to them and their parents. Needless to say we caused quite a sensation and the photographers, who take pictures of the children, took our pictures together. They asked Peter how it was that he spoke Cree and he told them, in front of everyone, that he and his Father lived up North and that his Dad was a bush pilot. He was so proud and excited and, to tell you the truth, so was I. Then they asked him if I was his grandmother. You could have struck me with a feather. Peter replied, "Yes, this is my grandmother." Well I was so flabbergasted, I couldn't speak." she went on.

"Did you deny it mother?" I asked. "Of course not, right there in the Bay? They all knew who I was," she said. "Well, that wasn't all. Your father came over with Mr. Chester, the head of the fur trade, and introduced Peter as his Grandson. Then the photographer wanted to take another picture of all the store management, who were watching from the sidelines, and Peter standing with his grandparents. They are sending us the photos when they're ready," she said.

"Were you embarrassed?" I asked, sort of looking for a reason to argue with her like I usually did.

"Well, if Peter calls you his Dad, then we must be his grandparents."

I could hardly believe my ears. I put my arms around her, something I could never remember doing, and gave her a kiss. She started to cry and I guess we were both having a good go at it when Peter came in.

"I'm sorry about this afternoon, I didn't mean to embarrass you," he said.

"Peter, your grandmother and grandfather are happy to welcome you into our family. I hope you will accept us like you have your Dad."

She went on to tell me how much Peter had sparked her life and shopping with him had been the best fun she had had in years. She was proud to boast about her grandson from the North.

The party at uncle Fred's was a huge success with Peter being the centre of attraction. The crowning touch came when my godfather came in displaying the Winnipeg newspaper. On the front page was a Christmas story and it was all about mother and father and Peter and, of course, Mr. Chester the head of the Bay Fur Trade. There they were, all emblazoned on the front page in a large picture, captioned by the story of the boy from the North who spoke Cree and who had won their hearts spreading Christmas joy throughout the store. Grandson of the Store's Chief Executive. No one was more surprised than I.

The final touch came when my Godfather asked Peter to say the table grace in Cree. Without batting an eye he stood up, looked at me with a big smile on his face, and said the grace, repeating it in English.

"I give thanks for the food we are about to enjoy and I ask a special blessing for Skipper who, without him, I would not be here today. I am also grateful for my new friends, gathered here this evening. I am

thankful for my grandma and grandpa who I have just met."

There wasn't a dry eye around the table, especially me. Everyone accepted Peter.

Peter came into the living room and sat down on the rug beside mother's chair. He looked up at her, "grandma, thank you for everything today, I had the best time I have ever had in my whole life," he said. She leaned over and kissed him. I had never seen my father show any emotion at all but I watched him wipe his eyes as Peter said goodnight and gave him a hug and left for bed.

Nancy was watching over him as usual and guided him away.

"Mother, you could never in all your life have given me a more perfect Christmas present than what you are doing for Peter and me," I said.

"No Skipper, it is you who have stepped back into our lives like our son and brought that wonderful boy into our lives. You've brought Christmas back into this house. Thank you for coming, we really needed you both you know," mother said. We kissed and I said goodnight. Tomorrow was Christmas Eve.

Our phone never stopped ringing with well wishes and friends of mother's being completely stunned with the newspaper report. Mother just absorbed it like a sponge and I know she was enjoying it immensely. She wasn't defending herself at all, she just acted as though it was the most natural occurrence and why should anyone get so excited about it all? No, she wasn't planning on a party for us. We were spending a quiet Christmas, just the family together. I loved her for that. It was the best Christmas I had had since leaving the ranch.

Saying goodbye at the station was very hard for everyone and I had wished that we had never decided to do it here. The train was late which made it worse. Leaving the house was hard for Peter because he had grown quite attached to Nancy, and she to him. They hugged and she kissed his cheek wiping a tear from her eye.

"You write to me you scamp or else I'll never make you another chocolate cake ever, you hear?" she said.

Finally our boarding announcement came and we said our final goodbyes. I had never seen mother cry before but she had tears in her eyes as she hugged us both. "Please come home again soon you two, we need you, you know," she said.

"And we need you too mother, I replied."

"Thank you for being my grandmother," Peter said, as he gave mother a hug. "You gave me so many things I really don't deserve," he said, and he shook hands with my father. Father was never a demonstrative man but he gave Peter and I both a hug as we left to get aboard.

A moderately successful holiday I would say. I had to be joking. It was the "GREATEST" according to Peter.

NEW VENTURE

The airway agent was expecting me and immediately whisked me into the manager's office. Floyd Kenward was an ex-airforce officer. He had been with Coastal Command and had completed a tour of operations on the East Coast of Canada. He had been based at Goose Bay Labrador. Everyone knew about that place. Cold and desolate.

"Skipper, do you want to buy your own plane and haul supplies for the new mining company setting up near Birch Rapids?" he said.

"Wait a minute, I can't afford to buy a plane," I said.

"Skipper, the flying club has a brand new Cessna Crane T50 that they'll sell to you at a really good price. They had it given to them by the Royal Flying Club Association but they can't use a twin engine aircraft for training," he said.

I asked him if I would have a contract.

"Skipper, they'll give you a three year contract if you want it. You know Birch Rapids like the back of your hand, why not do it and you'll make yourself some good money," he went on. He and I drove over to the club. They had indeed agreed to sell it to me on a time basis, with them doing the financing. The aircraft was brand new but required a new C of A (Certificate of Airworthiness). Hoooolly! was I ever excited. I know I could have obtained the money from my parents but I thought I would like to do this on my own.

"It'll take them a few days to get the C of A done and in the mean time we got a trip to South End, why not say you'll take it, and you can get on your way," Kenward said.

I told him I would think it over. It was a big step.

I had to take off right away, so that meant I wouldn't see Peter to discuss the proposition with him. I called the school and gave them a message for Peter that I wouldn't be able to see him until I got back from my trip.

I stopped at La Ronge and walked to the Bay to tell Bill of the news and of my trip to Winnipeg. I knew he and his wife would be most anxious to hear all the gory details, at least that's what they

were expecting. Bill was away on a fur buying trip and wouldn't be back until the end of the week. I would have to wait. I did see his wife for a minute and told her a few minor details about the new offer. I wanted to talk to Bill when he returned.

Nurse Thompson caught me just as I was leaving the post.

"Skipper, you young mutt, you have to tell me all about your trip," she exclaimed.

"Later Liz, when I get back. I have to leave for South End," I told her.

"Are you flying SAN ?" she asked.

"Yes, and I have to get a move on," I told her.

"Well, I'm on your flight Skippy, so don't go without me," she added. We left the store together since she had already deposited her bag at the agent's desk.

"Come on Liz, let's go, I yelled at her as I walked down to the plane." I knew this trip was going to be a reliving of the Winnipeg trip for Liz's benefit. She sat in the right seat and we talked all the way.

That Peter, are you ever lucky Skipper to have that boy and that everything has turned out so well," she said.

"My boys sure missed him when you were away. They've become quite friendly you know,"

I knew.

Liz and I had to overnight in South End and that meant staying with the Resources Agent and his wife. We sat and talked until late, about the holiday and all the things taking place in the big city. Nothing like first hand news for everyone. Liz had several visits to make in the area and would not be returning with me in the morning.

"Have you thought about what you are going to do with Peter?" she asked.

"Well Liz, I guess I have done little else but think of him since we left Winnipeg. I discussed the matter with my parents and decided that my main goal was for Peter to get a good education, college, if he wanted and also to make sure he has a home, for as long as he wants to stay," I said.

"He has three more years until he is out of high school and, at the rate he is going, he'll have a few more scholarships. I'm not sure what he wants to do with them yet," I said.

"Well, I am certainly surprised at the reception he got from your

parents," she said. I'll bet you can still hardly believe it."

"Liz, I was the happiest guy around. I certainly let them know how much I appreciated what they had done for Peter and me. It was wonderful after so many years of being alienated from one another," I said.

"Mother really loves that boy and that's something. That, I found the most difficult to accept but then you know Peter, he can sure win them over," I went on.

"Johnny told me that Peter doesn't plan to live here after he's finished school," Liz remarked.

"That's right Liz, he has said the same thing to me, he doesn't want to come back at all. We'll be living at Birch Rapids for the summer, depending on how well things turn out," I said.

I returned to Prince Albert and went in to see Kenward.

"Okay Lloyd, I hope our deal is still on," I said.

"Skipper boy, you have just made the biggest decision of your life," he said.

I completed the deal with the flying club. They had already started on the inspection and I would take delivery on Saturday.

"Go and get some time in with Peter and we'll see you in the morning," Kenward said.

"Oh by the way, the operations manager of the mine is going to be here in an hour or so and I want you to meet him. Quite a guy. He's just about your age, lots of responsibility for a young guy," he said.

"Quite British you know, came over here when he was a kid and you can still hear his accent. He comes from your part of the country Skip, got one of those double barrelled names the English have, Michael Stacey-Barnes," he mimicked with a British accent."

"Hooooolyyy, you're kidding. I know Mike, he and I grew up together. We're practically brothers," I told him.

"Be back here in an hour and you'll meet him," he said.

THE REUNION

I t was sure a small world. Mike and his brother had moved into my old ranch house, the one I inherited from old Jim Cowie. Ken and I continued to care for them after their mother died. I remembered something about an uncle or someone coming and taking the boys back to England. Well, I would soon learn. What a surprise!

I was sitting in the hotel having my lunch when Michael came over to my table.

"Skipper you son of a gun, I can't believe my eyes," he exclaimed.

"And look at you, you're as tall as I am, remember when we both thought that you were doomed to be a midget?" he reminded me. We hugged. Two other chaps were with Mike and he introduced me as a brother from his ranching days. They sat down at my table while Mike proceeded to tell me all that happened to he and Eric after his uncle came and claimed them. I had already heard most of the story from Ken. Mike was a mining engineer with one year still to go. This was a field operation for him to start on as he required the experience. I told him that I had the contract to haul his operation into Birch Rapids. "This is going to be simply great working together again," Mike explained.

It was almost 5 o'clock when I arrived at the school and as I had phoned ahead, Peter was waiting for me at the door.

"You are in one big trouble spot, Mr. Scott, " he confronted me, with his most stern look.

"Hooooollly, what have I done now?" I asked.

"You went and left without telling me you weren't going to be back that night," he scolded.

"Peter, I got so busy and the day was getting on. I had to go to South End, what was I supposed to do? I knew you were in classes so I did leave word with the secretary," I apologized.

"Well Dad, you almost missed out on the biggest surprise of your life," he whispered, as though he didn't want anyone to share in his news.

"And what big surprise might that be?" I asked.

"Okay Dad, sit down and brace yourself. I met my other Grandpa today and he's staying at the Royal. He's waiting to take us out to supper," he said. Hooooollyy, now what the heck was going on? I wondered.

"You'll see. Are we ready to go to the hotel now? I want to show you my other grandpa," he was so secretive and was enjoying my curiosity to the fullest.

"Okay, Okay let's go, but this had better be good, whatever you have up your sleeve," I said. We went into the hotel, Peter led the way upstairs and knocked on the door to a room. I stood there, wondering what in the world was going on. I decided to go along with the prank.

The door opened and there stood my other Dad, Ken Wills, along with his wife Ellen.

"Gosh all Friday boy, can't you do anything right," he laughed. I was so surprised and shocked I just hugged him while I tried to compose myself.

We all went down for supper in the hotel and of course talked and talked and talked. I have never been happier in all of my life than to see my mentor, my other Dad, the man who influenced my life when I was growing up.

"I see you got stuck with a little worm just like I did," Ken said.

"But I'll tell you one thing, I think he is even smarter than you were. I'm glad to see something rubbed off on you besides Bull S---." he laughed. Peter just sat with a big smile on his face, taking everything in. I had told him of my days with Ken on the ranch and Peter just devoured it all, wanting to hear more. Ken went on, telling story after story about he and I and, of course, all the goings on in those days. We talked a little about our overseas experiences, but we had been in touch and knew what each other had been doing. We had tried several times to get together while we were in England but things never worked out that way.

"You know how I knew what you were doing over there Skipper?" Ken asked. "I met an old friend of yours in London and she told me she knew you just like her own kid. I was in hospital for an infection from a wound and this nurse is the head honcho of the hospital. From my file she saw I was from Millarville so she came up to see

who I was. She recognized me right away and I recognized her.

She said, "Hey, I know you, you're the little cowpoke's Dad. You're Skipper's Dad, aren't you?" Boy did we ever give you a going over,"He said.

I knew he was talking about Burchill, my best friend from Manning Depot days.

"She really wanted to adopt you, you know, " Ken said.

"Burch and I were very close at a time when I really needed someone," I said. Remember how you used to tell me I needed someone to wash behind my ears?" I laughed.

Ken told me all about their talk and how happy he was to know I was home in one piece. Ken reached over and grabbed a surprised Peter and flipped him over his knee and made like he was going to give him a paddling. Peter somehow knew it was play and went along with it, hollering and bellowing like a young bull.

They wrestled like that for awhile and he told Peter, "That's the only thing your Dad understood, a good whack on the bum," he said. "I sure hope he knows how to tan your britches," he warned Peter.

"Dad has never spanked me once," he said, bragging to Ken.

"You know why? I never did anything bad. Besides, grandpa, the only reason I'm alive and here today, is because of my Dad. Aren't you glad he saved me, 'cause look at the great grandson you got," He looked Ken straight in the eye. Ken got serious, gave us another hug, and told us how happy he was at seeing me again.

"Ken. Do you know that your other stepson, Michael, is in this same hotel right this minute?"I asked.

"Gosh all Friday, now you are putting me on, " he said.

"Peter, will you find out what room Mr. Stacey-Barnes is in and go and bring him here. Don't tell him why, just that I want to see him. Okay?" I ordered. Peter left and it wasn't too long before there was a knock on the door and in walks Mike and Peter. Ken had walked into the bedroom to hide.

"Well Skippy boy, this is your famous Peter I hear you talking so much about. I'll say this for him, he sure is a pleasant, well mannered little guy. Doesn't take after his Dad at all," he said, patting Peter on the shoulder. Where's grandpa?" Peter asked. Mike looked around to see who Peter was talking about and Ken opened the door and stepped into the room.

"Oh my God." Michael started to weep as he ran to Ken and hugged him. "Oh God, how can this happen to me and both on the same day? My Mentor, my friend, My Dad, my bum whacker and my brother," Mike went on.

"Did you get a spanking from grandpa too?" Peter asked.

"Well you might say that he got tired of using your Dad all the time, so he decided to use me. Remember Eric and the soap?" Mike reminded us.

"He has never forgotten that, talks about it often and how he had never had a spanking before in his whole life. Then Ken lays two of them on him inside five minutes. He said he never wanted another one," Mike was laughing now. We reminisced until late and Peter absorbed every word and I am sure committed he it all to memory. He had a way of storing little tid bits and bringing them up at the opportune moments when it would be to his advantage.

Ken and Ellen, had decided to make a little detour on their way home from the East just so they could see us. They were leaving the next afternoon for Calgary. I told them I wanted to show them our airplane and would they come down to see where I worked and the aircraft I flew. They were delighted.

"Dad, what about me? I want to see the plane too and I could miss the first periods in the morning. After all, I'm with my grandpa aren't I?" he said. He was a manipulator.

"Come on Skipper, the boy comes with us, right?" Ken said.

I made arrangements for Peter to spend the night with me and for him to miss the morning classes. Ken told me that he enjoyed Peter calling him grandpa and if I didn't mind then he and Ellen sure didn't. They were very impressed with their new grandson.

They thought the tour of the airways office and a trip to the flying club hangar was impressive and they enjoyed it.

The time went by all too quickly and we saw them off on the train. Peter had to say goodbye after lunch as he had classes to attend. "grandpa, you're exactly like I thought you would be. I am very happy to have finally met you and Ellen," he said.

"You're exactly as I expected you'd be too Peter and we're very proud of you. You're welcome at our home whenever you and your Dad want to come. I would like you to come and live there," he said.

THE RANCH

I took delivery of CF-ALL and Lloyd Kenward, Michael and I, flew up to Birch Rapids to look the situation over. The airplane even smelled new and it handled quite nicely, although it could have had a few more horsepower but then we can't have everything can we?

The airplane performed well on her new skis and it was a real joy to once again land at Birch Rapids. We agreed that we would start hauling right away as the warehouses had been built and were ready to take supplies. I was happy to see that Mike had several natives employed in the new warehouse. I knew them all and it was like old home week with everyone wanting to know about Peter.

I hauled steadily, often overloading the poor aircraft. I always made sure I had lots of take off space before I would consider overloading her too much. Lloyd Hass was very happy with my efforts and as a sub contractor I was happy too and the money started to come into our bank account. Peter continued to work hard and his marks reflected his efforts. Everything was going well on that front. He received a letter from my mother along with some spending money which he promptly handed over to me to put into our bank account.

"We need every penny we can get for our plane," he would seriously point out to me. Michael, Peter and I spent many spare hours together when we could talking about the good old days and how I made out while in Michael's country.

I would have gone to see you if I had known where you were living," I said.

"At that time Skipper, I was still in the States completing my degree. I was really lucky, don't you think, to have missed the war although I did feel badly about someone else fighting my battle, so to speak. I was really forced to continue my education at that time due to the scholarships I had received," he went on.

Spring arrived and with it came break up. I took the skis off the aircraft and restored her to a land bird again. There would be no work for her during the Summer until next Fall. I went back to working part time for Hass and he was happy with that arrangement.

Bill also had me helping him bale furs to be shipped out to Winnipeg for the fur auctions, so I was kept busy.

The Easter break saw Peter and I heading for Calgary, much to my mother's disappointment. I assured her though, that Peter could spend some of his summer holidays with her and my father at their summer place in Kenora Ontario. This was the longest trip "CF-Fall" (we called it FALL) had made and she performed flawlessly. Ken and grandpa were at the field in our old pasture to meet us and drive us up to the ranch. Ken was now operating grandma and grandpa's old homestead ranch. Peter and I had the room that grandpa Wills had made for me before I left for Winnipeg to finish my school. It was made of logs and was just beautiful. Grandpa was quite taken with what he called "his great grandson" and Peter was in his glory.

He got to meet many of my old school chums and their children. Lynn Spence my friend from Turner Valley was gone. He had died in an Airforce training accident. His aircraft crashed just outside of Calgary. Most of our neighbours had returned safely from the war.

Ken had a horse for us both and we were at liberty to go wherever we wished. "Dad, how come you can ride on a horse all day without getting a sore behind? I can hardly sit down I'm so sore," Peter complained.

"You'll get used to it," I told him.

"Funny you mentioning having a sore backside, so did your Dad as I remember it," Ken laughed, "and it weren't from riding a horse, huh son?" Peter followed Ken wherever he went and soon Ken had him roping or at least practising with one of my old ropes. Even I was throwing almost as good as I used to, funny how some things never leave you, I thought.

We went to Peggy's for supper and of course nothing would do but all the boys would have a swim like old times. I decided not to tell Peter about Peggy's little jokes and would see if she was still pulling them off on the kids. Skinny dipping of course was the rule, as always, and we had a splashing good time but things had changed. It wasn't quite the great fun we used to have, I guess we were grown up now and had more on our minds than just the cares of little kids.

"Supper time." Peggy hollered. We all got out and rushed to get dressed.

Oh God, Peggy! I had thought that I was too big for her to play this dumb game on any more but my clothes and Peter's were gone. "Dad, what have you done with my clothes?" he asked.

"My dear boy, your Aunt Peggy has taken our belongings and is going to make us sneak up to the house to get them," I informed him.

"Good grief Dad, I haven't anything on," he said.

"Nor have I," I replied

"Did you forget that Peggy likes to steal clothes from boys," I reminded him. Everyone was just killing themselves as they watched Peter and I in our dilemma. I got to the house and there were my clothes laying on a chair but Peter's were nowhere to be seen.

"Peggy, please can I have my clothes?" He was hiding behind the same corner I used to use. Peggy sneaked up behind him and picked him up and pinched his bottom, just like she used to do to me. Thank goodness I was too big for that sort of treatment now. Poor Peter was shocked but then started to laugh when she started to tickle him. She put him down and gave him his clothes. He was as red as a beet from embarrassment but was still laughing.

"Dad, I see what you mean. Peggy, I'll get you for this one day, " he said.

"Sure you will little one, sure you will," she laughed.

I wondered if we could really go back and relive old times and came to the conclusion that, yes we could, but only a little at a time for too much would spoil it all. Peggy was much older but still had her great heart and her love of a joke or two. She loved her family and we loved her.

Our holiday went all too soon but not before Peter had seen all the things I used to do and the places where I used to do them.

"Dad! We have to come back here," was all Peter said, as we prepared to leave. I had taken the whole family up for a flight around our valley for old times sake. But now it was time for us to go back to PA. Goodbyes are always so hard to say, especially when there is so much love abounding. You could feel it everywhere and we were allowed to take it with us.

We arrived back in P.A. to a stack of letters waiting to be read. Peter received his share mostly from school friends and two from his grandparents. They wanted confirmation that Peter would soon be on his way to Winnipeg. Peter was excited at the thought of going to

the summer place in Ontario. I had promised my parents he could spend the balance of his holidays with them.

I had to make a flight to Winnipeg in CF-ALL to pick up some engine parts for the airways,so this was a golden opportunity for Peter to get to Winnipeg. It didn't take us long to have him packed up and ready for his holiday with grandma and grandpa. Peter flew most of the way while I was engrossed in a book. He was happiest when I wasn't looking over his shoulder.

My parents were at the airport so meet us. It was their plan that, being as I only had a few days, we should leave for the Lake immediately.

It had been several years since I had been to our summer place, and everything had changed. A new house, we could no longer call it a cottage. There was a huge boat house over the water's edge which held the big cruiser and an outboard runabout. There was work room for maintenance and tools and fuel.

The top of the boat house held two guest rooms one of which had a balcony that jutted out over the water above the big doors. This room was relegated to Peter. He was speechless, and overcome by the beauty of the location which appeared much the same as his home area at Nutt Point on La Ronge. The water was crystal clear and very inviting for a young boy.

Nancy wanted to be the one to show Peter to his new room, and thrilled at his enthusiasm and delight for his room.

My father and I had some very special time together going over things of the past, and both of us trying very hard to keep the bitterness we felt, from entering into the conversation. We decided what was done was done, the future was all that lay ahead and we should make the most of it.

Father smoked a pipe and mother the odd cigarette. I was not a smoker in those days. The three of us sat out on the front balcony overlooking the lake. We could see parts of the boat house down below us. There were stairs down to the dock, and an inside stairway leading up to the balcony and the guest rooms. There was another walkway from the second floor of the boat house onto the top of the stairs which led down.

The pathway that led to the boat house upper floor, also led to our neighbour's home a quarter of a mile around the bay. This was

Dr Cormaties summer retreat. He had three daughters, Jean, Barbara and Chrisy. Very nice girls.

We weren't there more than an hour before the girls were over wanting to meet Peter. At this point in his life, girls played a small, if not a non-existent roll in his life. I had a feeling things were about to change.

Peter asked Nancy if he could go for a swim as it was so warm and the water looked so inviting, especially the balcony railing which offered an ideal diving platform.

"Why don't you do that Peter, you'll have lots of time before supper," she laughed.

"Peter I don't see a swim suit amongst your things. I don't think I packed any," she said watching Peter as he undressed.

"Nancy? Why do I need any its only you and me," he said laughing heading toward the railing. He was over the side and swimming and diving about before Nancy could voice any words of restraint.

"Good grief, what's the use," she chuckled as she stood looking down at the naked Peter having the time of his life.

"Here Peter, catch the ball," she said as she took the huge beach ball and dropped it over the edge. His grandmother arrived in the room and came over to stand beside Nancy as she watched the frolicking taking place below. She laughed at Peter's innocence, but beckoned him out of the water through the boat house and up the inside stairs.

"Hi grandma," he said his eyes sparkling from the water dripping down his face. "Want to come for a swim?" he asked.

"Peter you scamp, I don't mind you skinny dipping when we're alone but you should be cautious when we have guests. They might not be used to having a small naked boy flashing by the dock in front of them," she laughed trying to show some degree of authority." I bought you a pair of the new style swimming shorts. Not that old woollen thing you have. Will you try it on please? " Nancy was having a hard time keeping her composure as Peter, feeling no embarrassment whatsoever, stood in front of them both as he pulled on his new shorts. He looked quite dashing in them, at least those were mother's words describing Peter's response to the new rules.

"Go ahead and try them out," she suggested. Peter climbed up on the rail and dove into the water fifteen feet below. Nancy and

mother watched from above as Peter disappeared below the surface and his swimming trunks stayed floating on the surface. They were laughing so hard, they could be heard way up to the main house. Father and I wondered what was taking place and walked down so as not to miss any of the entertainment.

Walking to the railing, we both broke out in a fit of laughter as we watched Peter struggling to retrieve his new trunks and then trying to get into them.

Mother referred to Peter as a breath of fresh air, that the summer camp needed for years. She decided that Peter was Peter, she was going to leave his naturalness up to him and his own discretion. Peter after all was a very clever boy, who seldom let any points of protocol go by without making some sort of an evaluation as to their priority.

TIME TO QUIT

Through-out the Summer, Peter spent as much time as he could in the right seat of whatever aircraft he could hitch a ride on. The pilots knew Peter and his interest and ability in flying and allowed him to fly with them . They were happy to have him come along as he was "very pleasant company". I didn't mind because he enjoyed it so much. Red McKenzie wasn't joking when he said that Peter was a natural pilot. He now was boasting some 30 hrs of dual instruction and had several take-offs and landings to his credit. All his accumulated hours were just for experience and couldn't be logged officially.

I was very proud of him and what he had achieved. He approached everything with such enthusiasm including all the boring flight ground-school assignments. He was just at home on the little Stinsons as he was on the Norseman, even though each handled quite differently. The Stinson would rise onto the step and become airborne with little effort. The Norseman on the other hand required man handling from the moment you opened throttle until she became airborne. Sometimes it just didn't want to leave the water.

Stew Heatherington taught Peter the art of using aileron and rudder together to break the Norseman free of the water. It sounded simple but it had to be co-ordinated and done smoothly. He told me that Peter just had that certain touch, that certain feel to know just how much rudder was required to offset the pull of the float carrying the load when aileron was being used.

The company frowned on Peter's illicit flying time particularily when the pilots allowed Peter to sit in the left seat of the Norseman. There was only one set of controls and the wheel could be flipped from left to right just by pulling a spring loaded pin and swinging the whole column over to the other side. However, the other pilots and myself, of course, made sure the company was kept in the dark as to Peter's buckshee flying time. I'm sure they knew.

The company's insurance agents were also quite against the unauthorized flying by Peter and told Floyd to stop the practice immediately or they could lose their insurance and someone might get fired.

It wasn't too often that Birch Rapids had more than one aircraft at its dock at one time, however, such was the case this beautiful sunny August morning. Stew Heatherington arrived in CF-SAO loaded with empty fish trays for the fish packing operation. He was North bound to Black Bear Island Lake to bring Jean Foster and his wife out. I was busy stacking the trays away in the storage shed when Peter burst in all out of breath. "Dad, Stew says I can go with him to Jean's if you'll let me. I can get some time in 'cause he's empty." he said, trying hard to sell me. It wasn't hard. He was very convincing when he looked at you with those big blue eyes of his. He knew my weak spots.

"How'll you get home again? Stew is going back to La Ronge," I said.

"Well you'll be in La Ronge in a day or so and I can stay with Bill overnight," he went on. (Bill was the HBC post manager)

"Okay, be careful," was all I could say. "Peter, have you got any money?" I yelled after his disappearing body.

"Sure Dad, I still got twenty bucks from my pay. Bye." He ran down the stairs to the dock. Peter was a good saver and only spent money when it was absolutely necessary, and if he couldn't get anyone else to pay.

I heard Stew trying to start SAO and it sounded to me like he had a weak battery by the way the engine was cranking over. Finally, after I thought for sure he had run the battery down, it caught and belched a puff of white smoke as the engine roared into life. Peter was untying and stowing the last ropes aboard as they taxied out into the bay.

I was waiting and watching, wondering what was taking them so long. Usually they would have been off by this time. They seemed to be taking too long warming up and were taxiing farther down the bay than necessary. Then I knew what was going on. Peter had probably talked Stew into letting him do the take-off. I know I always gave Peter plenty of take-off space, just as an extra precaution. Sure enough, when I heard the run up and the mag test, I knew it was Peter at the controls. He always did his checks on the downwind taxiing leg before he turned into the wind for take off. It was a good practice. Some pilots chose to turn into the wind almost immediately and do the initial checks and run up as they commenced

the take-off run. Saved time. Sure enough SAO passed the end of the dock and Peter was at the controls. I waved but knew he was too busy to wave back. Because the aircraft was empty, it rolled onto the step and became airborne in seconds climbing in a low gentle turn towards Black Bear Island. It was a nice take-off proving Peter was getting very good. After all I thought, he is still only a child. Isn't he? Perhaps not.

This trip with Stew Heatherington was to be the most challenging trial of Peter's young life. An accident at Black Bear Island Lake, when Stew was hit by a turning propeller causing him to become completely disabled, and proved Peter to be more man than just a boy as he flew the Norseman with the severly injured pilot to La Ronge saving his life.

This became a turning point in our lives. Peter's grandparents were determined their grandson was going to complete his schooling at St John's College in Winnipeg. As he and I were undecided what I would do when I left Birch Rapids, we came to the conclusion that he might be better off with my parents, and have a little taste of city life and school in the big time.

Peter was reluctant to leave, not because he didn't want to go to Winnipeg and the college, but he didn't want to leave me. The feeling was more than mutual, however in the long run, Peter agreed to go for a few months just to try it out. His grandparents were beside themselves. After all Peter was still enjoying a great deal of notoriety over his Mercy Flight. The media certainly created havoc in our lives. He was up to it, and none of the attention he was receiving changed him at all.

"Grandma. I wish you wouldn't introduce me to your friends as your grandson who was in the papers. I'm just your grandson right?" Peter pleaded .

"I am so proud of you I feel like shouting and telling the whole world," she said.

After moving Peter into his new home, and getting him settled in the college, I thought it best that I not hang around too long and perhaps make it more difficult for Peter to adjust.

We went to enroll him in the college, and there was nothing we could say but grandma had to come along. After all she was Mrs A E Scott. Peter did not need any help from mother. His reputation had

preceded him, and he was welcomed with open arms. I was happy that the headmaster was more interested in Peter's scholastic ability than his heroics in La Ronge. Mother soaked up all the complimentary things that were being said about Peter, like a sponge. She was truly in her glory as the three of us were introduced to the other teachers.

This in itself caused some raised eyebrows, when I was intruduced as Peter's father. They didn't have to say what they were thinking, it was so obvious. I thought an explanation might be in order but thought better of it, and just allowed them to think what they wished. Peter always enjoyed watching the questioning looks on peoples faces when introductions were made. Me Too.

I decided to head back to the ranch for a while. After all I had several head of cattle of my own, and I wanted to help out. Besides I had little else lined up. I was slightly shaken when upon renewing my license, the doctor discovered I had high blood pressure, enough to treat with medication. I would not be able to fly until they discovered whether or not the medication worked. This was a blow more to my ego, than being a critical factor in my future. My family thought I had pushed my luck long enough, and it was time I looked elsewhere for employment, such as going back to the Bay Fur Trade. I could have a trading post of my own. It turned out that my license was not going to be renewed. My blood pressure was not responding to medication. I didn't mind so much, but I would rather it have been my idea to quit rather than being "Grounded"

In spite of all his busy schedules, Peter never failed to write me every week.

He was very upset when he heard the news of my grounding, but I assured him this way we would probably be together a lot longer, than if I continued to press my luck. The North no longer held its romance for me now that Peter was gone.

I would never forget my experiences, adventures and my many friends but it was truly time to move on.

Ken and I and Olie worked the two ranches, and our herds were growing each month. Peter's letters were still coming regularly but the sparkle seemed to be missing. He didn't sound like his usual bubbly self.

I received a letter from Mother asking me to take some time to

come and spend some time with Peter he was lonesome.

I convinced mother not to tell Peter I was coming home. It would be a surprise. It was a surprise all right. I drove to the college and had Peter paged on the school P.A.system. " Peter Scott to the Headmasters office." They repeated it twice. I stood where Peter could not see me until he had entered the room. The secretary was smiling as Peter entered with a questioning look on his face.

"Peter there is someone to see you," she said. Peter turned and shouted,"Dad." and ran to me. We hugged as the tears streamed down his face. I was having a hard time trying to hold my composure and hold my son at the same time. Oh God it was good to hold him again. Just like when he was little. It was hard to believe we had been together four years . Even at sixteen he was still my little kid.

Peter went on to get a degree in electrical engineering and was later appointed to a management position with Ontario Hydro. He married Jean Cromatie and have three boys of their own.

My Little Napyo